(an Atheling book)

A Kansas Pacific Railway broadside announces five million acres for sale. (Courtesy, Newberry Library)

Fifty Million Acres:

Conflicts over Kansas
Land Policy, 1854-1890

PAUL WALLACE GATES (1901-)

CORNELL UNIVERSITY

n/LC

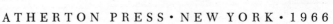 an Atheling book

ATHERTON PRESS · NEW YORK · 1966

Manufactured in the United States of America

Cover design by JoAnn Randel

FIRST ATHELING EDITION, 1966

Atheling Books are published by
ATHERTON PRESS
70 Fifth Avenue, New York 10011

Foreword to the Atheling Edition

THIS STUDY of "conflicts over Kansas land policy, 1854–1890" is neither an attempt to relate the more or less routine application of Federal land policy to a selected area nor an exercise in local history. There was little that was routine in the early development of Kansas; during the first years of its growth (as indeed during many of its later years as well), Kansas history *was* national history, its very name a byword and a slogan throughout the country. On the contrary, Paul W. Gates has contributed to the understanding of mid-nineteenth-century American history in two major ways. This book, first of all, adds a significant new dimension to the story of the Kansas struggles of the 1850s, revealing developments that have frequently been overlooked and neglected by past writers but which must, if properly pondered and appreciated, serve as a valuable corrective to the traditional, even stereotyped, picture of the turbulence which characterized the early years of Kansas Territory. Second, this study illustrates in graphic, and oftentimes dismal, terms the functioning of United States land policies on a frontier that did not share in the normal pattern (insofar as any frontier may be said to develop in a "normal" fashion) of settlement, growth, and development. There were many sides to the Kansas struggle that distinguish it from the experience of other frontiers; these

v

7589

facets of Kansas' history have intrigued writers and historians for over a century. Yet, in spite of all the thought and energy that has been applied to it, the real story of Kansas' early development still remains to be told. Valuable insights have been provided by such historians as James C. Malin, whose pioneering work in early Kansas history has considerably altered older ways of thinking. Gates' *Fifty Million Acres* represents an important further step toward a badly-needed synthesis.

The Kansas story, Gates writes, is "a grotesque composite of all the errors involved in the growth of the American West." If other frontiers reflected some of the same "errors," it is their combination in Kansas that makes this a meaningful study. If the author may have exaggerated the "grotesqueness" of the events he describes, it is because the Kansas story is so urgently in need of revision. *Fifty Million Acres* is not, as Gates himself concedes, a complete and definitive analysis of the problems of early Kansas; it should, and undoubtedly will, however, serve, in the author's words, to "draw attention to these problems and stimulate interest in them." But Gates has done more than simply point the way for future historians. He has probed Kansas' early difficulties from a fresh perspective and has offered new clues to their comprehension.

The Kansas struggles of the 1850s have traditionally been described as primarily an episode in a great moral contest, a view that was first propounded by many of the actors in the drama itself. Even today echoes of this interpretation persist. Although efforts had been made to organize the area west of Missouri as early as 1844, the creation of Kansas Territory a decade later was immediately embroiled in a sectional conflict over the question of slavery. The story of the Kansas-Nebraska Act, the maneuverings, machinations, and stratagems that resulted in its passage, is extremely complicated, too often dismissed by simple explanations. Its passage came at a time when significant stirrings of the moral aspects of the slavery question were making deep inroads into American politics. Under ordinary circumstances the act would not have aroused much criticism. The pressures along the Missouri River for the organization of the area to the west had been mounting; most Americans regarded the opening of this vast area to settlement to be long overdue. But Stephen A. Douglas, the author and sponsor of the act, was committed to the principle of popular sovereignty, or self-government in the territories, not only as a boon to the frontier settler but also as a national solution to the slavery problem. In order to make popular sovereignty meaningful, Douglas provided in his bill for the repeal of the Missouri Compromise, thus, in effect, opening the new territories to the expansion of slavery. Douglas' confidence, however, "that the people would decide against slavery if left to settle the question for themselves" was drowned out by the indignation and resentment of many Northerners against what they regarded as an unwarranted concession to the Southern slave power. New fires of sectional discord were kindled by the act; from its inception, Kansas Territory became involved in the dialogue between those who regarded slavery as immoral and who wished to prevent its expansion and those who looked upon slavery as a positive good and who desired its extension.

The first "abnormality" in the Kansas question lay in the fact that the territory was virtually uninhabited when its government was established. Except for the Indians and scattered numbers of soldiers, missionaries, and traders, no significant population existed in Kansas. The decision as to whether or not slavery should exist in the new territory was, then, to be made by a prospective population. The implication was clear; each side, proslavery and antislavery, recognized its responsibility—to encourage and promote emigration to Kansas in order to insure a favorable decision. In the popular mind at least Kansas was merely a pawn in the deeper struggle over the moral question of slavery. The turbulence of the territorial period, as settlers from the free states of the Ohio and Mississippi valleys and from the slave states of the upper South poured into the newly-opened region, thus became intimately related to moral conflict. A new political party, rising out of the opposition to Douglas' act and dedicated to the restriction of slavery, made capital out of the turmoil and owed much of its early spectacular growth to it. Slavery and freedom vied with one another in a life and death struggle on the prairies of Kansas (at least in the oratory of politicians and in the Eastern press) and "Bleeding Kansas" became a watchword and rallying cry in the political contests of the fifties. As one historian has written, "Like so many other things in that day, Kansas became a symbol, and realities lost their significance."

The facts of Kansas settlement, however, pointed in another direction. To be sure, emigration companies, hastily organized in the North, sought to promote the movement of an antislavery population to Kansas in order to combat the influence of proslavery settlers from the border slave states. The activities of a small number of fanatics on each side, generally working in defiance of or outside the law, seemed to lend credence to the popular view. But the efforts of the emigrant aid companies fell far short of their anticipations and the actions of the extremists were soon recognized for what they were—disruptive movements that impeded the orderly growth of the territory. The great majority of those who moved into Kansas were not idealists, determined to do battle for freedom against the forces of the slave power. They were home-seekers, land speculators, entrepreneurs and town builders who saw in Kansas new opportunities for their own advancement and gain. The prize for which they competed was not the restriction or expansion of slavery; it was land. Their success depended upon the degree to which the land policies of the Federal government could be adapted to the peculiar circumstances of the territory.

The passage of the Kansas-Nebraska Act in 1854 was a great blunder, Gates maintains, not because it repealed the Missouri Compromise and opened portions of the West to slavery but rather because it opened Kansas to settlement before proper steps could be taken to insure an orderly disposal of the land. Not one acre of land, he points out, was available for sale when the act was passed. The situation did not improve quickly or easily. During the years that followed, the administration of land policy in Kansas was marked by confusion and conflict. The unwillingness to recognize Indian rights and the subsequent controversies over Indian titles and allotments, the slowness with which the surveys were authorized and made, the designs of speculators and railroad promoters all combined to create a situation that was ripe for violence. The Panic of 1857 and President Buchanan's sudden decision to order Kansas lands into the market were heavy blows to a population already laboring under an inordinate amount of confusion. Speculators had a field day; in fact, the prospect of profit surmounted the moral scruples of many Kansans as proslavery and antislavery individuals joined in their promotional schemes. Kansas did bleed, but the wounds were opened by conflicts over land claims. "Filibustering, banditry, and personal vendettas continued to flourish under the guise of conflict over slavery," Gates writes, "but underlying these activities were struggles over the promotion of towns, over the removal of the Indians and the opening of their reserves to purchase, over the staking of choice claims, and over the selection of railroad routes." With an unsympathetic national administration and inefficient and mediocre territorial officials seeking to apply what Gates has called "an incongruous land system" to an area already involved emotionally in a moral question, it is small wonder that Kansas Territory should have been racked by conflict and disorder. This pattern of confusion and turmoil in Kansas land policy, so important to an explanation of what became known as the "Kansas question" during the 1850s, persisted beyond the territorial period, providing a dramatic and disillusioning case study of the operation of Federal land policy during the latter years of the nineteenth century. Many of the roots of the agrarian discontent which brought Kansas back into the headlines late in the century may, Gates believes, be found in the persistence of these land problems.

The history of Kansas presents a baffling and complex picture to the casual student of the nineteenth century. At the same time, it serves as a constant challenge to the serious scholar. With his expertise in the history of American agriculture and land policy, Gates has offered a fresh interpretation and a new explanation of early Kansas history that will benefit both the casual student and the serious scholar in coming to grips with one of the crucial problems of the past century.

ROBERT W. JOHANNSEN

University of Illinois

Preface

WESTWARD-MOVING frontiersmen reached the bend of the Missouri by 1825 where for a quarter of a century they were halted by the Indian barrier and by false assumptions concerning the arable character of the Great Plains. The barrier was only slightly breached in the forties by migration to the Utah Basin and the Willamette Valley of Oregon and by the rush of miners to California. Between the scattered islands of settlement in the Far West and the Missouri Valley remained a vast area, crisscrossed by emigrant trails and routes of traders and trappers and only sparsely populated along the eastern front by Indians intruded from farther east and by the blanket Indians of the Plains to the west.

Suddenly, in 1853 and 1854 the Kansas-Nebraska country beyond the Missouri loomed up as a tremendously attractive area, and there erupted in Congress, the press, and the pulpit an ominous war of words over the questions whether one or two territories should be created and whether slavery should be sanctioned in or barred from the territory.

For the next forty years Kansas was the focus of greater public attention than any other western community because of its record of civil strife, the intemperateness of its journalistic warfare, the baseness of some of its leading politicians, and the colorful character of its agrarian revolt. The Kansas Struggle, the Lecompton Constitution, John Brown, Samuel C. Pomeroy (the Senator Dilworthy of Mark Twain's *Gilded Age*), droughts, grasshoppers, the Santa Fe Railroad, Mary Lease, Senator Peffer and his whiskers, windstorms, the sodhouse frontier, "In God We Trusted, in Kansas We Busted," Ed Howe, and William Allen White were all names and symbols familiar to the average American of the time. They are also familiar to the casual reader of history today, for memory of them has lasted.

Fifty Million Acres aims to explain these phenomena, not in terms of population makeup, the course of immigration, the puritan character, or Freudian psychology, but rather through the functioning of governmental policies, particularly Indian and land policies. Some critics may say that more attention is paid to the derangements of these policies than to the policies themselves.

Kansas was selected for study because the story of its development involves analysis of a complex maze of inconsistent and badly-drawn legislation complicated by blundering, stupid, and corrupt administration. These confusions, combined with the demoralization produced by the bushwhacking and jayhawking of the proslavery and antislavery groups and with the breakdown of the moral fibre of the population, make the Kansas story a grotesque composite of all the errors involved in the growth of the American West.

Particular attention is paid in the present study to the treaty method of disposing of Indian lands, to land grants to railroads, and to the sales, settlement, and tax policies of these railroads. This material provides the background for an account of the numerous conflicts that flared up in Kansas between squatter-settlers, who were seeking ownership of land, and the railroads, which sought title to surrounding lands in order to profit from the increased value railroad construction would give them. Too much attention has been paid in the past to rates as a reason for hostility toward railroads in the West, and questions of land ownership have not been considered enough.

I would prefer to send this study out as a complete analysis of land policies and problems in Kansas, but the task is too great and other obligations make that goal impossible to achieve now. I cannot even claim to have covered completely the limited period from 1854 to 1890. Among the topics lightly dealt with or not touched upon are the management and disposition of speculators' holdings, grants to railroads, the management of school, university, agricultural-college, and internal-improvement lands, the role of the money-lender in pioneer Kansas, the development of large estates as distinguished from speculative holdings, the emergence of tenancy, and the relations of government land policies to the actual developing pattern of land use. All these questions call for intensive investigation, since we know very little indeed about them. This study may draw attention to these problems and stimulate interest in them.

In the course of my research, which has ranged over nineteen years of fairly continuous but scattered work, I have had the assistance of numerous officials in the General Land Office (now the Bureau of Land Management) and in the Office of Indian Affairs in the Department of the Interior, of the National Archives, the Kansas State Historical Society, the State Historical Society of Iowa, the Historical and Art Department of Iowa, the Indiana Historical Bureau, the State Historical Society of Wisconsin, the Library of Congress, the Detroit Public Library, the University of Virginia Library, and the Cornell University Library. I recall with special fondness the gracious hospitality provided by Kirke

Meachum, Nyle Miller, Martha B. Caldwell, and Mrs. Lela Barnes in the Kansas State Historical Society. Memories of their fine co-operation in the midst of a hot political campaign, when the East met the West and took it into camp, will always be cherished. Other notable directors and staff members of historical societies who were patient and helpful in meeting demands on their time and thought are Christopher B. Coleman, Edgar Harlan, Joseph Schafer, and Benjamin F. Shambaugh, all long since passed beyond the great divide, and Nellie A. Robertson, Dorothy Riker, and Alice Smith. Stephen Gilchrist, then custodian of the biographical files of James F. and Henry B. Joy at Grosse Point, Michigan, was more than generous in providing space for work and discussing with me problems of mutual interest. In my search for manuscript materials in private hands, I was bested in one instance by Lester J. Cappon, then of the University of Virginia, who unearthed and brought to Charlottesville the very choice collection of material on the large land-and-loan business of James S. Easley and William W. Willingham just before my letter of enquiry reached the owners of the papers. Needless to say, the papers were opened to me even before they had been properly processed.

Visits to 35 Kansas county seats, where I searched the deed, mortgage, and probate records with the tolerant permission of numerous but somewhat mystified officials, paid off in exciting new material. A year's research in Washington and frequent summer trips to the Sunflower State were made possible by a fellowship and grants-in-aid of the Social Science Research Council and a number of grants by Cornell University. To those who pioneered in securing funds and developing extensive programs of research grants my great obligations, and those of most scholars in history and the social sciences, are due.

Lewis C. Gray, the great authority on southern agricultural history, gave me much material of practical value during his course in Federal land policies at the Brookings Institution. From Lewis Gray, Eric England, and many other younger men then in the Division of Land Economics, Bureau of Agricultural Economics, United States Department of Agriculture, came acquaintance with many land-policy problems that otherwise might have escaped me. I cannot refrain from mentioning also Everett E. Edwards, for long years editor of *Agricultural History,* who through that journal, his own bibliographic contributions, and his suggestive articles contributed to the high position which agricultural history holds in the scholarly world.

Everyone who has studied the history of Kansas and its part in the history of the trans-Missouri country is familiar with the intensive and thoughtful articles and books of James C. Malin. Though we are not entirely in accord in matters of interpretation and emphasis, I have great respect for the volume, originality, and fresh approach of his work. His publications and those of his students have been most useful; his stimulating criticisms have induced careful reconsiderations.

Four of my graduate students contributed peripherally to this study, though I have borrowed only from their conclusions: David M. Ellis on the movement to forfeit the railroad land grants, Allan Bogue on farm credit in Kansas and Nebraska, Lee Benson on the nature of western agrarianism, and Charlotte Erickson on the American Emigrant Company.

Parts of the first three chapters of this book were read at the St. Louis and Madison meetings of the Mississippi Valley Historical Association in 1944 and 1949, and a portion of Chapter Two appeared in a different form in the June, 1951, number of the *Political Science Quarterly.* Professor John Krout has kindly given me permission to reproduce the latter material.

P. W. G.

Ithaca, New York, July, 1953

Contents

Maps and Illustrations

Introduction

"NEVER in all history, so it would appear, has the insatiable land-hunger of the white man been better illustrated than in the case of the beginnings of the sunflower state." [1] Whether or not Annie Heloise Abel was sufficiently familiar with "all history" to be able to generalize to this degree, few would dispute today that it was "insatiable land-hunger," rather than any idealistic notion of making Kansas a free or a slave state, that drew the bulk of the 100,000 people who rushed across the Missouri line in the period from 1854 to 1860. True, far larger numbers of people in the same six years were moving for the same reason to Iowa, Illinois, Wisconsin, Michigan, and Texas; but in none of these states was the impact of immigration so explosive in local and national affairs.

In Kansas two kinds of society seemed engaged in conflict, each attempting to establish its pattern of social institutions. That slavery could flourish on Kansas soil few could

[1] Annie Heloise Abel, *The American Indian as a Slaveholder and Secessionist* (3 Vols., Cleveland, 1915–1925), III, 23–24.

1

maintain, and nobody ever claimed that the plantation system, with its emphasis upon a major cash crop demanding a great volume of labor, could exist there.[2] But even though climate, soil, and geography forbade the introduction of slavery to Kansas, proslavery Democrats in Missouri and other southern groups tried desperately to make Kansas a slave state or to secure its assimilation to the southern point of view on slavery.[3] For political reasons which were operative in the 1850's and for many years to come, the struggle was pictured simply as between slavery and freedom—whatever each might connote. More recently attention has been focused upon other causes of conflict, for example the patronage that new territories and states provided to political parties,[4] the pleasures of distributing a rapidly multiplying

[2] Senator George E. Badger, of North Carolina, in arguing for the adoption of the Kansas-Nebraska bill said: "I think . . . it is in the highest degree probable that with regard to these Territories of Nebraska and Kansas, there will never be any slaves in them. I have no more idea of seeing a slave population in either of them than I have of seeing it in Massachusetts; not a whit." *Cong. Globe, Appendix,* 33 Cong., 1 Sess., p. 149.

Similar expressions were made by Edward Everett of Massachusetts, Stephen A. Douglas and James C. Allen of Illinois, Sam Houston of Texas, John Kerr and Andrew P. Butler of North Carolina. Avery Craven summarizes the issue: "The senseless talk of making Kansas a slave state arose, not from any sound hope of slavery expansion, but from a determination to preserve southern equality." "The Price of Union," *Journal of Southern History* (Feb., 1952), XVIII, 8.

[3] The ablest defense of Senator David Atchison and his fellow "Border Ruffians" (to use an expression he constantly employed) is in James C. Malin, "The Proslavery Background of the Kansas Struggle," *Mississippi Valley Historical Review* (Dec., 1923), X, 285–305.

[4] One of the most voracious patronage seekers of the 1850's, George W. Jones, Senator from Iowa, in a gossipy letter to Howell Cobb of Feb. 11, 1853, said that the Democrats in Congress were making efforts to create positions for defeated House members of the

number of offices paying generous salaries and profitable fees, the desire to control public offices such as territorial and educational institutions, a general hunger for lucrative mail, trucking, Indian, and army procurement contracts, and the granting of lands and loans to railroads. Also of prime importance in the Kansas political struggle was the search for land and for means that would make it valuable. All these issues existed elsewhere, just as in Kansas, and there is nothing unique about them there except perhaps the greater concentration of the people upon them.

The distinguishing features of the Kansas struggle are that the territory was opened to settlement at a time (1) when there was not within it an acre of land that was available for sale, (2) when along the eastern border a formidable array of Indian reserves remained, to which the owners clung tenaciously though unsuccessfully, and (3) when there was emerging the most complex and confusing array of policies affecting the distribution of the public lands and the transfer to white ownership of Indian land-rights that has ever emerged in the continental United States, save perhaps in Oklahoma. This complex and confused character of the land-disposal policies greatly increased the opportunities for administrators to seek plunder and special privilege. Hence land, slavery, plunder, and patronage combined explain the intensity of the political fight in Kansas as compared with that in Minnesota and Nebraska.

---

party. Two bills providing for the division of Oregon and the creation of Nebraska territory were approved by the House which, Jones said, when passed by the Senate, would make available "several fat offices of Governors, Secretaries, Marshalls, Attorneys, Judges, etc., etc., to bestow. I believe all who are going out of Congress voted for these bills. I said *Nay* to both." Ulrich B. Phillips, ed., "The Correspondence of Robert Toombs, Alexander H. Stephens, and Howell Cobb," American Historical Association, *Annual Report,* 1911 (Washington, 1913), II, 324.

The central issues in the Kansas struggle may be summarized as: (1) the slavery question, which motivated federal patronage appointees and Missourians, whether they intended to become residents of Kansas or not; (2) the struggle within Kansas itself over patronage appointments; (3) the scramble for public and Indian land; and (4) the rivalry of railroad groups for land grants and for loans from local and national government bodies. Though the slavery question loomed large at the opening of the territory, it became increasingly blurred, and the sharp division between the proslavery and antislavery factions gradually dissolved. Filibustering, banditry, and personal vendettas continued to flourish under the guise of conflict over slavery, but underlying these activities were struggles over the promotion of towns, over the removal of the Indians and the opening of their reserves to purchase, over the staking of choice claims, and over the selection of railroad routes.

For three-quarters of a century, democratically-inclined people had labored to create a system of land distribution that provided easy means to ownership for emigrants willing to undergo the hardships of pioneer life. Settlers had been granted the right to buy land at low prices, the right to enter upon and select the public land before speculative monopolists could anticipate them, and the right to have at least a year of residence and development before they had to pay for their tracts. And by the fifties it had been established that one-eighteenth of the public lands would be given to new states to aid in financing the development of elementary schools. Other extensive grants of land were being given to the states for building canals, river improvements, and railroads, all of which were anxiously sought by residents in isolated frontier communities. By the mid-nineteenth century the government was extending beyond one year the period of grace allowed settlers to raise funds for the purchase of their tracts, and there seemed a good prospect for the adoption of a free-grant measure to provide donations of 160 acres to anyone who would develop them.

Just when settlers' interests were prevailing in legislation and the management of the public lands, the Pierce and Buchanan administrations, under the pressure of southern conservatives and land-jobbing speculators, attempted to turn the clock back a full generation in two notable steps. One of these steps served to throw into discard the land-reforms of a generation by blocking the road to further re-ductions in the price of land, not to mention free homesteads, halting land grants to railroads which the West so ardently wanted, and limiting to a year the period of grace during which one might occupy public lands without paying for them. Large acreages of land on which squatters had resided from one to three years were pushed into market, thus forc-ing the claimants to borrow at extortionate interest.

By the national administration's action in pushing the pub-lic lands into market before settlers had completely invested them, Kansas was saddled with large speculative holdings of absentee capitalists and a mountain of debt. Nothing con-spired to repel Kansas from the Democratic Party more than the efforts of Democratic leaders to extract revenue from the lands. When they were first given the opportunity to cast their votes in a presidential election—in 1864—Kansas moved almost *en masse* into the Republican Party, whose record on liberal land-policies was far better than that of the Demo-cratic Party in the past decade.

The second of the Pierce-Buchanan policies was to revive the treaty-making method of disposing of Indian land. The traditional process of divesting the Indians of their right to occupy land was to draw a treaty providing for the sale or cession to the national government of the Indian right; when the treaty was ratified by the Senate, the land thus ceded be-came public domain and subject to the public-land laws. But in some older states, notably Indiana and Illinois, land was granted by treaty to chiefs and headmen in the form of individual reserves which might be sold directly to whites with the approval of the President.[5] Elsewhere in Mississippi and Alabama a number of million acres were allotted to individual Indians and in turn sold by them to speculators acting singly or in groups. None of these tracts were at any time a part of the public domain or subject to the public-land laws.

Allotment of Indian land by treaty was most frequent in Kansas during the Pierce-Buchanan administrations, though it was also of importance in Nebraska [6] and Minnesota. Eighteen Kansas reserves, ranging from the tiny 2,571-acre tract of the Christian Indians to the great Osage reserve of 8,841,927 acres, were forever barred from becoming a part of the public lands of the United States and subject to such laws as Homestead and Pre-emption.[7] Instead, these reserves became the booty of speculators, land companies, and railroads, with substantial benefits accruing to helpful politicians.

Through the treaty process the reserves were ceded in trust to be sold in large or small tracts for the benefit of the Indians, were allotted to individual Indians, or were held as diminished reserves until some future time when they might either be sold to whites or allotted to Indians. A fourth of the area of Kansas, and by all odds the best fourth, passed

[5] J. P. Kinney has summarized the allotment policy, if it can be called that, for the period before 1887 in *A Continent Lost—A Civilization Won: Indian Land Tenure in America* (Baltimore, 1937), pp. 81 ff. George D. Harmon, in his *Sixty Years of Indian Affairs* (Chapel Hill, 1941), also has useful information on allotments.

[6] Addison E. Sheldon provides statistics documenting the sale of 599,018 acres of Indian land in Nebraska in *Land Systems and Land Policies in Nebraska,* Nebraska State Historical Society, *Publications,* XXII, (Lincoln, 1936), 204–209, 332–334.

[7] Homestead, adopted in 1862, allowed free land to settlers; preemption, as of 1854, permitted squatters to buy their claims, prior to public auction, at $1.25 per acre.

by the treaty process from Indian ownership to individuals, land-speculating companies, and railroads without becoming a part of the public domain or becoming subject to Congressional control.

Treaty allotment of those Indian lands which, because of location and soil, were most desirable produced a scramble for the tracts that was accompanied by confusion over titles and assessments and much litigation. None of the ceded trust lands were subject to pre-emption, though squatters were sometimes permitted to buy their tracts, after long delays, at the appraised price, not at the basic Western land-price of $1.25 an acre. On other occasions great tracts on which individual settlers had already established claims were sold on sealed bids to favored speculators, among them high officers of the government. Most unsatisfactory to Kansans were the acts of land-speculating and railroad groups in drawing treaties which provided for the sale to them of entire reserves. Officials of the Indian Office and of the Department of the Interior were induced to approve, and the Senate to ratify, these treaties as a result of generous gratuities in the form of cash and lands. Mark Twain long ago described the boodling career of Senator Samuel C. Pomeroy, but less well known are the activities of Orville Browning, James Harlan, and even Edmund G. Ross in supporting questionable deals for Kansas reserves.

The treaty method of disposing of Indian land gave scant regard to settlers' rights and interests. It permitted speculators and railroads to buy the land before settlers had an opportunity to pre-empt or otherwise acquire them; the speculators and railroad groups thereby became middlemen in the distribution of lands and took the profit which immigration and the demand for land made possible. Disposal of land by treaty denied settlers the benefit of the Homestead Act of 1862, toward which democratically-minded reformers had worked for years. It gave paramount influence in shaping Indian relations to the Commissioner of Indian Affairs and the administration majority in the Senate. The popularly elected House of Representatives, where land-reform sentiment was strongest, was denied any part in policy making. Disposal of land by treaty produced violent antirent wars against the railroads and, combined with resentment against their high rates, led to enactment of radical measures to curb and control the practices of railroad magnates.

Because the railroads were snapping up much of the Indian land, in addition to the great grants of land given to aid in their construction, they were becoming the principal proprietors of the West, gaining all the profit which construction of their lines would assure to owners of land in the way of added value. The more the railroads anticipated the settler in the acquisition of land from Indian tribes or the national government, the more they made a mockery of the Pre-emption and Homestead Laws. Land reformers became increasingly distressed at the proportion of land being acquired by railroads, as well as land companies and other speculating groups and individuals, and at the high cost to settlers of middlemen intruding between them and the government. The reformers sought to halt the use of the treaty-making power in distributing Indian lands; they sought to end the flow of grants to railroads and to stop the unrestricted sale of public lands to large capitalistic interests.

Pioneer settlers moving into the area of public lands were themselves not squeamish about violating the Pre-emption Law, making illegal deals with Indians, and taking advantage of the loopholes in the Homestead Law. They were doubtless as guilty as the large interests of breaking the law and abusing political power. But they were the people, the sovereign citizens, the builders of Kansas, and they demanded the right to share in the rising land values which improvements and settlement assured. The absentee owners, whether James F. Joy and his Boston associates, the members of the "Indian Ring" in Washington, the American Emigrant Company with its charter from Connecticut, or Chick and Northrup of Kansas City, were attempting to rob the Kansas citizen of the right to acquire cheaply a tract of land which he could transform into a valuable investment.

The Kansas conflict between settlers and railroads, first arising in the fifties over the purchase of Indian reserves, flamed anew in the later seventies and eighties over railroad sales and pricing policies, especially over the delay in pushing railroad lands into market and in permitting them to be taxed. These issues and the emotions they engendered kept Kansas in turmoil fairly constantly in the "Gilded Age," and they provide much of the background for the story of agrarian movements. In Topeka and in Washington, Kansans demanded legislative and administrative action that would permit the lands to be settled without too much burden to settlers. They wanted withdrawn and unearned but reserved lands [8] restored to the public domain; they wanted the earned lands made taxable and their price put at a level that would attract buyers and permit their development. They were unhappy over numerous court decisions in which the judges seemed to lean over backward to read into the law rights that Congress had not intended to give the railroads until they had been earned.

At the same time the homestead and land-reform elements were calling for a thorough reorganization of the land system in order to assure settlers and farm makers an easier

[8] Withdrawn lands were public lands which had been opened to settlement and later were withdrawn from entry to permit railroads to make their selections of alternate sections. Once the line of the railroad was determined and construction under way, the officers of the companies would select their lands, which were thereafter reserved until construction was completed and the cost of survey paid by the railroad when the patents would issue. Withdrawn and unearned reserved lands as well as earned but unpatented railroad lands all appear prominently in western agrarianism.

9

path to ownership and to prevent cattle, mining, railroad, lumber, and other companies from benefiting by loosely framed and improperly administered laws. To these reform elements should be added the conservationists who wanted to create national forests and the eastern merchants who were shrilly demanding the revival of railroad competition and the establishment of rate regulation to assure low freight rates.

Despite the strength of the "Robber Barons," the fervor of the free enterprisers with their social Darwinism, and the threat of hostile court action, numerous changes, reforms, and radical innovations were actually carried through. Some unearned land grants were forfeited and great areas of withdrawn lands were restored to public entry. Railroad lands were made taxable; the cash-sale law, which permitted unlimited purchase of public lands in certain areas, was repealed. The National Forest Reservation Act was adopted. The power of aliens to acquire large estates was curbed in the territories and in many of the states. An Interstate Commerce Commission was created and given authority over the country's network of railroads.

In no other state did disillusionment with railroads and clashes with them appear so early and continue so constantly as in Kansas. Representatives of Kansas fathered scores of bills to safeguard settler claims against railroad rights, to require the railroads to take title to their earned lands and to have them placed on the tax roll, to have unearned land grants forfeited, and restored to the public domain. They were in the van of the movement for reform, but not in any way that would restrict the small man's right to take advantage of the land system.

The struggle for land in Kansas brought local issues to the attention of the public elsewhere, produced leaders for the national land-reform movement, and brought about final abolition of the treaty method of land disposal.

CHAPTER I

Land Problems in the Kansas Struggle: Allotments

IN THE first seventy years of its independent existence the United States developed a system of public land disposal that was well planned and logical, its various parts being reasonably consistent with each other. Among its basic and uniform elements were such features as the purchase of Indian title, the making of a rectangular survey, the holding of a public auction, the establishment of a minimum price, grants for education and internal improvements, and the privilege of retrospective and finally prospective pre-emption, which was a procedure for recognizing the rights of squatters, and for authorizing squatting on surveyed lands. Numerous questions arose that called for administrative interpretations, and at times confusion existed because of the lack of clarity in Congressional measures. Notwithstanding this confusion the system was understandable, the rights of individuals seeking land were easily determined, and where controversies arose between claimants adequate procedure existed to adjudicate them.[1]

In this early period the principal exception to the orderly character of the land system was the method of dealing in acquired areas with private land claims which dated back to preceding governments. Here the confusion was less due to Congress than to the chaotic nature of claims, rights, and titles to land dating from the early Spanish, French, and British occupation of Florida, Louisiana, and the Old Northwest. More than half a century was to elapse before many of these claims were to be settled.[2]

So long as the need for revenue was the basic influence underlying public-land distribution, no restrictions were placed in the way of large accumulation by speculators, land companies, and other nonsettlers; on the contrary, every effort was made to induce purchasing by them. As a consequence, many million acres went into the hands of these interests, which withheld them for prices beyond the reach of impoverished frontiersmen. Among the results of this speculator intrusion were the widespread dispersal of the population, the retarded growth of frontier areas, the delay in extension of local government, schools, and roads, the infrequency of social contacts among settlers, tenancy, farm

[1] Benjamin H. Hibbard, *History of the Public Land Policies* (New York, 1924), and Roy M. Robbins, *Our Landed Heritage: The Public Domain, 1776–1936* (Princeton, 1942), still remain the most useful general treatises on Federal land policy. They contain little on private land claims and are more concerned with political motivation than the actual functioning of the land laws. Much needed is a study of administrative policies and amplifying directives, which at times were as important in public land management as Congressional acts.

[2] There is no satisfactory historical study of private land claims.

mortgages, and greater pressure upon the Indians for their removal.[3]

Public-land policies were materially changed as the need for revenue from lands became less pronounced, and as the new states brought their influence to bear upon Congress in favor of more generous treatment of settlers. Pre-emption gave settlers at least a year's free use of the land before they had to buy their tracts. In 1854 graduation reduced the price to settlers of long-offered land as low as 12½ cents an acre. The Homestead Act in 1862 gave them free land. Western agrarians seemed to have won, and indeed did win, a major victory, but by no means the complete one they had sought.

At the very moment when Congress was promising free land to settlers, it was enacting measures which gave to railroads, in order to aid in their construction, an area three times the size of New York State. Congress was also giving lands to states as subsidies for education in universities, vocational, and grade schools. These lands were not to be given to settlers but instead were to be sold at the highest possible price. Furthermore, despite the advent of free homesteads in 1862 Congress neglected to repeal measures providing for unrestricted sale of public lands. Consequently, many million acres continued to be sold to speculators, lumber barons, cattle kings, and land companies, who secured the profits in rising land values that the Homestead Act had intended to assure the small man. In keeping old policies and superimposing upon them the new and more generous policies, Congress was moving away from the well-organized, consistent, and coherent policies of the past into a complex maze of inconsistent and inharmonious measures that mini-

[3] Paul W. Gates, "The Role of the Land Speculator in Western Development," *Pennsylvania Magazine of History and Biography* (July, 1942), LXVI, 314–333; Ray A. Billington, "The Origins of the Land Speculator as a Frontier Type," *Agricultural History* (Oct., 1945), XIX, 204–212.

mized greatly the benevolent character of the new program.[4]

This incongruity in the Federal land system was most pronounced in Kansas, where there emerged, in addition to the statutory system of public land policies, a second set of land disposal policies which applied to Indian reserves and was both framed and administered by the Office of Indian Affairs.

As far back as 1818 the Government had begun to divest the plains Indians or Indians whose claims extended well into the plains—the Osage, Kansas, Pawnee, Quapaw, Oto and Missouri tribes—of their right to land in present Nebraska, Kansas, and Oklahoma in order to provide an area in which eastern Indians might be colonized. While surrendering claims to vastly greater areas, the Osages retained a diminished reserve of well over eight million acres in southern Kansas, the Kansas or Kaw Indians retained a reserve of a quarter of a million acres in Lyon, Morris, and Wabaunsee Counties, and the Oto and Missouri withheld minute tracts. In western Kansas and parts of Oklahoma and Nebraska, aboriginal claims remained intact in 1854.[5]

[4] Paul W. Gates, "The Homestead Law in an Incongruous Land System," *American Historical Review* (July, 1936), XLI, 652–681.

[5] Indispensable for this study are the maps in Charles C. Royce, *Indian Land Cessions in the United States,* in Bureau of American Ethnology, *Eighteenth Annual Report,* 1896–97, part 2 (Washington, 1899). We may follow the Court of Claims' analysis of the types of land ownership in Kansas and Nebraska at the time these territories were open to settlement, as given in Pawnee Indian Tribe . . . v. The United States, Appeals Docket No. 11, decided Feb. 3, 1953.

1. Lands to which original Indian title had been extinguished and which had been regranted by Treaty in perpetuity to Indians removed from east of the Mississippi River. . . .
2. Lands to which original Indian title had been extinguished but which had not been regranted to other Indians, and title to which was in the United States.
3. Lands to which original Indian title had never been extinguished and which were still occupied by the indigenous tribes but without guarantees in perpetuity. . . .

The eastern portions of the ceded lands were either sold to Indians residing in states farther east, or were exchanged for their ancient reserves. Removal of these emigrant or intruded Indians was achieved by the promise that their new homes would be assured them "as long as the grass grew or water run." [6] No further moves were to be required. A total of 10,679 Indians whose ancestral homes ranged from Pennsylvania and New York to Wisconsin, Iowa, and Missouri had thus been established on reserves constituting a solid array along the Kansas-Missouri border.[7] The United States broke its faith with these Indians on March 3, 1853, when Congress authorized the Indian Office to negotiate "immediately" with the emigrant Indians for the cession of

[6] George W. Manypenny, Commissioner of Indian Affairs, quotes the Indians as using this expression in his *Annual Report,* in *Senate Executive Documents,* 33 Cong., 2 Sess., 1854–1855, I, part 1, 218.

[7] All the tribes with the "number of souls . . . made up from the best data in the possession of the Indian Office" are given in Commissioner of Indian Affairs, *Annual Report,* 1855, *House Ex. Doc.,* 34 Cong., 1 Sess., I, part 1, 575–576. Useful for government Indian policy and the establishment of the reserves are: Anna Heloise Abel, "Indian Reservations in Kansas and the Extinguishment of their Title," Kansas Historical Society *Transactions,* VIII, (Topeka, 1904), 72–109; James C. Malin, *Indian Policy and Westward Expansion* (*Bulletin of the University of Kansas, Humanistic Studies,* Vol. II, No. 3; Lawrence, 1921); and Grant Foreman, *The Last Trek of the Indians* (Chicago, 1946). Malin's maps are inaccurate and he misunderstood the treaties of 1853 and 1854. Foreman's account is based almost entirely on the *Annual Reports* of the Commissioner of Indian Affairs. The Delaware Treaty of 1829 is fairly typical of the numerous treaties that provided new permanent homes in Kansas territory for eastern Indians. It stated that the Kansas reserve therein being conveyed to the Delawares "shall be conveyed and forever secured by the United States, to the said Delaware Nation, as their permanent residence: And the United States hereby pledges the faith of the government to guarantee to the said Delaware Nation forever, the quiet and peaceful possession and undisturbed enjoyment of the same, against the claims and assaults of all and every other people whatever."

their reserves, and again on May 30, 1854 when it opened Kansas Territory to settlement.[8]

George W. Manypenny, Commissioner of Indian Affairs, could not have anticipated with pleasure the task of negotiating with the intruded Indians for their removal. He knew their opposition to removal and the difficulties involved in persuading them to give up their land. He stands out as one of the few commissioners who truly sought to protect and improve Indian welfare, no matter what the consequences. He held no brief for the usual methods of securing Indian treaties and cessions of land by the tricks of working through minority chiefs and half-breeds, who would be given special annuities or allotments of land, or through traders who would favor cessions provided their vastly inflated claims were taken care of, or through the use of liquor to soften up intransigent leaders. His first visit to the Kansas Indians in 1853 came to nothing because he could not bring himself to coerce or to treat improperly with them. Then too he found that the $50,000 appropriated for negotiations was inadequate to deal with more than ten thousand Indians, including half-breeds and others who had gone part of the road toward adopting the white man's ways.[9]

The renewal of negotiations in 1854, coupled with Manypenny's continued refusal to resort to the well known devices to break down Indian resistance, produced a situation that was fraught with much ill for the Indians, the incoming set-

[8] The act of March 3, 1853, appropriated $50,000 for negotiations with the Indians west of Iowa and Missouri to secure their consent "to the settlement" of citizens "upon the lands claimed by said Indians, and for the purpose of extinguishing the title of said Indian tribes in whole or in part to said lands. . . ." Perhaps it was the awkwardness of this measure that was partly responsible for the nature of the agreements later negotiated. 10 *U.S. Stat.*, 238, 277.

[9] For the failure of Manypenny's negotiations in 1853 see his *Annual Report*, 1853, in *Senate Ex. Doc.*, 33 Cong., 1 Sess., I, part 1, 247 ff.

tlers, and the Pierce and Buchanan administrations; indeed, the delay was responsible for no small part of the turmoil in territorial Kansas. The rapid expansion of white settlement westward and from the Pacific coast eastward spelled the doom of the Indian country, and by 1854 the Indians, like Manypenny himself to a certain degree, were convinced that instead of making further removals to more distant and less hospitable areas, they should be given smaller reserves and encouraged to cultivate them as white people did. Individual ownership of land might encourage them to show more enterprise in using and developing it, and diminished reserves and allotments were to be tried. Manypenny had thus moved far away from the frontier position, expressed in Kansas as elsewhere, that the Indians should be expelled from areas desirable for white settlement.[10]

Table 1. MANYPENNY TREATIES WITH KANSAS TRIBES, 1854–1855 [11]

Tribes	Date of Treaty	Ratified	Proclaimed
Oto & Missouri	March 15	April 17	June 21
Delaware	May 6	July 11	July 17
Shawnee	May 10	August 2	November 2
Iowa	May 17		July 17
Sac & Fox	May 18	July 11	July 17
Kickapoo	May 18	July 11	July 17
Kaskaskia et al.	May 30	August 2	August 10
Miami	June 5	August 4	August 4
Wyandot	January 31, 1855	February 20, 1855	March 1, 1855

The Manypenny treaties of 1854 revived two features of Indian-land policy which were fairly common east of the Mississippi but which had been largely abandoned in the

[10] Manypenny's *Annual Report,* for 1854, shows a considerable change of views in the past year. *Senate Ex. Doc.,* 33 Cong., 2 Sess., I, part 1, 213 ff. See also his later *Our Indian Wards* (1880).

[11] The treaties are in the United States *Statutes at Large,* but for purposes of convenience I have used Charles J. Kappler, *Indian Affairs, Laws and Treaties,* II, (*Senate Documents,* 58 Cong., 2 Sess., no. 319).

17

forties. The first, in accordance with the Commissioner's view that the Indians could not be persuaded to leave Kansas, provided for a reduction of the reserves by a surrender of a part and the retention for a small tribal community of a remainder that was ultimately to be distributed as allotments of 200 acres or less to individual Indians. Competent Indians with the approval of the Commissioner could convey their allotments but the allotments of incompetent Indians were to be held in trust. The other feature was the "cession in trust" whereby the land was placed in a category outside the public domain and independent of its administering agency, the General Land Office, being subject to disposal by the Office of Indian Affairs.[12]

Manypenny's hope that the Indians, when surrounded by white settlers, might "be saved and their complete civilization effected" was quixotic, to say the least. It showed no comprehension of the dynamic qualities of the western movement, for it assumed that the Indians could continue to live upon and farm their little enclaves, surrounded though they were by whites. Such an assumption was sheer folly and

[12] Numerous allotments in Indiana amounting to some 193,000 acres had been provided for chiefs in treaties with the Miami and Pottawatomie Indians which have been described in the introduction to the *John Tipton Papers,* edited by Nellie Armstrong Robertson and Dorothy Riker, *Indiana Historical Collections;* XXIV, (Indianapolis, 1942), 22 ff. Other allotments were given Indian chiefs and influential braves and half-breeds in Michigan, Illinois, and Ohio. The largest acreage of allotments was given the Chickasaw, Choctaw, Cherokee, and Creek Indians in Mississippi and Alabama. They bid fair to upset the entire public land system in these states. The biggest cession in trust was that of the Chickasaws amounting to more than four million acres in Mississippi. James S. Silver has some information on land speculation in this cession in *Journal of Southern History* (Feb., 1944), X, 84–92. The allotment question is an important one, and has not received its due attention. J. P. Kinney summarized the legislative history of allotments in his *A Continent Lost—A Civilization Won: Indian Land Tenure in America* (Baltimore, 1937) pp. 81 ff.

revealed little understanding of previous Indian-white relations. Worse still, the establishment of the diminished reserves aggravated an already bad situation in Kansas and made it possible for less worthy successors of Manypenny to despoil the reserves by selling them for inadequate sums to railroad and speculator groups. Furthermore, it forced the Indian Office into a position even more antagonistic to settlers than that which its normal responsibilities produced. The Secretary of the Interior in 1857 admitted the error, in part, when he said,[13] "The result has been disastrous. Trespassed upon everywhere, his timber spoiled, himself threatened with personal violence, feeling unable to cope with the superior race that surrounded and pressed upon him, the Indian proprietor has become disheartened. Many of them have abandoned their reserves, and still more desire to sell."

A major error in government policy toward Kansas was made when Congress opened the newly created territory to settlement on May 30, 1854, before any of the Indian treaties providing for cessions of land had been ratified or, indeed, before two of the most important had been completed, and before any provision had been made for setting off the diminished reserves or surveying the public lands. Furthermore, the Kansas-Nebraska Act had reaffirmed previous statutory prohibitions against encroachments upon Indian reserves, which were specifically excluded from the jurisdiction of the new territory. When, therefore, the first land-seekers crossed into Kansas in June, 1854, not an acre of land was legally open to them and they were subject to heavy penalties for invasion of the reserves. Four or five months after Kansas was opened to settlement, a petition of its settlers, actual or prospective, said: "It must be remembered that very little of the front of the Territory and of its best soil is really open to settlement." With the exception of the small Kickapoo and Iowa tract in northeastern Kansas, the petition stated that

[13] *Sen. Ex. Doc.*, 35 Cong., 1 Sess., 1857–58, II, 63.

19

"the naked prairies, forty or fifty miles back, are the nearest lands vouchsafed for the home of the white settler. Such a disheartening arrangement as this is already turning back the tide of emigration to States where valuable lands are offered, at prices from twelve-and-a-half to fifty cents an acre." [14]

The reserves, trust lands, and allotments could be protected against the bold intrusion of determined land-seekers only by the use of mobile cavalry units, as was later done in the Oklahoma country before its official opening. Such a policy of militantly safeguarding Indian interests Manypenny attempted to introduce, and for a time he seemed to have the support of the President. In his report of November 26, 1855, he said: [15]

Many . . . intruders have wholly disregarded the admonitions and warnings of the officers . . . and to compel obedience and to vindicate the good faith and authority of the government in this behalf the military arm has been invoked . . . and under instructions . . . of the President, it is expected that all persons remaining unlawfully upon any of the Indian reservations in Kansas Territory . . . will be forcibly ejected therefrom.

Had early and vigorous support been given Manypenny's efforts to expel intruders, it is possible that the trust lands, allotments, and diminished reserves might have been defended; but once squatters were firmly established on them, protection was out of the question. Political bickerings between the proslavery and antislavery factions, internecine warfare, confusion about the treaties and the lack of survey lines, and the unwillingness of Jefferson Davis, Secretary of War, to support Manypenny's requests for military

[14] Petition of 903 people "on behalf of the settlers upon lands in Kansas Territory. . . ." *House Ex. Doc.,* 33 Cong., 2 Sess., V, no. 50, 100.

[15] Commissioner of Indian Affairs, *Annual Report, House Ex. Doc.,* 34 Cong., 1 Sess., I, 328.

aid—all combined to prevent the enforcement of the Indian Intercourse Act and the defence of long-guaranteed Indian rights. Ironically, the Intercourse Act was only to be invoked later, when soldiers were used to eject squatters from lands owned or claimed by speculator and railroad groups; in some instances it would even become the basis of action against squatters on allotments.

Congress rectified one error and made a considerable step in the direction of meeting land-reformers' demands when on July 22, 1854, it extended the pre-emption privilege to settlers on *un*surveyed public lands in Kansas to which all Indian rights had been surrendered, thus sanctioning squatting on the ceded lands that were now a part of the public domain. The areas thus thrown open to settlement and on which previously established squatters could now rest content that their rights were recognized were the cessions of the Sac and Fox of Missouri and of the Kickapoo in northwestern Kansas, the cession of the Pottawatomie of 1846, the Delaware Outlet, and the Shawnee cession.[16] Of these tracts only the Sac and Fox and Kickapoo cessions of some 720,000 acres were on the eastern border, and settlers on them as well as those making claims on the Shawnee cession were in danger of finding when the survey lines were run that their improvements were on lands retained by the Indians. The only other lands subject to pre-emption and within convenient reach, were to be found in the Delaware Outlet some 150 miles from the Missouri River, in the area north of the Outlet, in the Pottawatomie cession 18 miles beyond the Missouri border, and in the Shawnee cession 36 miles west of the border.

It is thus seen that on May 30, 1854, when Kansas terri-

[16] The Pre-emption Act of 1841 had provided only for pre-emption rights on surveyed lands. Pre-emption on unsurveyed lands had previously been extended in California, Washington, and Oregon. 10 *Stat.,* 246, 268, 305, 310.

tory was opened to settlement, not an acre of land was available for pre-emption or purchase. After July 22, 1854 settlement on the eastern front was valid only on the Kickapoo and Sac and Fox (Missouri) cessions, the boundaries of which had not been determined. Farther in the interior, the cessions of the Shawnees and Pottawatomies, the Delaware Outlet and the area north of the Delaware Outlet were open to pre-emption. Interspersed with these areas were large and small tracts ranging from a few sections to several hundred thousand acres and including all the front of the territory south of the Kansas River. To these areas various Indian tribes possessed rights; and these areas were not, therefore, a part of the public lands now opened to pre-emption. These Indian tracts included 860,163 acres of cessions in trust; 320,000 acres of allotments authorized but not selected and of allotments already selected, few or none of which were alienable; 12,259,321 acres of diminished reserves and reserves which had not been reduced; and 1,790,000 acres of an original reserve, whose status was in doubt. Altogether 15,230,430 acres, amounting to 28 per cent of the area of Kansas stretching westward from the Missouri border, were closed to settlement.

The existence in Kansas of the reserves, the trust lands, and varieties of allotments resulted in a heterogeneous complex of land-disposal policies and land-administering agencies—all afflicted with their own conflicting and overlapping controls—so confusing that few immigrants were able to understand them. Contributing to the confusion were the immigrant guides which were widely published and widely used by immigrants in their search for homes. The author of one Kansas immigrant guide wisely advised immigrants to have with them copies of the Indian treaties—of which there were nine in 1854 and 1855—if they "would 'squat' intelligently," but did not help by adding that all Indians would shortly be removed and no one need fear unduly that pre-

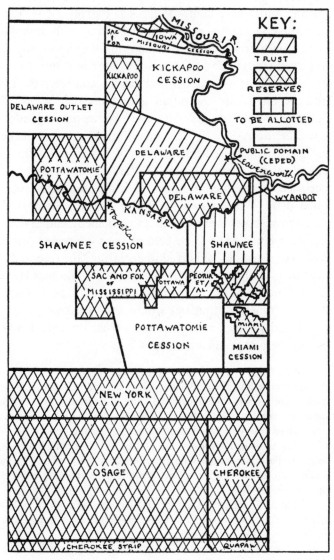

Eastern Kansas territory, 1854–1855. (Drawn by Mary Young)

emption rights would not be granted on their land.[17] Three leading antislavery men—Marcus J. Parrott, A. H. Reeder, and Mark Delahay—produced in 1856 a small pamphlet to attract immigration which was not at all enlightening so far as Indian lands were concerned. Despite the numerous claims on the Delaware, Confederated Peoria, and Iowa trust lands and the intrusions on Indian allotments they wrote: "The Settlements in Kansas Territory are on the public lands, with few exceptions. . . ." [18] No mention was made of the nearly solid array on the eastern border of Indian land which was closed to settlement. Nathan H. Parker, who had gained experience by producing guides to Iowa and Minnesota, implied in his *Kansas and Nebraska Handbook for 1857–8* that the reserves were closed to settlement and stated that the trust lands were to be sold at their appraised prices for cash, not warrants, but erred in declaring "the reserved lands are but a small portion of the Territory." [19] Thomas H. Webb in his *Information to Kansas Emigrants* expressed doubt that the government authorities would keep their plighted word to the Indians by barring squatters from the trust lands and selling them at public auction.[20]

[17] Max. Greene, *The Kanzas Region* (New York, 1856), p. 38. In this discursive and generally inaccurate account Greene gives information concerning the "aboriginal" and immigrant tribes in Kansas, their reserves, and the treaties of 1854 and 1855 with the cessions and diminished reserves. In addition to predicting the certain extinction of Indian titles in Kansas by the end of 1856 he held that pioneers might settle upon Indian land provided they were willing to pay "a small fee, ten dollars *or* so" to propitiate the owning tribe. *Ibid.*, pp. 38–39, 99–102.

[18] Marcus J. Parrott, Gov. A. H. Reeder, and M. W. Delahay, *Kansas: A Description of the Country—Its Soil—Climate and Resources* (no date, no place), p. 5.

[19] Parker, *Kansas and Nebraska Handbook* (Boston, 1857), pp. 34–35.

[20] Webb's guide, published in Boston, 1856, was reprinted in *The Garden of the World, or The Great West: Its History, Its Wealth, Its*

The counties of eastern Kansas. (Drawn by Mary Young)

Other authors of immigrant guides delineated the boundaries of Indian reserves which they said contained some of the most desirable parts of the territory and expressed optimism concerning the speedy removal of the Indians.[21] Those who predicted that pre-emption rights would be granted on the trust lands were to be proved wrong, though some squatters were finally conceded the right to buy their claims at appraised values. A more astute critic who participated in framing one of the treaties Kansans regarded as the "most iniquitous," wrote of the complexities of land-law in Kansas: [22]

The law in relation to Indian titles has to be collected from a mass of contradictory statutes and precedents which it is impossible to reduce to anything like a system. And the evil has been aggravated by the indirect aid, afforded to the speculators by Congress, so that each case instead of being settled *upon a fixed principle,* has been decided according to interests or caprice.

For a generation there were two major land-agencies in Kansas, the General Land Office having jurisdiction over the public domain to which the Indians had surrendered their full rights, and the Office of Indian Affairs having responsi-

---

Natural Advantages, and Its Future. Also Comprising a Complete Guide to Emigrants (Boston, 1856), p. 216.

[21] C. B. Boynton and T. B. Mason, *A Journey Through Kansas: With Sketches of Nebraska* (Cincinnati, 1855), pp. 152–155; Thomas H. Webb, *Organization, Objects and Plan of Operations of the Emigrant Aid Company: Also a Description of Kansas for the Information of Emigrants* (Boston, 1854), p. 11. Webb's two pamphlets were written to attract capital for investment in Kansas lands.

[22] Guy Bailey was secretary to the Commissioner of Indian Affairs, Alfred B. Greenwood, who with Perry Fuller and Bailey negotiated the Sac and Fox Treaty of October 1, 1859, which was ratified after this statement was made. Bailey, Interior Department, April 9, 1860, to R. M. T. Hunter, in Charles H. Ambler, ed., "Correspondence of Robert M. T. Hunter, 1826–1876," American Historical Association, *Annual Report,* 1916, II, (Washington, 1918), 319.

bility for the lands of the emigrant and other Indian tribes, whether original reserves, diminished reserves, allotments, or trust lands. The policies applicable to the public domain were established in law, though it should be added that legislation was frequently vague and ill-defined and required numerous amplifying regulations to be issued by the General Land Office. By 1854 public-land policies had become sufficiently liberalized to make for easy acquisition of land by actual settlers or at least by those who could meet the basic price of $1.25 an acre. But the allotments, diminished reserves, and trust lands were subject to the rule of men, not law. With Manypenny as a remarkable exception, the officials of the Indian administration were a low set appointed for political purposes and out for the main chance. Over the next two decades they took full advantage of the power over the Indian land given them by treaty.

In no part of eastern Kansas was confusion more thoroughly confounded throughout the territorial period than on the Miami and New York Indian reserves. The Miami Reserve in present Miami and Linn Counties was not actually opened until the very end of the period though even before the adoption of the Kansas-Nebraska Act whites had crossed the line to establish claims. The reserve was swiftly overrun by the most cantankerous and belligerent array of bogus claim makers, speculators, and settlers in all Kansas. The Missourians who early slipped across the line to make out claims came, said a local historian, "to keep away from progress" but after selecting their tracts they sought to "keep progress away from them." [23] Negotiations for the reduction of the Miami Reserve were not completed until six days after the territorial act was passed, and the resulting treaty was not confirmed until August 5. The Miamis agreed to surrender 429,360 acres, but before these lands could be opened

[23] A. T. Andreas, *History of the State of Kansas* (Chicago, 1883), p. 1102.

to settlement and sale the entire tract had to be surveyed, a full section was to be set aside for school purposes, and 70,-000 acres were to be reserved—partly for allotments of 200 acres to each member of the tribe, and partly for a diminished reserve to be retained until some future time when the tribe might wish to sell it. Since the allotments were to include the present residences and improvements of the Miamis, their selection after survey was certain to be time-consuming. A glance at the detail in Royce's map freely reproduced on page 23 will afford some indication of the problem in setting aside the area for allotments and the diminished reserve; it will also show how difficult it was for settlers to know, even after survey, what lands were open to pre-emption and what were not. After the first inrush of settlers and the assignment of allotments, speculators did their best to buy the Indians' 200-acre tracts, thereby precipitating a sharp conflict with the squatters.[24] Years later settlers on the diminished reserve of the Miamis, in a petition for the right to buy their lands, commented on the "greatest confusion and uncertainty" which prevailed in the territorial period as to the availability of lands open to settlement. The petitioners mentioned the great areas of lands that were claimed in various ways by the Indians whose rights were not well defined or easily understood even by the most astute persons. In this chaos of confusion and complexity, the squatters said, they had settled upon their lands which now, ten or twelve years later, they were still trying to buy.[25]

The process of allotting the land had proceeded sufficiently by 1857 so that 162 allotments containing 32,400 acres had been selected. In 1858 73 more allotments of 14,600 acres

[24] Robert Brackenridge, Ft. Wayne, Jan. 9, 1860, to H. W. Jones, and H. W. Jones, undated but 1860, to G. W. Ewing, in W. G. & G. W. Ewing MSS., Indiana State Library.

[25] Petition of settlers on the Miami National Reserve, Jan. 19, 1867, in Indian Affairs, National Archives.

were selected. Other Miamis seemed reluctant to take their land, and not until 1869 were the remaining allotments containing 13,000 acres selected.[26] Meantime, because of the delay in making selections, because of the presence of squatters or claims of bogus squatters on practically all the land, and because of an indecisive, incompetent administration in the land office, still further hindered by a territorial administration sent in from outside to aid the Missourians in securing their land, the Miami Reserve became a center of petty battles and bloody affrays.

The first intruders—Missourians—were warned off in 1854, but little was done to evict them. In 1855 they were again warned to remove or suffer expulsion by military force, but few left and none were evicted. In 1857 the register at the Lecompton land office mistakenly, so it was said, allowed individuals to pre-empt a portion of the Miami lands without authority. Officials in Washington cancelled the certificates thus issued and again warned the intruders that they must abandon their claims, but without effect. Then followed in 1859 more vigorous action against the intruders, some of whom had been on the land for five years; but, it should be noted, most of these squatters were no longer the proslavery border ruffians. Instead, actual settlers had replaced, at least to some degree, the earlier bogus squatters. Five hundred indictments for trespass were said to have been brought against the settlers. A quick roar of protest was made by the squatters and friendly settlers in other areas, a protest which softened the treatment of offenders by the territorial officers and judges. Fines of $5 were levied, but the squatters were permitted to return to their claims and resume occupation.[27] During these difficulties George Craw-

---

[26] *Miami County Republican* (Paola), Jan. 14, 1871.

[27] A. B. Greenwood, Secretary of the Interior, Dec. 29, 1859, to S. Medary, Kansas State Historical Society; *Kansas National Democrat* (Lecompton), July 21, 1859; *Fort Scott Democrat*, Dec. 22, 29,

ford urged President Buchanan to hurry the Miami and New York Indian lands into market, as bandits were enjoying a more profitable business than horse stealing in driving off actual settlers and securing their claims.[28]

Pre-emption entries were accepted on the ceded lands of the Miamis in 1857–1859, and the tracts thus entered were mortgaged to absentee investors. It was not until 1860, however, that the status of the ceded lands was clarified, and they were fully opened to pre-emption and purchase. Meantime, the Miami allotments were hawked around among speculators and agents of the Indians, and the usual liens were filed against them.[29] In May, 1861, the Commissioner of Indian Affairs found it necessary to issue a special circular describing the procedure for "reservees" or their heirs and legal representatives to follow in arranging for the sale of their allotments.[30] This and other amplifying executive orders failed to define the rights of the state and the local government in determining problems of taxation and ownership of allotments and liens on them. For years thereafter there was bickering and litigation concerning the ownership of the allotments. Gradually, the approval of the President was given for the transfer of titles from the Indians to white men

---

1859; *Lawrence Republican,* July 14, Dec. 15, 22, 1859, and Feb. 8, 1860; *Emporia News,* Dec. 24, 1859; *Miami County Republican* (Paola), Jan. 14, 1871.

[28] George Crawford, Kansas City, Mo., Jan. 4, 1859, to James Buchanan, Kansas State Historical Society, *Collections,* V, 579.

[29] Mortgage records of Linn and Miami counties reveal mortgages on the ceded lands of the Miamis as early as August, 1857. The deed and mortgage records of these two counties provide information concerning the transfer of Miami allotments and the part played by Baptiste Peoria as a middle man.

[30] William P. Dole, "Rules and regulations to be observed in the execution of conveyances of land in Kansas which have been assigned in severalty to Miami Indians. . . ." *Sen. Ex. Doc.,* 37 Cong., 2 Sess., I, no. 1, pp. 677–679.

of influence, but many Miamis clung to their allotments even though they were unable to live upon them or draw rents from them.

The squatters, meantime, continued to add to their improvements and to oppose every effort at eviction. Though they lacked title and consequently the opportunity to borrow upon their equity, they gained extensive support in their conflict with the Indian owners.[31] A new danger loomed in 1869 when James F. Joy, now rapidly emerging as the railroad king of the trans-Mississippi country, sought to acquire the remaining Miami lands and the Cherokee Neutral Tract for a railroad he was building south from Kansas City.[32] Joy's failure to get control of the Miami lands was followed by another effort of the Indians in 1871 to recover control of the allotments which had been for so long in the hands of squatters. John Roubideaux, Head Chief of the Miamis, presented a well-reasoned argument in behalf of his followers, wherein he pointed out that the squatters had built their improvements from the timber on the lands and had enjoyed the land rent- and tax-free for ten or twelve years. The honest squatters, he held, had bought their claims and paid satisfactory prices, but the three or four hundred, including women and children, who remained on the allotments and sought to acquire their lands at the values of 1854 or 1860, were trying to rob the Indians.[33] Continued talk of expelling the squatters together with firm resistance to sale by a few of the Miamis led to a compromise in 1874 when Congress provided for the appraisal and sale of the remaining lands.

[31] *Fort Scott Monitor,* Dec. 29, 30, 31, 1870 and Jan. 6, 1871.

[32] James F. Joy, March 1, 1869, to K. Coates, Joy MSS., Burton Historical Collections, Detroit Public Library.

[33] *Miami Reserve Matters. Statement of John Roubideaux, Head Chief of the Miami Indians of Kansas,* a 6-page pamphlet printed in Paola, Kansas, 1871, copy of which is in the College of Emporia Library.

Prices as high as $15 an acre were paid in 1874 for the last of the lands.[34]

The New York Indian reserve was a long narrow strip approximately twenty miles wide and extending more than one hundred miles from the Missouri border into the interior. Few of the thousands of Indians for whom the reserve was intended moved to it, and when the territory was opened hundreds of people rushed into the tract, laid out their claims without regard to Indian rights and in fact drove off the Indians, destroyed their homes, and fought with each other for the maintenance of claim rights that had no basis in law. Each of the first comers took up two claims as sanctioned by territorial law, and protected his rights in them through a "Protective League." Antislavery jayhawkers coming in later refused to acknowledge the rights of squatters, who were often absentees, to hold two claims. Claim warfare followed, with the jayhawkers and the bushwhackers involved in numerous forays against each other.[35] Government pressure was brought against settlers not known to be proslavery, and 500 writs were served against "trespassers" who were taken to Fort Scott, tried, and fined heavily for illegal settlement.

Notwithstanding harassment by government officials, continued warfare over claims, the failure to open the lands to settlement and purchase, and political strife, immigration continued to flow into the reserve of the New York Indians. In 1860 the number of settlers on the tract was estimated at nearly 5,000. There still remained much unoccupied land which the *Fort Scott Democrat* hoped would fall into the

[34] 17 *U.S. Stat.*, 631. Congress provided that the lands should be sold on sealed bids. For the bids see numerous letters of prospective buyers of February, 1874, in Miami File, Indian Affairs, National Archives.

[35] Donald W. Stewart, "Memoirs of Watson Stewart: 1855–1860," *Kansas Historical Quarterly* (Nov., 1950), XVIII, 395 ff.; *Fort Scott Democrat*, May 26, July 21, Aug. 18, 1859.

hands of immigrants and not "the grasp of the speculator." [36]
After years of indecision, the 1,824,000 acre tract was declared public lands and thrown open to sale and settlement in
December, 1860. Only a small tract of 10,240 acres was
reserved for Indian allotments. [37]

There followed a generation-long conflict between the
squatters on the small reserve and the Indian allottees, a conflict that is similar to the bickering, strife, and litigation
between similar groups on the 640-acre allotments of the
Kansas half-breeds, and on the Kansas, Miami, and Shawnee
lands. Congress attempted to cut through the difficulty in
1873 and 1874 by authorizing the settlers to buy their claims
at their appraised value, which was not to be less than $3.50
an acre, with two years' time in which to complete payments. [38] Settlers complained of the high price, and attorneys
for the allottees or their heirs maintained that their clients
were not getting true value for their rights. [39] The issue
dragged on for more years, with much court action, frequent
investigations and reports by congressional committees, and
continued unrest and uncertainty on the small tract. Gradually the claimants or their tenants and the allottees or their
heirs came to agreement, but not before nearly a half-century
had passed. [40] Finally, in 1898 and 1899 the Supreme Court

[36] *Fort Scott Democrat,* March 1, May 26, 1860.

[37] The tract was opened to pre-emption on June 17, 1860. Joseph
S. Wilson, Commissioner of the General Land Office, Aug. 16, 1860,
to Register, Fort Scott, Land Office Papers, Kansas State Historical
Society. For a summary of the issues see the case of New York Indians v. United States, decided April 11, 1898, in 170 *U.S. Reports,*
pp. 1–36.

[38] Act. of Feb. 19, 1873, 17 *Stat.,* 466 and June 23, 1874, 18 *Stat.,*
273.

[39] Commissioner of the General Land Office, *Annual Report,* 1878,
p. 141 ff.

[40] *Brief on Behalf of Settlers in Kansas, Upon Lands in Which it is
Claimed That Certain New York Indians Have an Interest Under the*

of the United States declared that the action of the President in calling the New York Indian lands public domain and in opening them to sale in 1860 was improper. The Indians were held to be entitled to compensation for the entire tract of 1,824,000 acres at the rate of $1.25 an acre with offsets for the allotments and other allowances.[41]

North of the Miami reserve was the reserve of the Confederated Peorias, Kaskaskias, Weas, and Piankeshaws, consisting of 256,238 acres. According to the treaty signed by these Indians on the day of the passage of the Kansas-Nebraska Act, 41,440 acres were to be allotted among the Indians themselves, 6,400 acres were to be held as a diminished reserve, 640 acres were to be given to the American Indian Mission Association, and the remaining 207,758 acres were to be sold as trust lands for the benefit of the Indians. All were quickly overrun by squatters. The trust lands were among the first lands to be sold in Kansas.

The Shawnee reserve just south of the Kansas River at its junction with the Missouri and the Wyandot reserve just to the north of that spot were uniquely attractive because they contained a good part of the timbered land in the territory and were located just across the boundary from teeming Kansas City and populous Platte, Clay, and Jackson Counties, Missouri. Like the Miamis, the Shawnees and Wyandots were among the more civilized of the intruded Indians and instead of being forced to move they were to be given allotments on which, it was expected by Manypenny, they might settle down and become self-supporting farmers.

Eight months after the adoption of the Kansas-Nebraska

Treaty Made With the Six Nations of New York Indians, January 15, 1838, by Charles and William King, n.d., n.p., *House Reports,* 50 Cong., 1 Sess., I, no. 15, 1–7.

[41] The award called for the payment of $1,967,056. 170 *U.S.,* 1, 614 and 173 *U.S.* 464. The two cases were decided on April 11, 1898 and March 20, 1899.

Act a treaty was negotiated with the Wyandots which provided for the allotment of their valuable and much sought-after reserve of 25,000 acres among the 554 members of the tribe. Competent Indians were to receive an "absolute and unconditional grant in fee-simple" while "those not so competent" were to be given patents to their allotments which should expressly reserve the right of alienation for five years; thereafter these allotments could be sold only with the approval of the President. Exemption of all these allotments from taxation was assured for five years after Kansas became a state, or, as events fell out, until 1866, unless the Federal Government authorized their taxation before.

It was not until April 13, 1859, that the Wyandot allotments were surveyed, assigned, and approved by the government.[42] The squatters who rushed upon the allotments and made their claims were in conflict on the one hand with Indians attempting to defend their rights and on the other with speculators who bought or otherwise acquired rights to or liens on the lands. The confusion was compounded by individual Indians who sold their land to more than one party, by the transfer of "competent" Indians to the "incompetent" list, by the insistence of municipalities that tax exemption applied only to state and county taxes, and by the persistence of the state in taxing the lands well before 1866. All interested parties, including the tax authorities and settlers living in the neighborhood of the allotments, were greatly annoyed and harassed by the long-lasting conflicts that developed over ownership and taxation.[43]

[42] The Wyandot allotments and those of the Shawnees in Wyandotte County are shown on maps in Kansas State Historical Society, *Collections,* XV, 103 ff.

[43] Abelard Guthrie, Quindaro, May 26, 1859, to Commissioner of Indian Affairs, Indian Affairs, National Archives; Guthrie, Quindaro, Dec. 3, 1864, to Wm. P. Dole, Pratt MSS., Kansas State Historical Society; Alfred Gray, Quindaro, March 10, 1859, to Chas. Farley, Alfred Gray Letter Book, 1857–65, *loc. cit.; Kansas Laws,* 1861,

There is little evidence that the 1861 order of the Commissioner of Indian Affairs, establishing the procedure for alienating allotments of both competent and incompetent Indians, aided materially in clarifying the numerous issues that kept the allotments of the Wyandot and other Indians in a state of chronic confusion over many years.[44]

Before the Kansas territory was opened to settlement the Shawnee Indians concluded with the United States a treaty wherein they surrendered title to a tract of 1,600,000 acres that fronted twenty-five miles on the Missouri border and extended 120 miles westward. The United States agreed to withhold the eastern 419,713 acres until the Shawnees had selected allotments of 200 acres for every member of the tribe. For four or five years the diminished reserve was legally barred to settlers and land speculators, despite its location in the heart of eastern Kansas. After the tract was surveyed, some 690 Shawnees located their allotments, amounting to 138,146 acres in almost solid array in the timbered lands along the Kansas River and its minor tributaries. At the same time the Black Bob band, preferring to hold their land in common, selected a small reserve of 33,392 acres adjacent to the Missouri border; this land was to be a center of conflict among Indians and whites for a generation thereafter. In addition, 24,138 acres were set aside for absentee Shawnees, most of which would be sold in 1869 and 1870 at $2.50 an acre. Finally, 4,488 acres were allotted to chiefs, presumably because they had approved the treaty of cession or assigned to missionary organizations.[45] Three sections or 1,908

p. 165; Commissioner of Indian Affairs, *Annual Report,* 1866, 19, 53.

[44] "Rules and regulations to be observed in the execution of conveyances of lands which have been or shall be assigned in severalty to Indians within the Territory of Kansas. . . ." approved on May 27, 1861. *Sen. Ex. Doc.,* 37 Cong., 2 Sess., I, no. 1, 676–677.

[45] Map showing Shawnee Reserve and Allotments, Division of

acres of the land thus allotted fell into the hands of Thomas Johnson, Superintendent of the Shawnee Manual Labor School, and influential proslavery Democrat.[46]

Even before the Indian allotments were selected, John W. Geary, Governor of Kansas Territory, reported a plan under way in Westport, Missouri, for 1,000 men to invade the reserve and make claims on the land.[47] The expected rush followed, and by March, 1857, a reporter for the *Missouri Democrat* estimated the number of claims at 2,700. Many claims were identified only by a foundation of four logs, or stakes; others had no stakes or other identifying marks.[48] When actual settlers tried to find land here, they refused to concede that absentee ownership of claims conformed to the frontier code, and jumped those without marks or which showed no sign of settlement. Bitter strife followed, though no legal rights to settle had yet been gained by anybody, for it was not until July 9, 1858, that the unallotted and unreserved land, amounting to 219,713 acres, was opened to pre-emption.[49] Subsequently 83 settlers living on the land of the Absentee Shawnees petitioned the government for their lands, stating that they had made improvements, erected

---

Maps and Charts, National Archives; Abstracts of Cash Entries, Topeka Land Office, 1869–70, General Land Office Records, National Archives.

[46] Martha B. Caldwell, *Annals of Shawnee Methodist Mission and Indian Manual Labor School* (Topeka, 1939), pp. 95, 107, 118, 120.

[47] John W. Geary, Leavenworth, Dec. 22, 1856, to Franklin Pierce, *American Historical Review* (Oct., 1904), X, 126.

[48] *Missouri Democrat* in *National Intelligencer,* March 23, 1857; *The National Era* (Washington, D.C.), April 16, 1857. For a petition of 122 settlers on the Shawnee lands asking for pre-emption see *Sen. Ex. Doc.,* 35 Cong., 1 Sess., I, no. 8, 59–60. The settlers claimed to have erected dwellings and to be *bona-fide* occupants.

[49] A. Arnold, Indian Agent, Washington, D.C., March 23, 1857, to Geo. W. Manypenny, Indian Affairs, National Archives; 16 *Wallace,* (Washington, 1873), 439.

houses, and opened up large farms. They also complained of party strife and sought to assure the officials that they were on the right side.[50]

The allotments, the lands withheld for Absentee Shawnees, and the Black Bob reserve were all overrun by claim makers and squatters, and the Indian owners were rudely thrust aside. When the allottees protested and attempted to secure legal redress, they were scorned by whites who demanded to see their patents; but the patents had not been forthcoming, either to competent or incompetent Indians. Having no evidence of title that would stand in the "ticky courts" of the territory, the allottees looked to the Indian agents for aid, only to find them "better Judges of Brandy than their duty." [51] Indian deeds, tax titles, judgment titles, settlement rights, and other liens all produced an almost impenetrable maze that kept ownership in litigation for years. Taxes on the allotments were assessed and collected from 1860 to 1867 but were later invalidated and ordered refunded by the United States Supreme Court. Whether this decision applied to probate sales and other judgment titles remained for further litigation.[52] The law was thus declared, but the court by its action did little to bring order out of the chaotic situation. Confusion caused by a welter of conflicting claims was worst of all on the Black Bob tract which remained a center of controversy and bickering between In-

[50] Petition of eighty-three settlers on the land of the Absentee Shawnees, Jan. 14, 1859, to Secretary of Interior, Indian Affairs, National Archives.

[51] Samuel M. Comatzer, Council Creek, Shawnee, Johnson County, July 8, 1858, to Jacob Thompson, Indian Affairs, National Archives.

[52] C. A. Colton, Indian Agent, Osage River, May 15, 1867, to Thomas Murphy, Superintendent of Indian Affairs; and Thomas Murphy, Atchison, Kansas, June 7, 1867, to N. G. Taylor, *loc. cit.* Reimbursement was provided by the Kansas statute of March 6, 1873, in *Laws of Kansas,* 1873 (Topeka, 1873), p. 220.

dians, speculators, creditors, settlers, and various other title claimants for the remainder of the century.[53]

Another tract of allotments which from the first opening of the Kansas territory attracted the cupidity of speculators because of its location was that assigned to half-breed children of the Kansas tribe under a treaty of 1825. To twenty-three half-breeds were assigned 640-acre allotments extending for twenty-three miles on the north bank of the Kansas River from a point above present Topeka to a few miles below Lecompton.[54] Being well-wooded lands in a region largely devoid of timber, they were valuable and therefore in demand at the outset. But as on the New York Indian tract and the Miami tract, the lack of survey lines and the ill-defined character of land ownership produced much confusion, uncertainty, and bitter rivalry for control of the Kansas half-breed allotments. Territorial officials (including Governor Andrew H. Reeder, Judges Rush Elmore and Saun-

[53] *Sen. Ex. Doc.,* 35 Cong., 1 Sess., no. 8, pp. 59–60 and no. 11, pp. 457–458; *Missouri Democrat* quoted in *National Intelligencer,* March 23, 1857; *The National Era,* April 16, 1857; Lecompton *Kansas National Democrat,* April 1, 1858; *Olathe Mirror,* Feb. 20, 1868, June 13, 1872; *Fort Scott Monitor,* March 31, 1870; A. T. Andreas, *History of the State of Kansas* (Chicago, 1883), p. 625.

Miss Abell traces the long continued struggle between the settlers, the Indian patentees, and speculators who had bought the Indian rights, and emphasizes the political significance of the issue. "Indian Reservations in Kansas and the Extinguishment of Their Title," Kansas State Historical Society, *Transactions,* VIII, 93–97. Not to be overlooked is the account of the way the settlers were able to finance their purchases of the Black Bob allotments from speculators in 1884. Allan G. Bogue, "Farm Land Credit in Kansas and Nebraska, 1854–1900," doctoral dissertation, Cornell University Library, p. 255 ff.

[54] The twenty-three section allotments are located on a map in the Commissioner of the General Land Office, *Annual Report,* 1860. They were too small to be shown in the map on p. 23.

ders W. Johnston, District Attorney Andrew J. Isaacs and antislavery leaders Charles Robinson, Thomas Ewing, and Samuel C. Pomeroy) sought to buy one or more of these half-breed tracts; and two companies made offers of $5 and $6 an acre respectively for the twenty-three sections. In October, 1854, Reeder, Elmore, Johnston, and Isaacs negotiated with the owners of four tracts for the purchase of 2,300 acres at $2.50 an acre.[55] Numerous deals were made with the half-breeds but were disavowed by the government, though only after great difficulty in which Manypenny's rigid stand against greedy Kansas officials brought him increasing political disfavor and angry attacks. Squatters inevitably found their way to these lands; at one time it was reported that there were sixty or seventy dwelling on the sections. John Montgomery, agent to the Indians in this area, after ordering squatters to leave the allotments, called out a contingent of the army to evict them and destroy their huts, on the ground that they were violating the Intercourse Act by intruding upon the reserves, driving off the Indians, and cutting down their timber. In retaliation he was arrested for arson and threatened with tarring and feathering; and some of the Indians he was trying to protect were brutally assaulted.[56] Later efforts of the agents to remove the squatters were as unsuccessful as the first, for the squatters simply

[55] George W. Clarke, Indian agent, Pottawatomie and Kansas Agency, Nov. 7, 1854, to A. Cumming, Superintendent of Indian Affairs, St. Louis, *House Ex. Doc.,* 33 Cong., 2 Sess., V, no. 50, 51–52; copy of letter of R. McClelland, Secretary of Interior, to A. H. Reeder, July 30, 1855, formerly in Land Files, Indian Office, now presumably in National Archives. Other material on efforts to buy the half-breed tracts is in the Emigrant Aid Company papers in Kansas State Historical Society and there are numerous transactions recorded in the conveyance records in Jefferson County.

[56] John Montgomery, Indian Agent, Lecompton, June 30, 1856, to A. Cumming, Superintendent of Indian Affairs, Indian Affairs, National Archives.

withdrew into the adjoining Delaware reserve until it was safe to return to the half-breed tracts.[57] Attorney General Isaacs and Governor Geary actually prosecuted the Indian agent for his efforts to protect Indians rights.[58]

Government policy toward these half-breed allotments well illustrates the confusion and vacillation that so greatly complicated the settlement and title situation in Kansas. Manypenny and the Indian Office tried to protect the rights of the Indians by keeping off squatters and refusing to recognize any sales of the tracts. Territorial officials and the United States Attorney General, on the other hand, maintained that the title in the half-breeds was absolute and alienable.[59] Meantime, squatters and rival groups of speculators fought among themselves and against the Indians to establish rights on these choice tracts. One speculator-trader who himself bought the Butler allotment for $640 (allowing the Indians to draw for $200 in goods which are listed in the request for patent, and giving two notes for the remainder), complained bitterly to the Indian Office of the "squatters," "land pirates," and "freebooters" who were "encouraged in their stealing propensities by the dirty popular sovereignty demagogues of the day. . . ." Never, he held, was there "such barefaced robbery" as was being committed by these squatters.[60] Robert S. Stevens, who claimed to be the representative of the half-breeds, though it is probable that he was acting for a group of speculators which claimed some rights derived from purchases, similarly denounced the squatters and demanded that the Indians should be given the full right to their tracts,

[57] *House Ex. Doc.*, 35 Cong., 1 Sess., I, no. 1, 679–682; *Sen. Ex. Doc.*, 35 Cong., 1 Sess., VI, no. 17, 84–86. Geo. W. Clarke to B. F. Robinson, Aug. 6, 1856, Pratt MSS., Kansas State Historical Society.

[58] *Kansas Weekly Herald*, May 23, 1857.

[59] Lecompton, *Kansas National Democrat*, Nov. 12, 1857.

[60] Geo. W. Ewing, Westport, Missouri, Oct. 21, 1858, to Charles E. Mix, W. G. & G. W. Ewing MSS., Indiana State Library.

including the right to sell them.⁶¹ At the same time officials of the Indian Office received a number of petitions from the squatters asking for the right to purchase their claims and urging protection against the speculators who were trying to acquire control of the tracts without giving adequate compensation to the Indians for their land or to the squatters for their improvements.⁶²

After numerous sales and resales of Indian rights, after the establishment of 46 squatters on twelve sections and "a large number of settlers" on three other sections—after, indeed, the sudden appearance on still another section of the town of Rising Sun with 30 or 40 houses and two sawmills—Congress authorized two successive investigations into the status of the Kansas half-breed allotments.⁶³ At the first of these, conducted by Hugh S. Walsh, the squatters and Stevens sought to bar each other from the hearings, each on the ground that the other party had no valid rights to be heard.⁶⁴ As a result of the first investigation Congress disallowed all conveyances made by the half-breeds, vested full rights of ownership in the heirs of deceased half-breeds, and authorized the Secretary of the Interior to sell the allotments on request of the owners or of the Kansas tribe.⁶⁵

This Congressional action satisfied no one. The squatters had no reason to trust their case to the Indian Office, which might be expected to sell to favored individuals; earlier buyers of allotments thought the Act of 1860 was legalized

⁶¹ R. S. Stevens, Lecompton, Aug. 24, 1860, to C. E. Mix, Commissioner, Indian Affairs, National Archives.
⁶² A number of such petitions for the years 1857–1860, are in Indian Affairs, National Archives.
⁶³ *Sen. Ex. Doc.*, 37 Cong., 2 Sess., V, no. 58. The second report by William H. Coombs provides information concerning the squatters on the lands.
⁶⁴ Stevens, Aug. 24, 1860, to Mix, Indian Affairs, National Archives.
⁶⁵ Act of May 26, 1860, 12 *Stat.*, 21.

plunder; and the Indians were dissatisfied with the continued confusion. Two years later Congress made matters worse by withdrawing from the Secretary of the Interior the authority to sell the allotments of reservees or their heirs on their request, but seemingly left in the hands of the half-breeds the

NOTICE
TO INTRUDERS
ON THE
KANSAS INDIAN
RESERVATION.

All persons who have made, and those

attempting to make settlements, or otherwise intruding within the limits of the Reservation of the Kansas Indians in the Territory of Kansas, are hereby publicly notified that they must abandon all such Settlements, and attempts to settle, or otherwise to intrude, thereon and retire from said Reservation within twenty days from the date hereof; in default of which the undersigned will, as he has been authorized to do by the direction of the President of the United States, call to his aid the Military to expel all such persons from said Kansas Reservation.

JOHN MONTGOMERY, U. S. Agent.

Agency for Kansas Indians,
October 49, 1859.6

A government broadside designed to protect an Indian reservation. (Courtesy, National Archives)

right of direct sale.[66] Meantime, suits for ejectment, first brought against the squatters by alleged owners of some of the allotments in 1858, had been won in the Jefferson County Court; but the threats of the squatters so intimidated the officers of the law that they dared not carry out court orders. Judgments were secured against the squatters but they like-

[66] Act of July 17, 1862, 12 *Stat.*, 628.

wise were made of no effect. Taxes on the allotments became increasingly heavy, tax titles were issued and passed into squatters' hands, and the heavy costs of redemption and of carrying on the seemingly interminable litigation led to compromises between the purchasers and the squatters.[67]

A further complicating feature of the Kansas land maze was the existence of the Wyandot floats which could be used in the same way as land scrip. In an 1842 treaty with the Wyandots, 35 members of the tribe had each been given a right to acquire 640 acres of public land in what was to become Kansas. When the floats were made assignable in 1855 they came into great demand, and frantic efforts were made to secure them as a way of entering full sections for those town sites in the promotion of which it seemed most influential Kansans were engaged. The floats did not take precedence over pre-emptions, nor could their owners dispossess squatters, but owners had the advantage of being able to secure title to public lands before pre-emptors or cash buyers could complete the purchase of their claims. Representatives of an association of squatters on the Shawnee lands were alarmed at the activities of speculators owning floats; they particularly disliked Joel Garrett who was described as "an insolent purse-proud aristocrat as rich as Croesus. . . ." The squatters urged the government to protect them at the same time that they threatened drastic action if settlers lost their claims.[68] For a time the only legal way in which outright title could be secured to any land in Kansas was through the use of floats. The first transfer of a float was made the day after the treaty providing for their assignability was

[67] Letters of Thomas B. Sykes, T. A. Hurd, Hugh S. Walsh, H. W. Jones, Wilson Shannon, and M. Sweetser to Geo. W. Ewing, 1858–1864, W. G. & G. W. Ewing Papers, Indiana State Library, throw much light on the thorny problem of the half-breed allotments.

[68] Levi Clarke, Johnson County, Kansas, Sept. 5, 1857 to James Buchanan, Indian Affairs, National Archives.

ratified, the price being $800. Two other sales in 1855 were for $800 and $1,000. One cannot be sure, however, that the Indians holders actually received these sums.[69] In 1859 Wyandot floats were reported to be worth from $1,500 to $2,000.[70]

The Manypenny treaties had not only left a maze of Indian rights in land that assured confusion, bickering and conflict between "straw" and actual claimants, speculators, and Indians; they were also responsible for a vast deal of litigation and dispute concerning the question of local or county jurisdiction over trust lands, allotments, and diminished reserves, as well as concerning the exemption of allotments from liability to levy, sale, execution, forfeiture, and taxation. Judgments were continually being secured against Indian allotments, titles became encumbered, sales were held, and new ownerships established—and this whole process further complicated an already impossible situation. Further-

[69] The location of the 35 floats, the date of filing the entry and the names of the persons making the locations may be seen in *Annual Report,* Secretary of the Interior, 1857, *Sen. Ex. Doc.,* 35 Cong., 1 Sess., I, no. 11, 274–275. Seven floats were located in the name of Charles B. Garrett, two were located by Samuel C. Pomeroy on present Manhattan, and others were located by C. K. Holliday, Johnston Lykins and Benjamin F. Stringfellow on present Topeka, Lawrence, and Atchison.

[70] Johnston Lykins bought the Reed Float on February 21, 1855, for $800; William H. R. Lykins bought the Robertaile Float on March 24, 1855, for $1,000. Both these floats were used to acquire the site of Lawrence. George W. Ewing, perhaps the most persistent, the shrewdest, and the least moral of traders dealing in Indian lands bought the Clarke Float for $800. Douglas County Deeds, A:24, 47; G. W. Ewing to Major Richardson, Aug. 4, 1855, in W. G. & G. W. Ewing Papers, Indiana State Library. Samuel C. Pomeroy bought the Silas Armstrong Float for $1,000 on October 5, 1855. Pomeroy to A. A. Lawrence, October 5, 1855, Kansas State Historical Society; Thomas Ewing, Jr., (no relation to the Indianapolis Ewings) Leavenworth, March 14, 1859, Ewing Letter Book, Ewing MSS., Kansas State Historical Society.

45

more, the problem of inherited allotments did not ease the question. As a result properties were held or claimed simultaneously by Indian allottees, purchasers who had Indian deeds, holders of tax, foreclosure, or other judgment titles, and by settlers claiming squatters' rights.[71]

The Wyandotte constitution on which Kansas entered the Union in no way improved the status of Indian allotments for it avoided all the questions. The legislature, in the absence of any restrictions on its authority, proceeded to tax the allotments and to require the Indians to perform road work and all other duties of citizens.[72] The state court appointed administrators of deceased orphans, and incompetent Indians sold their allotments, ostensibly to pay debts. When the counties sold the allotments at tax sales, state courts sustained the action. By 1866 the Indian Office reported that much of the Shawnee and Wyandot allotments had been sold to whites for taxes and debts. Contrary to a specific prohibition against taxing the Wyandot allotments until five years after statehood, the land had been taxed since 1860 and sold for taxes almost yearly. Similarly, the Kaskaskia group "suffered greatly from the troublesome tax question which vexes and harasses so many of the Kansas tribes." [73] In 1867 the United States Supreme Court reversed the action of the state courts in holding that allotments were taxable, but the

[71] Benjamin F. Robinson, Delaware agent, tells of efforts (which he frustrated) by representatives of Leavenworth County to levy taxes and execute writs on the Delaware reserve. *House Ex. Doc.*, 35 Cong., 2 Sess., I, no. 2, 462. See also *Kansas Reports* (Leavenworth, 1866), III, 361; Abelard Guthrie, Quindaro, Dec. 3, 1864, to Wm. P. Dole, Pratt MSS., Kansas State Historical Society.

[72] J. W. Whitfield, Kickapoo, Nov. 25, 1859, to W. H. English, English MSS., Indiana Historical Society.

[73] Letter of principal chiefs of the Wyandot nation, Wyandot, Oct. 17, 1865, to John G. Pratt, U.S. Indian agent, Pratt MSS., Kansas State Historical Society; Indian Office, *Annual Report,* 1866, pp. 19, 245–246.

victory of the Indians was pyrrhic for their titles were so encumbered with liens, and the Indians had so little hope of holding their tracts that many had given up the struggle and gone elsewhere.[74]

[74] *Miami County Republican,* May 11, 1867. The cases were Blue Jacket *et al* vs. Commissioners of Johnson County and Yellow Beaver *et al* vs. Miami County. For a later discussion of allotments in Kansas see "Allotments of Lands in Severalty Among Indian Tribes," *House Misc. Doc.,* 47 Cong., 2 Sess., I, no. 18, *passim.*

CHAPTER II

Sale of the Trust Lands

NO GREATER blunder has been made by Congress than the one it committed in opening Kansas Territory to settlement on May 30, 1854, before removing the Indians or concentrating them in small carefully surveyed reserves and without clearly establishing the rights of settlers on trust lands and of Indians on diminished reserves. But, to aggravate the situation, Congress did not authorize the survey of the public lands until July 22, the first contract was not let until November 2, and the first plats were not forwarded to the office until January 12, 1855. Six months after the territory was opened to settlement, officials of the General Land Office wrote to a prospective settler that not an acre of land was subject to pre-emption or cash purchase, and warned that no private purchase of Indian rights or allotments was valid without approval by the President.[1]

On November 22, John Calhoun, Surveyor General for the territory, was instructed to survey the Kickapoo cession,

[1] Memorandum on letter of Vincent M. Bate, New York City, Nov. 22, 1854, to Secretary of Interior, Indian Affairs, National Archives.

which, with that of the Sac and Fox of Missouri, constituted the only part of eastern Kansas on which squatting was legal. The trust lands of the Iowas, Delawares, and of the Confederated Peorias, Kaskaskias, Weas, and Piankeshaws were also ordered surveyed.[2] After surveying had been under way for some time, it was discovered that an "enormous error" necessitated setting aside the work then accomplished, erasure of the corners, and running new lines. Slowness in commencing the survey, extensive illness among the crews, incompetent surveyors, and blundering administration so retarded progress that a year and a half after the territory was opened to settlement it was not possible to report that a single township had been completed.[3]

By October, 1856, however, nearly 3,000,000 acres had been surveyed and the plats submitted to the Washington office; but delay in examining them, setting up the local land offices, and advertising land for sale prevented an early public offering. The following year the surveyor general for Kansas and Nebraska reported the acreage of land surveyed had doubled, but still there was no sale of public land.[4] Despite this progress, surveys were still far behind settlers' needs, for the concentration of Indian lands in eastern Kansas had sent land-seekers far into the interior after good claims. The surveyors' progress had, however, established the corners and boundary lines of many thousands of potential quarter-section farms—18,750 at least by October 20, 1856.[5]

[2] John Wilson, Commissioner of the General Land Office, Washington, Nov. 22, 1854, to John Calhoun, *loc. cit.*

[3] Report of John Calhoun, November 8, 1855, in *Annual Report, Secretary of the Interior,* 1855, *House Ex. Doc.,* 34 Cong., 1 Sess., I, no. 1, 308–315.

[4] *Annual Report,* Secretary of the Interior, 1856, *House Ex. Doc.,* 34 Cong., 3 Sess., I, no. 1, 526; *Annual Report,* Secretary of the Interior, 1857, *Sen. Ex. Doc.,* 35 Cong., 1 Sess., I, no. 11, 262 ff.

[5] Interior, *Annual Report,* 1856, *House Ex. Doc.,* 34 Cong., 3 Sess., I, no. 1, 526.

To make the situation in Kansas more acute, the opening of the territory coincided with the longest and most active period of land speculation in the history of public-land disposal. The outpouring of California gold, the Crimean War, the demand for American wheat abroad, high commodity prices, huge immigration, and the rush of people to take up government land all contributed to a rapid rise in land values everywhere in the West. Stories of high profits being made by investors fed the boom and led to a rush of capital into western land. Speculators petty and large from all parts of the country, North as well as South, either personally or through the many western land agents, sought to acquire wild land wherever it was available at government prices. The rapid exhaustion of public lands in Illinois and the enormous entries of land in Iowa did not satisfy those who sought fortunes through land speculation, and with the opening of Kansas territory many rushed to acquire rights there. It is easy to concentrate upon the larger operators in land for they drew the hostile attention of local anti-monopolists and opponents of absentee ownership and were the object of bitter attack. Their advertisements appear in the local papers and their business records have been left in abundance for study and analysis by historians. The small investors in land, who were seeking one to three quarter-sections, even a full section on the frontier, are all-pervasive, but their activities cannot be traced through individual collections as easily.

Among the investors anxiously looking for opportunities of acquiring extensive lands in Kansas during the territorial period were William W. Corcoran, Elisha Riggs, and Charles W. Pairo, all Washington bankers; James S. Easley and William W. Willingham of Halifax County, Virginia, who ranked among the heaviest investors in western lands; the children of Thomas Ewing, Whig Secretary of the Interior in Taylor's cabinet; William H. Russell of the great trucking firm of Russell, Waddell, and Majors; New England capitalists organized in the Kansas Land Trust; [6] and Jefferson Buford, notorious for his bushwhacking raids in the territory. Thomas Ewing's family investments came to $11,300; those of Corcoran to $9,000; the New England Emigrant Aid Company invested $64,029 in town and city property and in the construction of buildings; Heedleback, Seasongood & Co., of Cincinnati invested $20,000; and Buford invested $10,000 in land.[7]

Corcoran, Riggs, and Pairo, the Ewings, and Easley and Willingham not only sought to anticipate future settlers' needs by cornering as much of the good land as their funds permitted; they also planned to make loans to settlers pioneering on their claims who could not otherwise raise the funds with which to pre-empt them. By the middle-fifties the business of lending money to credit-shy squatters (who had to pre-empt before the auction or chance the loss of all their labor on their claims) had reached high proportions in the

[6] Thomas H. Webb of the New England Emigrant Aid Company tried to raise money for investment in the Delaware lands in the fall of 1856. He was bothered by rumors that William H. Russell and other Missourians were planning to buy largely and expressed the wish to have $300,000 for investment in the lands, partly for profit which he was assured would come, and partly to keep the lands out of the hands of proslavery folk. Thomas H. Webb, Boston, Oct. 7, 1856, to Dr. Charles Robinson, and Webb, Oct. 11, 1856, to Wm. Willis, Portland, New England Emigrant Aid Co. Letter Book, 1856–1857, Kansas State Historical Society.

[7] Compiled from the abstracts of sales of the trust lands, National Archives, and W. W. Corcoran, Oct. 27, 1856 and Jan. 8, 1856, to Major George Deas, Leavenworth, Corcoran MSS., Library of Congress; Thomas Ewing, Lancaster, Ohio, Jan. 1, 1857, to Charles Ewing, Ewing MSS., Kansas State Historical Society; William H. Carruth, "New England in Kansas," *New England Magazine* (March, 1897), new series, III, 21; Samuel A. Johnson, "The Genesis of the New England Emigrant Aid Company," *New England Quarterly* (Jan., 1930), III, 95–122; Kansas *Weekly Herald* (Leavenworth), Dec. 13, 1856.

West. Interest rates ranged from 20 to 120 per cent, the common rate probably averaging close to 40 per cent. This trade promised as good return as land speculation and with as good security.

The first objective of most people who went to Kansas in the territorial days was to secure land-claims which might be sold profitably to other claimants, actual settlers, or town builders. So preoccupied were the people with claiming land that the ordinary routine of farm making which pioneers had to go through was neglected. One who observed at first hand the process of claim making drew up his indictment then and many years later again described the business; his words provide us with a useful summary: [8]

Besides the capitalist who invests in land, on the theory that a country rapidly increasing in population, will insure greatly enhanced value to land, we have another class of speculators. They are not capitalists, for their chief stock in trade is precedents. They are not "actual settlers," but they are middlemen, who go between the government and the actual settler who really, in good earnest, improves and cultivates the soil. They have been called "squatters." They are really dealers in that vague commodity— "inchoate titles." They do not squat for the purpose of making a home, but for selling claims. With them an affidavit is a mere form. They calculate to sell without preempting, partly because they rarely have money, and partly because it might interfere with their business in future transactions. If they do preempt at all, it is to close a sale, the terms of which are already made, and they move off to a new field to renew their operations. In the early settlement of Kansas, one armed company of thirty-two men took every timbered claim on a valuable stream that ran through three counties. They laid foundations of four logs, marked the trees on the claims, and had squatter organizations in each township. They hovered over them to and fro, occasionally building a rough cabin or plowing a few furrows, but their chief business was to find

[8] William A. Phillips, *Labor, Land and Law. A Search for the Missing Wealth of the Working Poor* (New York, 1886), pp. 340–341.

customers. The revolver and bowie-knife were the certificates of title. There was an unwritten legal fiction between them, however, that has entered largely into the pioneer land system of the United States: it is the doctrine that when a man discovers a tract of land that no other man has appropriated, he acquires a certain kind of right to it, acquired to the exclusion of all other persons in the United States. He acquires a right in it altogether independent of the question whether he intends to make a home of it; acquires it without the slightest reference to its ultimate and permanent improvement.

The same writer, describing the first group of Missourians who rushed across the line from Westport to establish claims, wrote: "Scarcely a merchant or storekeeper's clerk—in fact, scarcely any one about Westport and Independence—but had a 'claim staked out' . . . [which] rest on a bowie-knife-and-revolver basis. . . ." [9] Few of these Missourians were slaveholders, one may judge, since only 3 per cent of the population of the border counties held slaves.[10] They gave support to the movement to make Kansas a slave state, but their concern about land speculation in a small way was probably just as important in their minds, perhaps more so. Martha B. Caldwell found that only 41 per cent of the squatters who in 1854 registered their claims with the squatter association of the Whitehead District in Doniphan County were living in the area three years later.[11]

Professor James C. Malin makes the interesting point that the Missourians who early established their claims on the eastern front of Kansas sought out the timber and coal

[9] William A. Phillips, *The Conquest of Kansas by Missouri and Her Allies* (Boston, 1856), p. 14.

[10] Computed from *Eighth Census of the United States,* Vol. *Population* (Washington, 1864), pp. 274–277, and Vol. *Agriculture* (Washington, 1864), pp. 233–234.

[11] Martha B. Caldwell, "Records of the Squatter Association of Whitehead District, Doniphan County," *Kansas Historical Quarterly* (Feb., 1944), XIII, 22.

lands, command of which might make it possible for them "to control the territory." [12] There can be little question that the Missourians, as well as immigrants coming in from Illinois, Iowa, Kentucky, and other older states, sought out the timbered tracts close to the streams, for nowhere else before the coming of railroads and the building of roads could they get their building and fencing materials or their fuel. The most extensive timbered tracts were adjacent to the Missouri border, the first lands to which settlers came. In selecting their allotments, the Indians likewise sought out the forest-covered areas. Examination of maps showing the allotments of the Shawnees, Wyandots, Miamis, Kickapoo, Pottawatomie, Kansas half-breeds, and the Confederated Tribes (Peoria) shows that they uniformly located their allotments along the streams where the timber grew. [13]

Another transient element that joined in the rush for squatters' claims comprised the officers and enlisted men stationed at Fort Leavenworth, which was adjacent to the Delaware trust lands. By November, 1854, all the officers and many privates were said to have made claims on the Delaware lands. [14] The officers took a leading part in the claim association for the Delaware lands and in the establishment of the city of Leavenworth, though both actions were contrary to law. Claim associations, whether organized

[12] James C. Malin, "The Proslavery Background of the Kansas Struggle," *Mississippi Valley Historical Review* (Dec., 1923), X, 294, 305.

[13] Copies of maps in the Division of Maps and Charts, National Archives.

[14] B. F. Robinson, Kansas Agency, Nov. 14, 1854, to George W. Manypenny, Indian Affairs, National Archives. For details concerning squatting on the Delaware lands see "Letter from the Secretary of the Interior Transmitting Reports in reference to the carrying out of treaty stipulations with the Delaware Indians," *House Ex. Doc.,* 33 Cong., 2 Sess., V, no. 50, 110. This includes a list that purports to be names of settlers on the Delaware trust lands.

by military officers at Fort Leavenworth, non-resident Missourians, or actual squatters on the land, threatened punishment to any person so bold as to jump properly registered claims.[15] Some of the associations, in defiance of past frontier insistence that they should protect only legitimate settlers' rights, were so largely made up of non-resident Missourians that they held some of their meetings in Missouri.[16]

In the first territorial or "bogus" legislature the Missouri claim makers adopted an act "to prevent trespass on the

[15] The first squatter association was organized at Salt Creek, June 10, 1854, just 11 days after the Kansas-Nebraska Act was passed. It clearly did not consist of the usual frontiersmen, who organized to protect their claims only after substantial improvements had been made and in anticipation of the auction sale. They were non-resident Missourians who were seeking to protect their rights to land which few of them planned to improve. On June 24, July 8 and in November similar associations were organized at Whitehead, Stockbridge and Leavenworth. Constitutions of these associations are in "Report of Special Committee to Investigate the Troubles in Kansas," *House Reports*, 34 Cong., 1 Sess., II, no. 200. See the Liberty *Democratic Platform*, June 29, July 21, August 10, Sept. 7, 1854, and Lawrence, *Herald of Freedom*, Oct. 21, 1854. These settlements, if they can be called that, were partly on the Delaware and Iowa trust lands which were closed to all white use until the sale which was to be held two years later. Efforts to prevent these intrusions (in which military officers at Fort Leavenworth participated) brought Manypenny into sharp conflict with Jefferson Davis. See Manypenny's strictures on the illegal settlement in his *Annual Report*, 1854, *Sen. Ex. Doc.*, 33 Cong., 2 Sess., I, no. 1, part 1, 217.

[16] The first two meetings of the Leavenworth Association were held in Weston, Missouri, on June 23, and July 1, 1854, the third was held on July 7 on the "Tract" of the Association. (Minutes of Leavenworth Association, Miles Moore Papers, Kansas State Historical Society.) The Kickapoo Town Association at its organization meeting on Aug. 28, 1854, agreed to meet thereafter each Tuesday in Weston, Missouri. (Record Book of the Kickapoo Town Association, Kansas State Historical Society.) The White Cloud City Company directors met in St. Joseph, Missouri, Oct. 23, 1857. White Cloud *Kansas Chief*, Nov. 12, 1857.

possessions of settlers on the public lands" authorizing 320-acre claims of which 160 acres might be timber and requiring that the boundaries should be distinctly marked and that improvements to the value of $50 should be made within six months after the claim was established. The law significantly added that "occupancy by tenant shall be considered equally valid as personal residence." Another statute attempted to protect speculators' or non-residents' rights to claims by making valid in law and equity all contracts for the sale of claims; quitclaim deeds and other conveyances were hereby made as binding and effective in law as in cases where patent titles were involved.[17] In such ways did Missourians make possible speculation in claims and monopolization without settlement of large tracts. The principal interest of many Missourians who continued thereafter to interfere in Kansas affairs was to protect their interests in claims and to add to the value of those claims, but not, one may argue, to make Kansas a slave state.

Since many Missourians were primarily concerned to establish and protect their claims and did not plan to give up their residence in their home state, it was not to their advantage to maintain claims far beyond the border, as did many of the permanent settlers who followed them.[18] Instead, they turned to the Kickapoo-ceded lands, the Delaware, Confederated Peoria, and Iowa trust lands, and the Shawnee, Miami,

[17] *Statutes of Kansas Territory*, 1855, pp. 301, 711–712.

[18] Samuel R. Ralston, a strong proslavery youth who migrated from North Carolina to Independence, Missouri, established a claim in Kansas, and with 2,000 other Missourians crossed into the territory in 1854 to elect a delegate to Congress while retaining his residence in Missouri. His letters reveal more about the interests of Missourians in Kansas than much of the formal historical writing. Darrell Overdyke, "A Southern Family on the Missouri Frontier: Letters from Independence, 1843–1855," *Journal of Southern History* (May, 1951), XVII, 230–237. The letter on page 230 was doubtless written on Jan. 28, 1855, not 1854.

New York, and Cherokee reserves and allotments. Only the Kickapoo and Sac and Fox (Missouri) cessions were open to pre-emption and that only after July 22, 1854, but the Missourians were not troubled about this, assuming as they did that the Indian right would shortly be acquired and the lands brought into the public domain. To conform to the pre-emption law, claimants made a foundation of four logs or inserted marked stakes. Others did not even make distinguishable marks, but counted on the effectiveness of the claim association to protect their rights until they were ready to sell. Some built on their claims shanties or huts which they rented to other migrants or left untenanted.[19]

With claims in such unrecognizable condition, there was certain to be conflict, which followed swiftly in a generous degree. Even among the Missouri claimants there was dispute, with some contending that the claims should be held for no more than two weeks without improvements, others insisting on twenty-five or thirty days, three months or six months.[20] Practically all accounts agree that there was much dispute and bickering over claims among the Missourians, but the open warfare that followed the coming of actual settlers from Illinois and other northern states was far worse.[21]

With the area along the border already claimed by Missourians or held by Indians, the later comers had to go farther afield in their search for land. One participant in the rush for Kansas land in 1856 later recalled:

One would very naturally suppose that to have found a first class claim in Kansas in 1856 would have been a very easy matter. Nothing, on the contrary, was further from the truth. Shrewd Yankees, stray Hoosiers, and enterprising individuals of a specu-

[19] *House Ex. Doc.,* 33 Cong., 2 Sess., V, no. 50, 47.
[20] The minutes, constitutions, and bylaws of the squatter associations created by the Missourians show these differences. *House Reports,* 34 Cong., 1 Sess., II, no. 200, 950 ff.
[21] *Ibid., passim; Sen. Ex. Doc.,* 35 Cong., 1 Sess., II, no. 2, 454.

lative turn of mind, from north, east, south and west . . . were already on the ground as far west as Fort Riley . . . and in possession, in person or by proxy, every eligible location to be found.

Many people, it was said, had as many as two, three, four, or even six claims.[22]

Continued immigration in the face of this solid array of claimed and Indian land on the border coupled with a natural reluctance to move very far away from navigable rivers led to many strains on frontier custom. Long hunts for land were impossible for pioneer settlers who had little capital and needed to begin at once farming on a small scale to provide for their own and their families' needs. Huts or cabins had to be built, small prairie tracts had to be broken and planted to corn or wheat without delay. Disregard of Indian rights was traditional on the frontier, and it did no violation to settlers' ethics to intrude upon Indian lands, whether trust, allotments, or reserves. But to encroach upon squatters' claims was another thing, for that was contrary to the common law of the frontier. Now, however, immigrants began to decide that claims marked by four logs or stakes and having no occupant were not held by *bona fide* settlers. Where claims had been made for speculation and there was no one actually living on them, settlers looking for lands were willing to challenge custom and jump them.[23]

The story of this conflict over claims is basic to Kansas history. The existence of numerous absentee or non-resident claimants and the pressure of incoming population looking for land led to claim jumping on a large scale. "Border Ruffians" or immigrants from slave areas, inflamed by stories

[22] *Manhattan Beacon,* May 30, 1872.

[23] The Atchison *Squatter Sovereign,* Jan. 29 and Feb. 5, 1856, criticized the numerous claims around Atchison on which no one dwelt and the only improvements were a pole foundation or a pen about 3 by 6 feet. It spoke of the business in claims, fifteen of which had been sold by one man.

of the millions of dollars that were to be used by northern emigrant aid societies to buy up land, retaliated by seizing northern-held claims.[24] Throughout eastern Kansas, but especially south of the Kansas River, claim warfare spread until it threatened to engulf the people in chaos. The slavery issue was deeply involved in claim jumping, with the proslavery people repelling the "antis" and the antislavery people trying to drive off the "pros." Dispossession by the strong of claims by the weak was followed by operations of organized bands to put off rival claimants; then came murder, horse stealing, and pillaging, much of it being done in the name of the "higher law" or for the protection of "southern chivalry." Governor John W. Geary was well aware of the demoralizing effect which administration of the public lands was having on the fabric of society, as indicated by the following extract from a report to his superior on September 22, 1856: [25]

One of the greatest, if not *the* greatest, obstacle to overcome in the production of peace and harmony in the Territory, is the unsettled condition of the claims to the public lands. These lands are very considerably covered by settlers, many of whom have expended much labor and money in the improvement of their claims, to which, as yet, they have no legal title. These improved claims have excited the cupidity of lawless men; many of whom, under pretence of being actuated by either anti-slavery or proslavery proclivities, drive off the settlers and take possession of

[24] Russell K. Hickman describes the "Speculative Activities of the Emigrant Aid Company," in *Kansas Historical Quarterly* (Aug., 1935), IV, 235–267.

[25] John W. Geary, Governor of Kansas Territory, Lecompton, K. T., Sept. 22, 1856, to W. L. Marcy, Secretary of State, *House Ex. Doc.*, 34th Cong., 3d Sess., 1856–7, I, no. 1, p. 130. The Howard Committee Report on the Troubles in Kansas, *House Reports,* 34th Cong., 1 Sess., II, no. 200, contains the greatest amount of material relating to the Kansas troubles and the part claim disputes played in them.

their property. The persons thus driven off, having no legal title to their claims, have no redress at the hands of the law, and in many instances have patiently and quietly submitted to their wrongs, and left the country; while others, and a still greater portion have retreated to the towns, combined together, and prepared themselves to defend and maintain what they justly conceive to be their rights, by meeting violence with violence. There is an easy remedy for this great and growing evil, and this remedy consists in the immediate opening of the land office, that settlers may record their claims (and have them legally confirmed) to the public lands on which they have settled and made improvements. This done, incendiarisms will be far less frequent, and the original settlers may return with comparative safety to their homes. Hence, the opening of the land office, at the earliest possible moment, is of incalculable importance to the well-being of the Territory.

Geary feared serious trouble when the Delaware trust lands were offered for sale, for the squatters, who had made substantial improvements, would exert every effort to prevent competitive bidding.

The frequent conflicts over claims and their effect in exacerbating the feelings both of the proslavery officials of the territory who were struggling to make Kansas a slave state and of the antislavery party that questioned every action taken by the officials, are topics worthy of some exploration. As early as February 13, 1855, the *Squatter Sovereign* of Atchison said: "It is a historical fact that almost all the contentions which result in bloodshed in the settlement of a new country, have their origin in some dispute over land claims. . . ." On May 15 the same paper denounced bogus claim makers, deplored the amount of claim jumping in the vicinity, and held that actual residents should be given every protection on their claims. The White Cloud *Kansas Chief* quotes another paper as saying of claim jumping, "There is no more fruitful source of difficulty, in Kansas . . . than this. Each week adds to the list of murders in Our Territory, mostly growing out of this one thing; and there is no law to come to the rescue and settle the differences arising between parties on this point." [26] The murder of Gaius Jenkins by Jim Lane, which was the occasion for the outbreak of the Wakarusa War, followed by successive murders in Douglas, Franklin, and other counties, not to mention continued and chronic claim warfare on the Miami, New York, and Confederated Indian lands and on the public lands as much as seventy or eighty miles west of the Missouri border, all attest to the disturbing character of the claim disputes.[27]

The management of the trust lands, of the allotments and of the diminished reserves harked back to an earlier period when revenue rather than settlement was the basic concern of policy. Under the pressure of settlers and speculators the diminished reserves were whittled down to small proportions. Allotments were pressed upon the Indians, who still had little appreciation of the white man's land system, by a combination of greedy traders and speculators, thieving bureaucrats, and restless settlers; and, as soon as the lands were patented, they quickly passed out of the Indians' hands for small considerations. The trust policy and its later development, disposal by treaties with Indians, threatened for a time to displace the public-land policy in Kansas. For example, in the first year in which government-held land, whether public domain or Indian trust holdings, was available for sale, in the fiscal year 1856–1857, only 17,351 acres of the public domain were sold, but 363,270 acres were entered with

---

[26] *Kansas Chief,* July 16, 1857.
[27] Wilson Shannon, Shawnee Mission, Nov. 27, 1855, to Gen. H. I. Strickler, *House Ex. Doc.,* 34 Cong., 3 Sess., 1856–1857, I, no. 1, 54; *Kansas National Democrat* (Lecompton), May 9, 1857; *Herald of Freedom* in *Elwood Advertiser,* July 2, 1857; *Kanzas News* (Emporia), Sept. 19, Oct. 17, Dec. 19, 1857; *Kansas Chief* (White Cloud), April 22, 1858; *Fort Scott Democrat,* Aug. 25, Dec. 8, 1860.

land warrants, and 860,163 acres of trust lands were purchased.[28] During this same period numerous allotments, Indian floats, and a small reserve were being sold. Kansans generally deplored the chaotic land situation, but some of the territory's most prominent politicians were its favored beneficiaries and they supported it with new variations for a generation.

Increasingly the custom of setting aside trust lands, which were to be sold and the income invested for the benefit of the Indians, took the place of annuities or special cash grants as a way of meeting Indian obligations. The trust lands were managed by an agency having no tradition of respect for settlers' rights and claims, as had the General Land Office, and which, if it served its wards well, had to place itself squarely in opposition to settlers' interests. The Office of Indian Affairs had to resist demands for Indian removal, expel intruders from reservations and trust lands, destroy their crude improvements, prevent illicit trade and business relations between the two races, and insist on competitive bidding for lands. The Indian trust and surplus reserve lands were treated with no degree of uniformity; their sale was subject to departmental decrees rather than Congressional acts. This inconsistency opened the door to fraud and preferential treatment, against which settlers' complaints were to be directed in vain.

Three cessions in trust were included in the Manypenny treaties of 1854. A small tract of 94,450 acres in extreme northeastern Kansas was ceded by the Iowa band; a tract of 557,955 acres west of Fort Leavenworth and north of Topeka was ceded by the Delawares, who retained a diminished reserve of 318,484 acres west of the Wyandot reserve and extending along the Kansas River; and 207,758 acres south of the Shawnee diminished reserve and extending west from

[28] Compiled from *Annual Reports* of the Commissioner of the General Land Office and of the Commissioner of Indian Affairs for 1856 and 1857.

the Missouri border were ceded by the Confederated Peoria, Kaskaskia, Wea, and Piankeshaw Indians, who retained a diminished reserve of 48,277 acres for allotments.

Table 2. TRUST CESSIONS AND DIMINISHED RESERVES, 1854–1855 [29]

Tribe	Trust lands (acres)	Diminished reserves (acres)
Christian		2,571
Delawares	557,955	318,484
Iowas	94,450	14,080
Confederated Peorias	207,758	48,277
Miamis		70,631
Kickapoo		152,417
Oto & Missouri		32,000
Shawnees		419,713
Totals	860,163	1,058,173

According to rulings of the Indian Office, trust lands were to be appraised and minimum prices established for each tract before the auction; if not purchased at the auction at or above the appraised price they would then be held for $1.25 an acre. Military land warrants (then generally used to make entries after public sales because the low price for which they could be purchased made possible a substantial reduction in the cost) could not be used to acquire trust lands. Nor was pre-emption, which permitted squatters to buy before the auction at the minimum price, allowed on the trust lands. To the settlers this was the greatest hardship involved in the sale of the trust lands. In addition, the rules requiring reservations for common schools and 5 per cent

[29] Compiled from many sources, including *Reports* of the Indian Office, the General Land Office and the Department of the Interior, Royce, *op. cit.*, Abel, *op. cit.*, and checked with table in Daniel W. Wilder, *The Annals of Kansas* (Topeka, 1875), 640.

donations to the state of the net proceeds from the public lands did not apply to the trust lands. As viewed by the settlers, the trust policy was a backward step which not only made a nullity of the principle of pre-emption but revived the old efforts to prevent by military force intrusions of squatters and to exact the greatest possible income from land sales.

The diminished reserves, like the trust lands, never became a part of the public domain but were (1) gradually allotted to individual Indians, whether competent or incompetent, (2) sold on sealed bids in large tracts to insiders, (3) conveyed to land speculator or railroad groups by treaty or through direct sale by the Indian officers, or (4) appraised and sold to squatters who had long since settled on them. The ill-defined and temporary character of the diminished reserves along with their advantageous location and fertile soil made them the center of almost continuous conflict between groups and individuals struggling to acquire control of small claims or large tracts. On the Delaware, Shawnee, and Miami diminished reserves were fought many of the clashes that marred early Kansas history.

The reserves that were untouched by the treaties of 1854 and 1855 (and therefore remained closed to settlement when the hordes of land-seekers swept across the Missouri River after the opening of Kansas territory) likewise became the center of conflict between bushwhackers and jayhawkers, and between powerful economic interests aiming to acquire ownership of them. Of these the Cherokee, Pottawatomie, and Sac and Fox reserves were to be largely acquired by railroads and politicians, while most of the others were slowly to become available to farm makers through allotments and resale or division into small tracts and sale. How to protect the reserves against speculators and assure their division among squatters upon them became a major political issue in Kansas in the sixties. For all the reserves but the Osage tract and the Cherokee outlet were covered by squatters in the territorial period; and every squatter had a vote.

Table 3. RESERVES UNTOUCHED BY TREATIES OF 1854–1855

Cherokee Neutral Tract	800,000
Cherokee Strip	434,679
Chippewa	8,320
Kansas	256,000
New York	1,824,000
Ottawa	75,742
Osage	8,841,927
Pottawatomie	568,223
Quapaw	7,880
Sac and Fox	453,600
Total	13,270,371

The first public sale of land in Kansas was begun on November 17, 1856, more than two years after the opening of the territory, when the eastern portion of the Delaware trust lands were offered. There had been continued excitement and turmoil on these lands preceding the sale, and concern was expressed because the Indian Office refused to recognize squatters' rights. Raids, counter-raids, and the prevailing political unrest had made farm making and crop raising difficult and may have led some persons who were anxious to settle down upon a tract to change their plan and wait for a favorable opportunity to sell out. More upsetting was the almost hysterical scramble after Kansas lands for speculation. This was in no sense a phenomenon peculiar to the territory; but because of the unparalleled publicity given to the area by the antislavery forces in northern newspapers and also because of the rapid exhaustion of public lands in Illinois, Iowa, and southern Minnesota, there was a rush to Leavenworth of capitalists aiming to secure a share in

65

lands they thought were certain to increase rapidly in value. The Leavenworth *Kansas Weekly Herald* reported that at the opening of the sale a perfect jam of settlers, speculators, land-lookers, and visitors estimated at three to four thousand had crowded beyond capacity every hotel and boarding house. The newspaper maintained, with some exaggeration, that no less than $5,000,000 had been brought in for investment in lands or loans.[30]

Considerable funds were raised by antislavery people to invest in the trust lands with the idea of keeping them out of the hands of the proslavery forces, but most of the larger sums invested in purchases and loans were owned by people who sought profits only.[31] A correspondent of the *St. Louis Republican* observed that at the sales "no party cries have been raised, and the 'pro' and 'anti' men seem to blend harmoniously for the time, but, after the claims are secured they [sic] may, and doubtless will be some individual feuds." [32]

Manypenny had been troubled that squatters had rushed

[30] *Kansas Weekly Herald* (Leavenworth), Nov. 15, 22, 1856.

[31] The Amos Lawrence MSS. and papers of the Emigrant Aid Company in the Kansas State Historical Society provide much information concerning the plans and purchases of the Kansas Land Trust and other antislavery groups and individuals at the Leavenworth and Ozawkie sales of the trust lands. The *Herald of Freedom* (Lawrence), Nov. 29, 1856, described in some detail the early sales of the trust lands at Leavenworth. George Collamore, an antislavery man, and Thomas J. Buford, William H. Russell, and Hines, Burnham & Co. bought respectively 4, 7, 5 and 8 or 10 quarter-sections that were not claimed on the first three days. The *Herald of Freedom* reported anxiety among the proslavery men to get as much of the land as possible in order to keep it out of the hands of their opponents. One may conclude, however, that economic considerations were paramount in the purchase of land. Since settlers lacked the means to acquire their tracts they had to rely for funds upon capitalists attending the sale.

[32] Quoted in *Danville Independent* (Danville, Illinois), Dec. 18, 1856.

on the trust lands, marked out their claims, and then created claim associations to prevent competitive bidding on them. He felt that justice to the Delawares required that the lands should bring their actual values as determined by competitive bidding and not the minimum appraised price. But the concerted opposition proved too powerful for him. It consisted of squatters, many of whom were influential Missouri claim grabbers, of speculators and money lenders who acquired interests in claims before the public auction, combined with the military officers at Fort Leavenworth and the territorial officials who also had financial interests at stake. Manypenny gave way to the point of permitting the *"bona-fide* settlers" to have their lands at the appraised price, and through his agent sought to sift out the "straw claims" which were held by non-residents or capitalists who had acquired the flimsy settlers' rights. But even this was too much to achieve in the face of the interests arrayed against him. As things fell out, the squatters, speculators, and lenders were able to dominate the sales and secure the tracts they sought at their appraised price. Notwithstanding settler opposition, Manypenny succeeded in securing for the Indians the appraised price rather than the pre-emption price of $1.25.[33] For example, William H. Russell, who bought thirty-four quarter-sections had to pay from $2.20 to $4.30 an acre. Similarly Jefferson Buford paid from $2.40 to $2.95 an acre for the eleven quarters he acquired. The average price which the 209,148 acres brought at the Leavenworth sale was $2.09. This was a triumph for Manypenny, but his insistence on getting every possible penny from the land brought him into ill repute with the settlers and speculators

[33] Manypenny to Norman Eddy, Special Commissioner, Oct. 29, 1856, Pratt MSS., Kansas State Historical Society; Eddy to Manypenny, Nov. 29, 1856 and Jan. 5, 1857, Indian Office Records, National Archives. Seven quarter-sections and fractional quarters were unsold.

who together included most of the people in the territory.

Search of the deed and mortgage records of Leavenworth, Atchison, and Jefferson Counties reveals that a great deal of the land sold at Leavenworth passed quickly into the hands of speculators or was mortgaged to them on interest rates ranging from 25 to 40 per cent. The sales had done little to assure land to actual cultivators or secure a stable pattern of ownership. After the sale the *Kansas Weekly* blossomed out in numerous advertisements of land for sale; the tracts ranged in size from a quarter-section to 2,600 acres.[34]

On June 3, 1857, the second sale of trust lands in northeastern Kansas was opened at Iowa Point. Sol Miller, the territory's most scurrilous editor, wrote that every quarter had its claimant who secured his land at the appraised price; but after the sale was over, all the "settlers" left by boat for their residence elsewhere. Brown County had a big population through the sale, but after it was over and all had departed there was nothing left but deserted cabins. Money lenders and speculators here connived with claim grabbers to get control of much of the land, to the distress of those intending to remain in the community.[35]

---

[34] Substantial purchasers or persons lending a number of thousand dollars each at the Leavenworth sales were Jefferson Buford of Eufaula, Alabama; William H. Russell of the trucking firm of Russell, Waddell & Majors; Charles W. Pairo and William W. Corcoran, bankers of Washington, D.C.; and Hines & Burnham. All of the above were proslavery. Heedleback, Seasongood & Co., of Cincinnati; John R. Ford of Boyle County, Kentucky, and George W. Collamore of Boston were others. The latter was a strong antislavery man. *Kansas Weekly Herald,* Dec. 6, 13, 1856. The abstracts of cash entries in the National Archives give all the original entries but do not throw much light on those which were made in the name of squatters and immediately transferred in whole or in part to the capitalist providing the funds for purchase. These facts may be seen in the conveyance records of Leavenworth, Jefferson and Atchison Counties.

[35] White Cloud *Kansas Chief,* June 11, 1857. Substantial investments at the Iowa Point sale were made by William B. Victor of

The remaining Delaware trust lands in the western portion of the reserve, amounting to 348,810 acres, were offered at Ozawkie on July 15. Of the Ozawkie sale it was said: [36]

There was a large crowd there at the land sales, more than could be accommodated in the houses, hence many had to resort to tents. A company of dragoons were stationed there to protect the money arising from the sales. A motley crew was present, consisting of the honest squatters, speculators, sharpers, traders, etc., who were there on legitimate business. Then there were a large number of horse thieves, who tried their hand quite extensively. There were not a few gamblers present, with their banks, sweat-clothes, chuck-a-luck, and other games spread out to view.

According to the *Elwood Advertiser* [37] between 75 and 110 tents were set up to provide accommodations for the crowds that came to Ozawkie. They were occupied by the "most ill-favored gang of gamblers and horse thieves, on whom it was ever our fortune to look." Dr. Norman Eddy, commissioner to conduct the sales at Ozawkie, warned his superiors of "the various larcenies daily committed here, the Assemblage of Gamblers and other disreputable characters at this point . . ." and expressed fear that the government receipts might be in danger.[38] Eddy himself was accused of favoring "Border Ruffians" in cases where more than one person claimed the right to buy the same quarter-section.[39]

At the Ozawkie sales, as at Leavenworth and Iowa Point, claim associations functioned to protect the squatters, money lenders, and speculators, and there was little competition

---

Lexington, Kentucky; William S. Reyburn of Springfield, Ohio; Luther R. Smoot of Washington, D.C.; Omer Tousey of Lawrenceburg, Indiana; and Jefferson Buford.

[36] *Kansas Weekly Herald,* August 15, 1857.

[37] August 6, 1857.

[38] Eddy, Ozawkie, July 22, 1857, to J. W. Denver, Indian Affairs, National Archives.

[39] Emporia *Kanzas News,* August 8, 1857.

though every acre was sold. One Tennesseean loaned funds to forty-five squatters to acquire their lands, taking the title in his name but binding himself to convey title when the principal and interest at 5 per cent a month was paid.[40]

The fourth sale of trust lands was that of the confederated band of Peorias, Kaskaskias, Weas, and Piankeshaws at Paola. Like the Delaware lands, they were well-timbered. Missourians had early made claims on them but seemed to have devoted more energies to driving off others who came in looking for farm land than to erecting improvements themselves. A reporter in *The National Era* commented just before the sale began that there was no war on the tract but there was "a great deal of quarrelling and fighting which does not amount to much." [41] A free-state man who wrote of the sale criticized the "Fanatical Abolitionists" who were great trouble makers and embroiled all free-state men in difficulties.[42] When the sale was over, it was found that the transient squatters who had bought much of the land had transferred it to "land sharks." [43] In 1858 a Leavenworth land agent advertised 10,000 acres of the trust lands of the Confederated Indians and 5,000 acres of the trust lands of the Delawares and Iowas for sale.[44]

If Manypenny had failed to force competitive bidding at the sales, he had succeeded in having the appraised value of the lands established as a minimum, thereby bringing to the Indians an average of $1.84 an acre in contrast to the mere $1.25 that could have been expected from the same lands had they been public lands. Unfortunately, the $1.84 per

[40] Albert D. Richardson, *Beyond the Mississippi* (Hartford, 1869), p. 71.

[41] *The National Era* (Washington, D.C.), April 16, 1857.

[42] George A. Crawford, to Horatio King, July 13, 1857, in *Mississippi Valley Historical Review* (March, 1927), XIII, 543.

[43] *Centropolis Leader* in Emporia *Kanzas News*, August 22, 1857.

[44] *Leavenworth Daily Times*, August 11, 1858.

Table 4. KANSAS INDIAN TRUST LAND SALES, 1856–1857 [45]

Date	Place	Indians	Acres	Receipts
Nov. 17, 1856–Feb. 12, 1857	Leavenworth	Delaware	209,145	$438,982
June 3–9, 1857	Iowa Point	Iowa	94,450	184,437
June 25–July 13, 1857	Paola	Kaskaskia	207,758	346,671
July 15–Aug. 11, 1857	Ozawkie	Delaware	348,810	587,337

acre was not justified in terms of the economic progress and transportation facilities of the territory. When the panic of 1857 occurred, and immigration declined sharply, followed by the great drought of 1859 and 1860, the bottom fell out of the market. Speculators could not unload their now-unwanted wares, debtors could not carry their mortgages with interest rates of 40 to 120 per cent, and the "loan sharks" were unable to meet their taxes or to force collections. Because of the debt left by the public-land sales which are described in the next chapter, Kansas was in a deplorable condition during the last years of its territorial status.

[45] Volume, "Indian Trust Sales, Kansas, 1856–7," General Land Office, National Archives.

CHAPTER III

Public Land Sales in
the Territorial Period

PUBLIC lands in Kansas which were subject to the regularly established land laws—in contrast to the Indian trust lands, diminished reserves and allotments—were brought into market slowly as a result of the incompetence of the political charlatans handling surveys, the slowness with which Indian rights were surrendered, and the inclination of the land officers not to press the lands into the market until the people on them were ready to buy them.

The appointments by Pierce and Buchanan to positions of surveyor general and register and receiver of the public land offices were not calculated to make for efficiency, good administration, and fairness in the management of the lands.[1]

[1] Of all modern writers Allan Nevins is the most critical of the land and territorial officers in Kansas in *The Emergence of Lincoln* (2 Vols., New York, 1950).

Much of the time and energy of these officials was devoted to political activities, and their office work suffered. Furthermore, they were involved in speculative schemes, though it should be added that this was a common practice for land officials as well as territorial bureaucrats. Serious and well-substantiated complaints were directed against these officials for their neglect of official duties and for using their offices to favor Missouri non-resident claimants and pro-Democratic speculators against *bona fide* settlers and speculators not identified with the Democracy.[2]

Leadership in the land reform movement had during earlier periods been mostly in the hands of the Democratic Party with the Whig Party providing conservative opposition. After the passage of the general Pre-emption Act of 1841, the attitude of the government toward western settlers had grown increasingly benevolent. It had become the practice to survey great tracts far out on the frontier and to delay for years advertising them at public auction. Between survey and sale

[2] Emporia *Kanzas News,* Aug. 8, 1857. Sol Miller, one of the most uninhibited of the territorial editors, who belabored the Republicans almost as much as the Democrats, said in the White Cloud *Kansas Chief,* June 16, 1859: "We do not believe that nature ever spewed out a more contemptible set of politicians than Kansas and Nebraska contain. One-horse is too dignified a térm for them. They have not sufficient calibre, to make respectable demagogues." His views of the election of Lane and Pomeroy as Kansas senators are equally interesting: "But such things are not to be wondered at, after all, when we see how Kansas is overrun and cursed with one-horse politicians. Bankrupts in politics, law, medicine, theology, and rascality—who could not, at the East, obtain a respectable vote for Constable or Overseer of the Poor—come out West to become great, and to frame laws for the people. Poor devils, whose purses have for months been innocent of the sinful lucre, sell themselves and betray their trusts for enough money to buy them a clean shirt—and that money stolen from the charity box! Rather a sorry picture, but a true one. If this is a fair sample of Kansas Republicanism, an occasional dose of Democracy might be beneficial, just for a change." *Ibid.,* April 11, 1861.

73

squatters could settle upon them, erect a simple home and make such improvements as their means permitted. In effect they had the free use of the public land for a time, during which they could raise a number of crops and perhaps accumulate enough cash to buy their claims.

In the basic public-land act of Kansas of July 22, 1854, squatters were permitted to settle upon *unsurveyed* land, a privilege first extended for two years in 1853 in California and made permanent in 1854 throughout the territories of Oregon, Washington, Kansas, Nebraska, and Minnesota.[3] The statute applying to Kansas required pre-emptors to file a declaratory statement within three months after the survey "had been made in the field" and to prove up and pay for the land before it was offered at public sale.[4] The slowness with which lands were surveyed thus worked to the advantage of settlers by delaying the day when they had to pay for their land, but it made for conflicts over boundary lines and claim ownership.[5] Conflicts over claims flared up throughout east-

[3] Benjamin H. Hibbard, *History of the Public Land Policies,* p. 167, was aware that pre-emption on *unsurveyed* lands had been allowed in a number of territories but Roy M. Robbins, *Our Landed Heritage, The Public Domain,* p. 237, did not know that this privilege had been extended prior to the Homestead Act of 1862. As late as 1950 the United States Court of Claims awarded a judgment of more than $16,000,000 to an Oregon Indian group in a decision that is partly based on the erroneous assumption that pre-emption was not extended to settlers on *unsurveyed* lands till 1862. See Alcea Band of Tillamooks, Etc. v. The United States, United States Court of Claims, no. 45,230, p. 10.

[4] In contrast the statute extending pre-emption to the unsurveyed lands in Washington and Oregon provided that pre-emptors had to file within six months after the survey was "made and returned. . . ." The difference in minimum time allowed for filing the declaratory statement was of course considerably more than three months. 10 U.S. *Stat.,* pp. 308, 310. The measure applying pre-emption to unsurveyed lands in Minnesota followed the Kansas statute.

[5] A dispatch from Kansas in the *Baltimore Sun* for Dec. 8, 1856, saying "All the settlers in the country are looking anxiously for the

ern Kansas on both the trust lands and the public lands and were the basis of much of the bloodshed in the so-called Kansas Crusade. One paper said of these conflicts in 1857: "There is no more fruitful source of difficulty, in Kansas, as in all western countries, than this. Each week adds to the list of murders in our Territory, mostly growing out of this one thing; and there is no law to come to the rescue and settle the differences arising between parties on this point." [6] Claim associations undoubtedly aided materially in solving numerous arguments over claims; and, equally important, they provided an extralegal method of transferring and recording claims prior to the patenting of lands and the beginnings of official county recording. But because of their vigilante, extralegal character they easily fell prey to the Missouri nonresident claimants or to rabid abolitionists who used them for other than their established purpose.

Before the opening of the land offices and the appointment of the registers and receivers, persons planning to preempt their claims were permitted to make their filings with John Calhoun, Surveyor General for Kansas and Nebraska. By October, 1856, Calhoun reported that 3,036 declaratory statements had been filed on pre-emption claims, a substan-

---

opening of the Land Office at Lecompton, to enable them to pre-empt their lands," can be taken with a grain of salt. Undoubtedly, they wanted to file declaratory statements which would protect them and their rights until the public sale but it was a rare case on the frontier when settlers were ready and anxious to pay for their land.

[6] *Kansas Leader* in White Cloud *Kansas Chief,* July 16, 1857. For other comments on the numerous claim conflicts and the part they played in the Kansas War see the Atchison *Squatter Sovereign,* Feb. 13, May 15, 1855; White Cloud *Kansas Chief,* April 22, 1858; Emporia *Kansas News,* Sept. 19, Oct. 17, Dec. 19, 1858; Lecompton *Kansas National Democrat,* May 9, 1857; Lawrence *Herald of Freedom* in *Elwood Advertiser,* July 2, 1857; *Fort Scott Democrat,* Aug. 25, Sept. 15, Dec. 8, 1860; and Wilson Shannon, Headquarters, Shawnee Mission, Kansas Territory, Nov. 27, 1855, to Gen. H. I. Strickler, *House Ex. Doc.,* 34 Cong., 3 Sess., 1856–1857, I, no. 1, 54.

tial portion of which, one may assume, were made by bogus squatters. By the act of filing bogus as well as actual settlers gave added protection to claims which were already listed with the claim associations. But the declaratory statements were in no sense indications of improvements, permanent settlements, or even intention of settlement. Many preemptions were made for speculation and sale before the preemptor had to prove up and purchase. Because of Calhoun's neglect of duty, his carelessness and incompetence, the filings were irregularly made, duplications were permitted, and entries were accepted for land not open to pre-emption.[7] Continued mismanagement and failure to keep open the principal land office at Lecompton led Wilson Shannon, former territorial governor, to urge the "absolute necessity" for a change and the appointment of men as register and receiver who had some business capacity.[8] It was this carelessness and incompetent management of the land officers, together with the transitory character of many of the early claimants, that produced more "litigation, expense, and bad blood" than an equal number of pre-emption filings in any other land office, said a Kansas historian.[9]

The period of grace between the time of settlement and the public sale before which all pre-emptors must have made the payment on their land was so well established by 1856 that it was publicly declared as a policy by the Commissioner of the General Land Office, Thomas A. Hendricks, a Hoosier Democrat, in these words: [10]

[7] Report of Calhoun in Secretary of the Interior, *Annual Report, House Ex. Doc.*, 34 Cong., 3 Sess., I, part 1, 526–528; Albert R. Greene, "United States Land-Offices in Kansas," Kansas State Historical Society, *Transactions* (Topeka, 1904), VIII, 1–7. Greene had formerly been an employee of the General Land Office.

[8] Wilson Shannon, Lecompton, Sept. 25, 1858, to Geo. W. Clark, Indian Affairs, National Archives.

[9] Greene, *op. cit.*, p. 7.

[10] *House Ex. Doc.*, 34 Cong., 3 Sess., 1856–1857, I, part 1, 190.

In regard to the new lands in and near the valley of the Mississippi, the progress of actual settlement has been so rapid under the pre-emption system, and the propriety of dealing with this class of our citizens in the most liberal spirit so obvious, that it has not been deemed advisable to precipitate public sales of these lands . . . it is believed to be the true policy of the government to secure the public lands to actual settlers thereon, and withhold them, as far as practicable, from speculators.

In his annual message to Congress in December, 1857, Buchanan seemed to countenance and indeed support the policy of favoring settlers in the acquisition of public lands. He spoke of the importance of the public lands in "furnishing homes for a hardy and independent race of honest and industrious citizens who desire to subdue and cultivate the soil." The lands should be "administered mainly" to promote "this wise and benevolent policy." The cardinal principle should be "to reserve the public lands as much as may be for actual settlers, and this at moderate prices." [11] In his slap at speculators and his support of pre-emption he gave encouragement to Kansans who were led to think, in the words of John Everett that "the land sales would be put off till the land was all in the hands of actual settlers." [12]

In 1856, for the first time in many years, no public lands were advertised for sale by the Federal government and in 1857 only a little over a million acres were advertised, none being in Kansas. The territorial squatters had, with this period of grace, as much as two, three, or four, and even five years before they were compelled to buy their claims to prevent speculators or others from acquiring them. Unfortu-

[11] James D. Richardson, *Messages and Papers of the Presidents, 1789–1902* (1904), V, 459–460. Buchanan recapitulated the old Jacksonian position without conviction for he recommended no action that would effectively protect settlers and curb speculators.

[12] John Everett, Osawatomie, April 24, 1858, to his father, in *Kansas Historical Quarterly,* (August, 1939), VIII, 294.

nately the time lag between settlement, survey, and public sale was not clearly defined, being subject to determination by administrative officials.

The end of the benevolent treatment of squatters coincided with the panic of 1857 and the sharp business contraction that followed. At the same time the opening of the Buchanan administration brought the displacement of Robert McClelland of Michigan, Secretary of the Interior, by Jacob Thompson, a large planter and slave owner of Arkansas who has been characterized as relentless, vindictive, ambitious, calculating, a Mississippian and southerner before he was an American.[13] For the next four years the enlightened and relatively liberal land policy that had led to the benevolent treatment of squatters on the public domain, to the lowering of the price of land, to the use of cheaply priced land warrants as the principal means of entering land, and to liberal railroad and internal-improvement grants, was abandoned. In its place was substituted a policy of attempting to exact from the public lands and from the squatters upon them as much revenue as possible to aid in balancing the budget and thereby to avoid the necessity of raising the tariff. In order to implement this policy the price of newly offered land was not to be reduced or graduated, no matter how poor it might be, the period of grace was to be limited to one year, millions of acres of land were to be pushed into the market despite depression conditions and regardless of the drain of funds from the public-land area, railroad landgrants were to be denied new areas, and free homesteads were to be unalterably opposed, notwithstanding the popular clamor for them.

This return to past policy in public-land disposal has been overlooked by historians, and its significance has been neglected. The party of Jefferson, Jackson, Benton, Douglas,

[13] Roy F. Nichols, *Disruption of American Democracy* (New York, 1948), pp. 79–80.

78

and other advocates of distributing the public lands as cheaply as conditions justified in order to assure widespread ownership had gradually eliminated the pursuit of revenue as the basis of land sales. While the Democrats pursued the goal of cheap land and advocated the use of the public lands to build up the West through grants for canals, roads, railroads, schools, and colleges, they assured to themselves increasing support in the West. Now with the Democratic Party's titular leader and its machinery in the hands of southern conservatives who frowned on the rapid growth of the new and radical states of the upper Mississippi Valley, a sharp turn in land policy was inaugurated that would retard the growth of the West and make it contribute a larger share of the cost of government. Buchanan's reversal of land policy was a dangerous expedient, for it was certain to repel from the party the Upper Mississippi Valley. It contributed to the breakup of the Democratic Party in 1860, and to the election of Lincoln.

In the midst of the economic catastrophe that struck in the panic of 1857, Buchanan, like a later Republican President in a similar crisis, believed the powers of the Federal government too weak to meet the crisis effectively. Rather than recommend action to alleviate suffering, he urged that no new public works be undertaken, that Congress be sparing in making appropriations, that nothing be done to interfere with the sale of public lands at a fair price to the government, and that the tariff be adjusted upward for both revenue and protective purposes.

"The Old Public Functionary," as Buchanan's western enemies were beginning to call him, was surrounded by a horde of hungry cormorants in the form of politicians who were seeking opportunities to make money in speculative enterprises which might be benefited through his aid. The President was under heavy obligations to William W. Corcoran, the "angel" of the Democratic Party, who was reputed to have spent between $10,000 and $20,000 in its behalf in the campaign of 1856.[14] For years Corcoran had financed, and during the years 1857–1860 he was still carrying on, large business ventures, mostly in western real estate, for prominent members of the Democratic Party, including Jacob Thompson, R. M. T. Hunter, John C. Breckinridge, Robert J. Walker, and others. In return he had been granted valuable government favors that aided materially in making him and his partners Elisha and George Riggs the most successful bankers and brokers outside New York and Philadelphia.[15]

By ordering the western lands into the market, the administration could repay Corcoran for his generosity to the party and at the same time provide many of its leaders with a splendid opportunity for investing at high interest rates. Corcoran, Riggs, August Belmont, John Slidell, W. R. W. Cobb, Eli Shorter, Breckinridge, Robert W. Johnson, Sally B. Floyd, consort of the Secretary of War, and others did not let the opportunity pass.

Nor should it be forgotten that by ordering the Kansas lands into market in the midst of a depression, the administration could strike a heavy blow at people who were persistently refusing to accept the southern position on territorial policy. Indeed, as many thought at the time, the land sales were ordered in an effort to coerce the people or to strengthen the administration's bargaining position.

In the expectation of bringing additional funds into the treasury, Buchanan, Thompson, and Hendricks, who clung to his position as land commissioner but reflected western

[14] *New York Tribune*, Feb. 12, 1859. In his *Disruption of American Democracy* (New York, 1948), p. 46 and *passim* Roy Nichols has shown the part played by Corcoran in the campaign but mentions only one contribution of $1,000.

[15] Numerous letters in the Corcoran & Riggs MSS., Library of Congress, bear on the mutual favors Corcoran gave and received.

opinion in a diminishing degree, ordered into market 46,-422,583 acres in 1858, 1859, and 1860. Never before in any comparable period had such a huge volume of land been dumped on the market. Since there already were offered and available for sale 80,000,000 acres of public lands, it could not be maintained that there was any need or demand for bringing the additional acreage to sale.[16]

At least 7,966,090 acres in Kansas were ordered into market in the three critical years 1858–1860. Announcement of the sale, though made well in advance of the auction, threw the squatters into great excitement, for it required them either to raise the $200 for the purchase of their quarter-section claims or to suffer the loss of all improvements on them. Though some had been on their claims long enough to have enjoyed the benefit of at least two crops, possibly three, they had invested most of their profits, if any, in land improvements, livestock, and farm machinery, being lulled into a feeling of false security by the period of grace and the early reassuring statements of Buchanan and Thompson. Few had ready cash or credit.

Land offices were opened in 1857 for the filing of declaratory statements by pre-emptors: the first was opened at Lecompton on April 30, the second at Ogden on October 12, and the third at Doniphan on October 13.[17] Persons with means, including speculators who had bought claims, then completed their entries. Others (and by far the larger number) postponed filing until the last moment before the auction sale made action necessary.

[16] Data on public offerings are computed from the *Annual Reports,* Commissioner of the General Land Office, 1857–1860.

[17] The first pre-emption entry was that of Julius Newman on the SW section 25, town 5 south, range 20 east. The dates of the opening of the offices are from the abstracts of cash entries for the three districts, in the National Archives. *Cf.* the *Lecompton Union,* April 25, Oct. 29, 1857, for slightly different dates. The Ogden office opened in the fall of 1857, *Kansas Weekly Herald,* Oct. 17, 1857.

The first Kansas sale was announced for July, 1858, in the midst of a major depression. That the squatters could not without great difficulty raise the funds necessary to buy their claims was clear. The destructive effects of the panic of 1857, with its calamitous decline in prices of wheat and corn, combined with the draining of funds to the East and the poor crops, made the West the most depressed part of the United States; and within the West the territory of Kansas was most seriously affected.[18] One squatter from New York described the plight of himself and his fellow sufferers in May, 1858:

The great majority cannot pay now without ruinous sacrifices or more ruinous interest. We are just feeling the effect of the money crisis. It is harder times for money than it has been since we have been in the territory. Money on mortgage will be worth here from 50 to 100 per cent between now and July.

Again in August, 1858, he wrote: [19]

It is very hard times here for money now. Nothing is to be had at the stores except for money. At the same time if one has any thing to spare to neighbors it is a chance if he gets money for it. It seems as if all the money had gone to the land office. It is impossible to borrow money except at ruinous rates. I do not know any chance of borrowing money on bond and mortgage at less than 5 per cent *per month* and at that rate you would be obliged to let it run for a year. On other security money has been loaned in Lawrence as high as 15 & 20 per cent *per month*.

The West's natural and persistent opposition to the auction sale, now aggravated by the economic plight into which it

---

[18] Van Vleck, *op. cit.,* p. 83 *et seq.,* shows that the Middle West was the section most seriously affected by the panic. I base my statement about Kansas on the understanding that a larger proportion of the people of this territory were debtors and for 1859 and 1860 on the desperate situation resulting from the drought.

[19] Letters of John Everett, Osawatomie, April 24–August 12, 1858, *Kansas Historical Quarterly,* VIII, 294–300.

had fallen and the hope that a free homestead measure might be passed, induced it to make a concerted drive to secure postponement of sales.

Announcement of the public sales in Kansas strengthened antiadministration feeling in Kansas. The cry was raised that Buchanan was using the threat of public sales as a club to force the people to accept the Lecompton constitution. Having failed in that, he was taking revenge upon the territory by requiring that the sales be held.[20] Public meetings were held at which indignant resolutions were adopted condemning the President, and participants took oaths to do everything in their power to prevent speculators from buying their homes. Kansas was in the vanguard of the movement for land reform at this time, some of its leaders going so far as to favor the end of land grants to railroads as well as the abolition of sales to speculators.[21] At the same time a strong movement was under way in Congress to suspend the public sales announced for Kansas as well as other western territories and states.[22]

As a result of the outcry against sales, a number of postponements were made in 1858 and 1859. Poor crops, sickness, floods, and "the scarcity of money [that] was everywhere prevalent and paralyzing" were given as reasons for the postponement. Sales announced in Kansas for July, 1858, were put off till October, and when conditions did not improve were further postponed to July, 1859. Then, said the pompous Jacob Thompson, the "exigencies of the public treasury demanded the free offering and sale of lands. . . ." In justification of his action in ordering the lands to sale, Thompson said:[23]

[20] John R. Everett, May 20, 1858, to his sisters, *Kansas Historical Quarterly,* VIII, 297.

[21] Emporia *Kanzas News,* June 6, 1857; Atchison *Squatter Sovereign,* April 3, May 8, 1858; White Cloud *Kansas Chief,* April 8, 1858.

[22] *Cong. Globe,* 35 Cong., 1 Sess., 1857–1858, pp. 135, 324, 1703.

[23] *Annual Reports* of Jacob Thompson, Secretary of the Interior,

These requests [for postponement] could not be acceded to without interrupting the harmonious operation of the laws constituting our land system, which requires the public lands to be brought into market from time to time, in proportion as surveyed lands are disposed of and other lands surveyed.

The fact remains that previous administrations had increasingly restricted land purchases to actual settlers by limiting the amount of land offered for unrestricted entry and allowing settlers to pre-empt at their pleasure without the threat of the auction sale being held over their heads to force them to buy. Thompson's fatuous statement was simply an effort to explain away by empty rhetoric what was becoming a punitive as well as a reactionary policy.

The government's insistence on bringing the public lands into market in Kansas at a time when the welfare of settlers, already jeopardized by the depression, was in 1859 and 1860 further deteriorating as a result of the drought, brought upon Buchanan a stream of shrill invective and vituperation that has rarely been equalled in the annals of American politics. The Council Grove *Kansas Press* denounced "Old Buck," the "Old White House man," who was responsible that "Men are in rags, women and children barefooted, with starvation staring them in the face,—many of them could not raise ten dollars to save their souls from perdition." [24] The Emporia *Kansas News* said: "It does seem that the four years page of meanness, so nearly finished . . . is full enough of sin, without inflicting upon the squatters, the distress of this malicious attack upon their homes." [25] Other papers spoke

---

for 1858, 1859, and 1860, in *House Ex. Doc.,* 35 Cong., 2 Sess., II, part 1, 75; *Sen. Ex. Doc.,* 36 Cong., 1 Sess., I, no. 2, 93; *Sen. Ex. Doc.,* 36 Cong., 2 Sess., I, no. 1, 30. See also White Cloud *Kansas Chief,* May 13, Sept. 23, 1858; Atchison *Freedom's Champion,* May 15, June 12, Sept. 25, 1858.

[24] Council Grove *Kansas Press,* July 30, 1860.

[25] Emporia *Kansas News,* June 11, 1860.

of Buchanan's "fiendish malignity," his "iniquitous policy" that "has wreaked a terrible vengeance upon us for refusing the Lecompton swindle," a "tyrannical, desperate, and revolutionary power . . . that stifles the voice of an indignant and suffering people." [26] The "Democracy of to-day is bastard," said the *Elwood Free Press.*[27] At the Osawatomie convention of the Republican Party in May, 1859, it was resolved "That the President, in ordering the public lands in this and other Territories to be sold during a season of universal depression, thus impoverishing thousands of our fellow-citizens, has been guilty of an act of injustice without parallel in the history of a free Government. . . ." [28]

The *Freedom's Champion* of Atchison summed up the situation in strong but effective language: [29]

Long since, while smarting under the rejection of the English bribe and as a punishment to the people who dared denounce it, the vast body of lands comprised within the Delaware and Pawnee districts, and embracing the whole of the Eastern portion of Kansas, was by order of the President, sold at public auction, and greedily purchased by a horde of hungry speculators. Thousands of honest, hard-working farmers, who had invested their all in a few improvements, trusting to have an interim of some years between filing their declarations of settlement and the sale, and hoping in that time by industry, economy and perseverance to make enough to pay for their quarter-section, were by this act of persecution and oppression cheated out of their land, or forced to borrow money at high rates of interest, which will untimately compel them to sell it, or keep them poor for years. And now, following this outrage rapidly, is another order of sale, embracing the whole of the arable lands in the Western and Southern portion of our State. What suffering, what privation, what years of toil

[26] *Kansas News,* May 19, June 7, 1860; *Lawrence Republican,* Oct. 4, 1859; *Freedom's Champion,* July 14, 1860.
[27] June 25, July 2, Aug 28, 1859.
[28] Daniel W. Wilder, *Annals of Kansas* (Topeka, 1875), p. 203.
[29] June 23, 1860.

this new act of villainy and bad faith will entail, only those who have lived a pioneer's life in the wild west can conceive. Thousands will be rendered homeless and houseless, and left to struggle on against a hard fate and the most bitter privations; and it will be long years before Kansas will recover from the effects of this act, while many of her citizens will never rise from it.

The President was attempting, the West was convinced, to extract every possible dollar from land sales; furthermore, he was indifferent to, if not motivated by, the fact that in forcing land on the market he was playing into the hands of financiers and speculators who could take advantage of the western situation to make large profits. Nor, thought the West, did he care that forcing land upon the market could have only evil results; settlers who saved their claims would henceforth stagger under a mountain of debt and those claims which were not saved would become part of a large speculative holding—a speculator's desert—which would long retard settlement, immigration, and community development. The slave power and Buchanan, its tool, must be fought as enemies of the West with every weapon. Said Preston B. Plumb's Emporia *Kanzas News:* "We are at war with Slavery because that institution crushes labor and degrades industry." The policy of selling land was "injurious" to the West, the *News* declared, because it permitted large-scale engrossment and forced settlers to go to the loan sharks; land grants to railroads and sales to speculators should stop and a free homestead measure should be adopted.[30] Spurning the administration, the West appealed to Congress to assume control of land policy by halting all land sales and providing free homesteads.

The anguish of the Kansas Democrats at the conduct of the administration was most acute. The land-reform movement had been one of their principal issues and their greatest source of strength on the frontier. None but thorough ad-

[30] June 6, 1857.

ministration men—and they were mostly confined to appointed officers—could afford to defend Buchanan's position on land sales. At the Democratic territorial convention held in Leavenworth in November, 1858, the party "most respectfully but urgently" took issue with Buchanan by asking that all public lands be withdrawn from the market for three years during which time no sales should be permitted and that preemptors be permitted to buy their land for the cost of survey, which would be less than ten cents an acre. At Tecumseh, in May, 1859, another Democratic convention urged that sales of public land be postponed for at least a year and that a free homestead be given to every actual settler on the public lands.[31] Even proslavery Democratic organs such as the *Topeka Tribune* found it necessary to deviate from the party line by commending a free-homestead measure which, so the paper said, would end the ceaseless agitation over slavery.[32] They accused the Republicans of stealing their political thunder.[33]

At a nonpartisan railroad convention called to meet in Topeka in October, 1860, to urge that land grants be given to aid in the construction of railroads, local Democratic officials had to eschew the Buchanan and southern position on land questions. Not only did they favor land grants which the President had declared unconstitutional, but they were forced by circumstances to support unanimously a resolution that "without distinction of political opinions" urged the postponement of sales for an additional year. That Samuel Medary, who was Buchanan's final appointee as Territorial Governor of Kansas, Benjamin F. Stringfellow, Peter T.

[31] Wilder, *op. cit.*, pp. 191, 200.
[32] March 17, 31, 1860.
[33] The *Kansas National Democrat* (March 22, 1860), unlike the *Topeka Tribune,* expressed doubt concerning the constitutionality of free homesteads and maintained that they would be highly injurious to the railroad interests of the territory.

Abell, and Wilson Shannon joined in supporting this resolution shows how embarrassing was the position of the national Democratic leaders to the local following.[34]

The Democratic Party, threatened with division, loss of the presidency and also of the attendant spoils, was trying to find common ground on which to stand, and in its search it let the land question drop. Neither the Breckinridge nor the Douglas wing of the party took a stand in behalf of cheap or free land in 1860. Advocates of land reform had then to turn to the Republican Party for aid.

The move to strip from the President the power to order public-land sales came to a head in the House of Representatives on May 22, 1860, when a bill was passed to prevent any but actual settlers from acquiring public land for ten years after it was surveyed and to permit settlers a full ten years in which to raise the funds necessary for the purchase of their claims.[35] Republican leaders, fully aware of the intensity of feeling in the West, had by now taken over the leadership on the land question previously held by the Democrats. Their bill would have given the squatters on the frontier four to eight years more in which to complete the purchase of their claims. In the Senate, where administration support was stronger, no action was taken on this measure,

[34] *Freedom's Champion,* Oct. 27, 1860. It is worthy of note that Henry Barricklow who was loaning substantial sums to settlers with which to purchase their claims was a member of this convention.

[35] *Cong. Globe,* 36 Cong., 1 Sess., 1860, III, 2252–53. Bills to postpone or suspend land sales had been introduced by Grow, Seward, and Johnson in the previous Congress. The Grow bill provided that the sales then advertised should be postponed until fifteen years had elapsed after the lands had been surveyed. *Cong. Globe,* 35 Cong., 1 Sess., I, 135, 324; II, 1703; *Freedom's Champion,* June 12, 1858. Horace Greeley regarded the land question as so basic in 1859 and 1860 that he included in *The Tribune Almanac* for those years detailed analyses of the progress and failure of Congress in dealing with it.

but another bill loomed up that could not be so easily rejected.

This was the bill to provide for free homesteads. A strongly Republican House passed the measure but in the Senate the advocates of land reform were much weaker and were outmaneuvered by their opponents. Free grants were dropped entirely, but squatters on the public lands were given a two-year extension before the public land sales would be held. In other words, the squatters were allowed two more years in which to raise funds for the purchase of their claims, and the price they had to pay was reduced to 62½ cents an acre. Heads of families who thereafter made homes for themselves on the public land could buy their quarter-section after five years of residence for 25 cents an acre.[36] To Senator James S. Green of Missouri, a proslavery leader and opponent of land reform, the Homestead bill was so "eviscerated" that it had become simply a measure to reduce the price of land, and therefore he and other southern spokesmen of public-land states could support it. While Greeley and the land reformers thought the bill a "miserable makeshift," it did offer relief to the embattled squatters.[37]

Buchanan now dealt his final blow to the West by vetoing the Homestead bill, which was distasteful to the southern slaveowners if not to the southerners in Congress from the newer states. In what is perhaps the most irrational, ill-conceived and amazingly inaccurate veto message that has emanated from an American President, Buchanan struck down the measure on the following grounds:

Donations of land are unconstitutional.
The bill discriminates against the first settlers who have paid $1.25 an acre for their land.

[36] For analysis of the House and Senate bills and the final enactment see *Cong. Globe*, 36 Cong., 1 Sess., IV, 3178–79.
[37] *New York Tribune*, May 11, 1860.

It does injustice to veterans, whose land warrants will depreciate in value.

"It is a boon exclusively conferred upon the cultivators of the soil."

It would deprive the older states of their fair share of benefits from land sales.

It would enhance speculation in land.

It would discriminate in favor of alien immigrants.

It would give an advantage to existing pre-emptors as against future pre-emptors.

It would sharply reduce income from public lands.

It would impair or destroy the "present admirable land system." [38]

The bill was far from a perfect measure, but Buchanan's strictures are not directed at its weakness, and his sophistries are apparent to any student of land policy.

If Kansas, Nebraska, Iowa, Minnesota, and Wisconsin, where most of the settlers on the public lands were then living, were embittered by the action of Buchanan in ordering their claims into market and refusing to postpone sales further, they were infuriated by the President's veto of the Homestead bill. To be sure, there was strong feeling against the veto elsewhere in the North, but it was natural that the squatters on the public lands should have the most intense feelings because their homes were in jeopardy; the veto meant the end of their hopes. Public sales would permit large-scale purchasing by non-residents, a development that no western community wanted. Speculators, "land sharks, counterjumpers, and those who are too young to leave mama" were warned not to come West to buy claims since they would "be taxed so steeply and . . . harassed so vigorously" that they would "gladly enough dispose of them as readily as they would drop hot potatoes." [39] Now, driven to greater

[38] *Cong. Globe,* 36 Cong., 1 Sess., IV, 3263–64.

[39] *Neosho Valley Register,* Burlington, Kansas, Jan. 10, Feb. 21, 1860.

violence and disregard of law by their conviction that Buchanan as the representative of the slave power was using his
authority to strike at and destroy free states, they advocated
mass action to prevent sales. The *Freedom's Champion* said:
"This act of oppression and disregard of the interests of the
people would . . . sink the administration of James Buchanan in infamy as long as it will be remembered." [40]

Kansans had successfully fought the efforts of the slave
power working through the Pierce-Buchanan administrations to make their territory a slave state. They had endured
the corruption of the carpetbag administrators sent in from
the older states to fill territorial positions; they had struck
back at the pillaging of the "border ruffians" and in turn had
done considerable bushwhacking of their own; they had
stubbornly insisted on admission to the Union as a free state
and were now about to win that fight.[41] Though Kansas succeeded in that struggle, it lost another. It failed to gain ownership of land for its settlers without a mountain of debt.

The land sales were held in 1859, 1860, and 1861. Let
us see what became of the argument offered by the administration that the necessity for raising additional revenue
required bringing the lands into market. Well before 1857
military-bounty land-warrants given veterans of previous
wars had largely displaced cash in the making of land entries.
It is true, warrants could not be employed at the auction
in place of cash, but after the land had been offered and not
taken at the auction it was subject to "private entry" for
warrants or cash. Furthermore, squatters could use warrants
either before or after the public sale to make their entries.
Since the warrants were currently quoted at 71 to 94 cents

[40] July 7, 14, 1860. See also the *Dubuque Herald,* June 27, 1860,
as quoted in George M. Stephenson, *Political History of the Public
Lands from 1840 to 1862* (Boston, 1917), p. 217.

[41] G. Raymond Gaeddert, *The Birth of Kansas* (Topeka, 1940),
is an excellent account of this struggle.

an acre, squatters could be counted on to use them in lieu of cash. The only hope for a substantial return from land sales was, therefore, that at the public offering speculators would come forth to take large tracts. This doubtless was what Buchanan and Thompson counted on, a fact which shows their lack of understanding of the way speculators were acquiring land in the territory. In the territorial period the large holdings were acquired more generally by hiring squatters to file the pre-emption claims and make payment with land warrants. A speculator thereby saved as much as $84 on a 160-acre tract.

Table 5. ACREAGE OF PUBLIC LAND ENTRIES WITH CASH AND WARRANTS IN KANSAS AND THE UNITED STATES, 1855–1860

	Kansas		United States	
Year	*Cash*	*Warrants*	*Cash*	*Warrants*
1855	——	——	15,729,524	1,345,580
1856	——	——	9,227,878	8,382,480
1857	17,331	37,584	4,124,744	6,283,920
1858	93,464	933,211	3,804,908	5,802,150
1859	29,052	870,923	3,961,581	2,941,700
1860	44,973	1,312,347	3,461,203	2,782,780
1857–1860	184,820	3,154,065	15,352,436	17,810,550

Speculators thus had little reason to buy for cash at the public sale. Of the first 10,000 acres offered at Lecompton in 1859, only 320 acres were sold, and of the more than 500,000 acres offered at Fort Scott only 80 acres were sold.[42] The table of public land entries in the United States and in Kansas for the period from 1855 to 1860 shows how small the Kansas cash purchases were in proportion to the total

[42] *Kansas National Democrat,* July 18, 1859; *Leavenworth Times* in White Cloud *Kansas Chief,* Sept. 8, 1859; *Lawrence Republican* in *Leavenworth Herald,* July 30, 1859; *Fort Scott Democrat,* Aug. 18, 1860.

Table 6. AVERAGE PRICE FOR WHICH PUBLIC LANDS SOLD IN
THE UNITED STATES

1856	95¢
1857	83¢
1858	55¢
1859	41¢
1860	53¢

number of sales and of what minor importance was the revenue derived from sales. A considerable portion of the cash
entries was for excess acreage where a 120-acre warrant, for
example, was used, and the other 40 acres had to be bought
or where a fractional quarter-section included more than
160 acres. In the older public-land states, where prices were
graduated, and it was cheaper to pay cash than to use warrants, only 18 per cent of the sales brought the minimum
price of $1.25 an acre, the average for all sales ranging from
41 cents an acre in 1859 to 83 cents in 1857. There is little
here to indicate that the policy of pushing the lands into
market was fruitful in producing revenue. A glance at the
return from the public lands for 1856 to 1860 as compared
with the total income of the Federal government further
illustrates this.

Table 7. RETURN FROM PUBLIC LAND SALES AND TOTAL
RECEIPTS OF FEDERAL GOVERNMENT [43]

Year	Receipts from public land sales		Percentage of total receipts of government	Total receipts of Federal government
	As given by Treasury	*By Land Office*		
1856	$8,917,645	$8,821,414	12	$74,056,699
1857	3,829,487	3,471,522	5	69,965,313
1858	3,513,716	2,116,768	4–7	48,655,366
1859	1,756,687	1,628,187	3	53,486,465
1860	1,778,558	1,843,630	3	56,064,608

[43] Compiled from the *Annual Reports* of the Commissioner of the
General Land Office, 1856–1860, the abstracts of warrants entries

Clearly the opponents of public offering of lands between 1858 and 1860 were correct in maintaining that the small returns to be expected from the sales would not justify the Buchanan-Thompson insistence on bringing the lands into market.

In advance of the public sales the squatters turned to the money lenders who long since had perfected a procedure by which funds could be loaned on fair security. Since the settlers' claims could not be mortgaged until the patent had been issued, the settler could not borrow on mortgage in advance of the sale. Instead, the squatter would make an agreement with an eastern money lender, in person or through his agent, according to which the latter would enter the land, take title in his name, and give a bond binding himself to convey the property to the borrower at the end of a year if the latter had paid the principal and a premium of some $40, $60, or $80, plus legal interest. The cost was high, but in the absence of other means, and with the loss of their homes staring them in the face unless they followed this procedure, the squatters had no choice. In Kansas and Nebraska the lenders and their agents took advantage of the plight of the squatters by exacting from 3 to 10 per cent interest a month on this kind of transaction.[44] Only under nearly ideal conditions could settlers meet such extreme interest demands. At the end of the year the contract might be ex-

---

for the Kansas land districts in the National Archives and *Historical Statistics of the United States,* 1789–1945 (Washington, 1949), p. 297.

[44] I have described this "time entry" business as it was called in my "Southern Investments in Northern Lands before the Civil War," in *Journal of Southern History* (May 1939), V, 162 *et seq.* The Lawrence *Herald of Freedom* (quoted in the *LaCrosse National Democrat,* July 13, 1858) mentions a money lender who received 10–20 per cent per month for the use of money and who said that he "had been paid at the rate of 20, 25, and 30 per cent per month to discount notes."

tended with interest added at the maximum rate allowed by law—20 per cent in Kansas—but because of continued financial difficulties on the frontier it was not easy for settlers to rid themselves of the heavy and increasing burden they had incurred. In many instances the contracts were forfeited, and the settlers lost their equity in the claims.

To take advantage of the 36 to 120 per cent interest that the West was offering for the use of capital and of the opportunities for speculating in land, there descended upon the public land offices where the sales were announced scores of financiers and their agents—"hordes of speculators" said the *Freedom's Champion*—from the older states.[45] In Lecompton there were from fifteen to twenty land agents who were making loans for people from the states. Lawrence and all the other towns in the territory were similarly well supplied with dealers and agents.[46]

Advertisements appeared in the local papers announcing, for example, that Thaddeus H. Walker & Co., real-estate brokers and dealers in land warrants, were prepared to locate warrants, make collection on land contracts, and make arrangements for "lands entered on time." [47] With capital provided by friends and associates in Salem, New York, the home of Walker, this firm entered either for speculation or for settlers 81,000 acres in Iowa and Kansas during 1859 and 1860. Reuben H. Farnham advertised that he could enter 50,000 acres on time for actual settlers, much of the capital being provided by Patrick M. Henry of Washington.[48] John Fitzgerald, of Winnebago County, Wisconsin, brought to Kansas land warrants to the amount of 30,000 acres and

[45] *Freedom's Champion,* June 23, 1860.

[46] D. S. McIntosh, Lecompton, Kansas Territory, April 25, 1859, to Cyrus Woodman, Woodman MSS., Wisconsin Historical Society.

[47] *The Conservative* (Leavenworth), July 18, 1861. Statistics of land entries were compiled from the land entry books in the National Archives in Washington and from the county deed records.

[48] Emporia *Kanzas News,* June 12, 1858.

after looking over the land to make sure that it was good arranged with some 187 squatters to enter their claims. Although the warrants could have cost him no more than 85 or 90 cents an acre, probably less, he exacted for each quarter-section a note for $230 (which was at the rate of $1.43 an acre) and required 40 per cent interest on top of that.[49] Wilson Shannon and Robert S. Stevens, staunch Buchanan supporters and beneficiaries of federal patronage, announced they would enter land on time for pre-emptors and in 1859 advertised 15,240 acres for sale.[50] Asaph Allen advertised that he would enter quarter-sections with warrants for pre-emptors for a mortgage of $250 payable at the end of a year, a contract which would give him 84 per cent profit if we disregard the small fees.[51] Mitchell and Weer of Lecompton went so far as to promise 25 per cent interest to any person who would send them funds or warrants to loan to squatters.[52] James C. Ayer, of Lowell, Massachusetts, famous for his "Cherry Pectoral" and "Ayer's Cathartic Pills," loaned extensively to squatters.

Charles Robinson, prominent free-state leader, and Thomas H. Webb, active in the Massachusetts Emigrant Aid Company, also were attracted by the high interest rates to enter the "time entry" business for settlers. Robinson wrote from Lawrence on September 14, 1857, that he could loan money on good security at 5 per cent per month or that he could purchase good claims and take half the land, which,

[49] Copy of letter of George W. Ewing, Ft. Wayne, Indiana, March 3, 1860, to H. W. Jones, Westport, Missouri, W. G. & G. W. Ewing Papers, Indiana State Library. There was no usury law in Kansas at the time. D. S. McIntosh, Lecompton, April 25, 1859, to Cyrus Woodman, Woodman MSS., Wisconsin Historical Society.

[50] Lecompton *Kansas National Democrat,* August 19, 1858, and Jan. 13, 1859.

[51] *Topeka Tribune,* May 26, 1859; *New York Tribune,* May 30, 1859.

[52] *Kansas National Democrat,* Dec. 10, 1857.

with improvements, was worth $5 to $10 per acre. For a 160-acre land warrant he could get a mortgage for $200 at 40 per cent. J. Lyman, to whom he wrote, was asked if he knew anyone who wished to invest in such opportunities.[53]

Prominent Democrats who came to Kansas, Nebraska, Minnesota, Iowa, and Wisconsin to lend money to squatters or to acquire extensive holdings of land were William W. Corcoran, George W. Riggs, John Slidell, John C. Breckinridge, Williamson R. W. Cobb, and Eli S. Shorter. Slidell alone had a half-interest in 45,000 acres in Iowa and Wisconsin. So great was the investment of southern capitalists at the Kansas land sales that Kansas Senator Jim Lane lamented in 1862, "We have in Kansas a larger proportion of rebel property than any other state in this Union." [54]

Proslavery leaders in Missouri had employed every effort to acquire and hold land for speculation in Kansas since the opening of the territory in 1854. They rushed across the line, took up claims on which they made a minimum of improvements, organized claim associations to protect their interests, elected by ballot stuffing a proslavery or "bogus" legislature to control affairs in concert with the proslavery governor and national administration, and then returned to Missouri. They kept the territory in turmoil for years by their efforts to retain their false claims and to maintain their fraudulent political control. Among these proslavery Missourians was Colonel W. Broadus Thompson of St. Joseph, who was the leading spirit in the Squatter Association of the Whitehead District, which resolved that "we will afford protection to no

[53] Charles Robinson, Lawrence, Kansas, Sept. 14, 1857, to J. Lyman, Lawrence MSS., Kansas State Historical Society; Thomas H. Webb, Boston, Sept 15, 1858, to M. F. Conway, Emigrant Aid Company MSS., Kansas State Historical Society; Cottonwood *Kansas Press,* May 30, 1859

[54] I have given considerable attention to these southern investments in public lands during the period from 1857 to 1861 in my "Southern Investments in Northern Lands before the Civil War," *passim.*

abolitionist. . . ." [55] Thompson's brother, M. Jeff. Thompson, an extensive land dealer of St. Joseph, in his *M. Jeff. Thompson's Real Estate Bulletin,* published in 1858, included a special section:

KANSAS AND NEBRASKA LANDS

The President having ordered a Sale of Public Lands in Kansas in the month of July and in Nebraska in the month of September, there will be a large amount of valuable lands thrown in the market, and splendid speculations will be made. I will select and purchase for clients either at the public sale for cash, or by locating warrants after the sale. Having surveyed a large portion of Kansas and Nebraska for Government, and having made a special examination of each and every piece of land, I will guarantee good selections.

* * *

My charge will be 10 per cent, or $20 per Quarter Section, and I pay all fees and office expenses.[56]

John P. Johnson, an active money lender operating in the Kickapoo and Sac and Fox cessions in northeastern Kansas, who was called a "skinner," and "Hog Eye Johnson" by Sol Miller, entered squatters' claims on halves or loaned 160-acre warrants that had cost him no more than $144, and then took mortgages for $285. According to Miller, Johnson ended the year by "getting the whole." [57]

Analysis of the deed and mortgage records of all the Kan-

[55] Martha B. Caldwell, "Records of the Squatter Association of Whitehead District, Doniphan County," *Kansas Historical Quarterly* (February 1944), XIII, 21, 23.

[56] I can find evidence of only two small surveying contracts that M. Jeff. Thompson had prior to the appearance of his pamphlet; they were both for land in Nebraska. See *House Ex. Doc.,* 34 Cong., 1 Sess., I, no. 1, part 1, 312–313.

[57] White Cloud *Kansas Chief,* Aug. 5, 1858. John P. Johnson and Mitchell & Weer of Lecompton, both extensive dealers in land at the auction sales, had government surveying contracts in Kansas.

sas counties in existence in 1861 and of the abstracts of land entries of the Kansas land offices now in the National Archives shows how extensively eastern and southern capital was invested in Kansas in the territorial period. From the first sales of public land in 1858 until the opening of the Civil War 3,417 mortgages were made on "improved" claims. Eighty persons from the East, the South, and the Middle West either provided funds for the purchase of four or more claims of 160 acres each or bought from 1,000 to 30,000 acres of land on speculation. Of the southerners who loaned a number of thousand dollars on mortgages the following are the more noteworthy: Septimus D. Cabaniss of Madison County, Alabama; James S. and Daniel B. Easley of Halifax Court House, Virginia; and Patrick M. Henry of Washington, D.C. Among the more numerous northerners whose investments were heavy were Henry Barricklow of Harrison County, Ohio; George Beach of Greene County, New York; Reuben H. Farnham and Robert S. Stevens of Batavia, New York; John Fitzgerald of Winnebago County, Wisconsin; Gustavus Kutter and G. J. Obrig of New York City; Ambrose Merrill of Hollowell, Maine; and James C. Ayer of Lowell, Massachusetts. Three Missourians who were active in making loans were Kirkbride Howard, William R. Pye, and Rollin Richmond, all of St. Louis.

Many mortgages were in default at the end of the first year when they were due and had to be extended with interest added. Foreclosures were not immediately pushed, for the land had little value, so depressed were conditions. With the outbreak of war and the inflationary effects of government buying, conditions changed, there was more demand for land, and debtors who could not pay were foreclosed. A writer in Gage County, Nebraska, reminiscing about pioneering during the territorial period, said that most settlers who borrowed at usurious rates lost their claims, some after paying interest for several years and of course after making heavy investments of labor.[58]

The veto of the Homestead bill, together with the forced sale of public lands, the drought, and the resulting crop failure forced thousands to abandon claims on which they had invested the labor of one, two, or more years.[59] It was estimated that during 1860, 30,000 people left Kansas, and smaller numbers left Nebraska, western Iowa, and other regions in the public land area. Those who remained were saddled with heavy debts bearing crushing interest. Through subsequent foreclosures many even of the survivors were to lose their claims. Petitions were circulated in Kansas to ask the governor to call a special session of the legislature for the purpose of enacting a stay law to prevent foreclosures, but this was opposed by the *Fort Scott Democrat* on the ground that such a measure would only delay the inevitable and would bring on expensive litigation.[60] Other persons sought relief through the enactment of a usury law making the legal rate of interest 10 per cent and stipulating that all contracts calling for interest in excess of 20 per cent were illegal and that only the principal could be collected on them.[61] Litigation under this measure was to annoy creditors, but the law could not effectively prevent the charging of fees and other costs that made real interest well above the legal limit.

To raise money for payments for their land, settlers parted with much-needed livestock, even the necessary horses and mules. They sometimes sold a portion of their claims, and denied themselves the necessary farm machinery. A Lyon County, Kansas, paper said in 1859 that there were but two

[58] Hugh J. Dobbs, *History of Gage County, Nebraska* (Lincoln, 1918), p. 169.

[59] Emporia *Kansas News,* July 7, 1860.

[60] *Fort Scott Democrat,* August 18, 1860.

[61] *Freedom's Champion,* March 24, 1860.

reapers and mowers in the county, the cradle and scythe being commonly used. Several farmers, it was stated, had been on the point of buying reapers but, instead, had to use their funds for entering their land.[62] Large land holdings had been created through forced sales and foreclosures, and actual settlers could but watch the process by which their improvements enriched the owners of these extensive tracts.

In territorial Kansas, as on all frontiers, there were men who came not to establish permanent homes for themselves but rather to acquire color of title or full ownership of land when it was available at its lowest price and to sell to later comers when the demand for land had pushed up its market price. Large capitalist speculators we have seen, but the small man who invested nothing but a slight amount of labor on a claim of a quarter-section was perhaps equally important. The Missouri non-resident claim makers were the most flagrant illustration of this type, for they made little pretence of living upon their land or conforming to the spirit of the pre-emption law. Many of them were either driven out, became discouraged in the face of the government auction, or succeeded in selling their claims, and after 1857 were less important in the Territory. Their place was taken by other migratory people who, lacking in stability and desire to make farms for themselves, sought only to conform to the minimum requirements of pre-emption so they could sell their claims as soon as the pressure on the land supply made that possible. Other migratory squatters, despite their natural frontier antipathy to absentee speculators, aided the latter for a small compensation in taking advantage of the pre-emption law to build up large ownerships. The large investors, by hiring pre-emptors and placing them on the more desirable land, were assuring themselves ownership and preventing actual settlers from establishing squatters' rights. Of the large sales at the Lecompton office in July, 1859, it was

[62] Emporia *Kansas News,* June 25, 1859.

estimated that one-half the pre-emptions had been acquired by speculators.[63]

Horace Greeley, visiting in Kansas on his way to Pikes Peak in 1859, made some acid remarks about the "twin curses" of the Territory, which he identified as the "manufacture of paper cities and bogus corner-lots," and the "grasping of whole townships by means of fraudulent pre-emptions and other devices familiar to the crafty and One-Horse Politicians." [64]

There are [he wrote] too many idle, shiftless people in Kansas. I speak not here of lawyers, gentlemen speculators and other nonproducers, who are in excess here as elsewhere; I allude directly to those who call themselves settlers, and who would be farmers if they were anything. To see a man squatted on a quarter section in a cabin which would make a fair hogpen, but is unfit for a human habitation, and there living from hand to mouth . . . with hardly an acre of prairie broken (sometimes without a fence up), with no garden, no fruit trees, "no nothing"—waiting for some one to come along and buy out his "claim" and let him move on to repeat the operation somewhere else—this is enough to give a cheerful man the horrors. . . .

As to the infernal spirit of Land Speculation and Monopoly, I think no State ever suffered from it more severely than this.

Greeley was convinced that not one-fourth of the preemptions had been made in good faith. His strictures were well made, but one may surmise that he was not sufficiently aware of the difficulty and cost of farm making under the conditions then prevailing in Kansas.

Sol Miller of the *Kansas Chief* paid his respects to the evasion of the pre-emption law for the purpose of petty speculation. Nine persons out of ten who pre-empted had violated the spirit if not the letter of the law, he was convinced. By

[63] Lecompton *Kansas National Democrat*, July 21, 1859; *Leavenworth Times* in White Cloud *Kansas Chief*, Sept. 8, 1859.
[64] *New York Tribune*, June 2, 9, 1859.

erecting sheds that were not fit for stables, placing worn-out straw beds, a bench or stoop, perhaps a broken stove and a dish or two in them, and either sleeping a night or eating a meal of crackers and cheese, they were enabled to swear they had conformed to the pre-emption requirements of residence and improvements. Miller went so far as to urge incoming settlers to jump claims not being improved.[65]

Population on the frontier was always much more unstable than that of well-established communities. Many of those who evaded the pre-emption law in their effort to get title to claims did so because they could not legally in the period of financial stringency, drought, and poor crops, raise the funds. They had to work through the money lender to whom they deeded their right and with whom they signed a contract to purchase it back. Others sold their claims and went on to try anew elsewhere. Some were professional claim makers or land lookers who spied out tracts that might soon attract buyers, made their claim marks, and sold as soon as purchasers appeared. Still others sought by claim making and claim selling to accumulate sufficient means to enable them to acquire and equip a successful farm. Few frontier residents entertained any scruples against shading or taking advantage of the land laws.

If we add the speculative purchases, large and small, to those of the trust lands made in 1856 and 1857, we have a considerable concentration of land ownership in eastern Kansas. One of these large holdings—that of Thaddeus H. Walker—included 76,000 acres. It is not possible to determine the extent to which large-scale and absentee ownership had been established, but we do have some figures that are at least suggestive. The census takers of 1860, whose figures are undoubtedly subject to question, though they do indicate trends, reported 1,778,000 acres of improved and unimproved land in farms in Kansas. As well over 4,000,000

[65] White Cloud, *Kansas Chief,* March 8, 1860.

acres had passed into private ownership through trust and public land sales, entries with military warrants, and sales of allotments, it would appear that at least one-half of this sum was held by speculators, large and small.[66] "Land monopoly," as the term was used at the time, was no phantom in the newly developing West.

As the territorial period of Kansas passed into history, it left as its heritage a nonstatutory method of Indian-land disposal that was to be abused by the two succeeding Republican administrations more seriously than it had been under Pierce and Buchanan. It also left extensive speculative ownerships by absentees, heavy debts bearing intolerably high interest rates, farms that were poorly developed because of inadequate resources and the concern of farmers with political and speculative activity, a host of Indian allotments whose ownership was in doubt, and several thousand squatters whose rights to their claims on reserves were in question, many never to be confirmed. For these evils it was natural and in a large degree proper to blame the Democratic Party and especially the southern proslavery wing.

While some of the northern states gave impressive votes in 1860 to Breckinridge, the candidate of the southern wing of the Democratic Party, the new public-land states which had been angered, like Kansas, by Buchanan's veto of Homestead and his insistence on pushing public lands into the market and forcing settlers to borrow under adverse conditions, gave him no more than one vote in 50.[67] Lincoln, whose party was promising to enact a true, not a sham, homestead measure, won these states with a clear majority, receiving 54 per cent of the total vote in Iowa, 56 per cent in Wisconsin, 57 per cent in Michigan, and 60 per cent in Minnesota. Kansas did not have an opportunity to vote for

[66] The acreage in farms is taken from the *Eighth Census of the United States,* Vol. *Agriculture* (Washington, 1864), 222.

[67] *Tribune Almanac,* 1861 (New York, 1861), p. 64.

a president until 1864 when it gave 79 per cent of its vote to Lincoln. This was a much larger proportion than was given the Republican candidates in any other state. For many years Kansas, Nebraska, Iowa, Minnesota, Wisconsin, and Michigan were strongholds of the Republican Party, and the people of these states were never permitted to forget, nor could they forget, that it was the GOP which had fathered the Homestead Act, and that the land policy of the Democratic Party had saddled the West with large speculative holdings and the settlers with heavy debts.

CHAPTER IV

Railroad Purchase of
Indian Reserves

THE KANSAS conflict had as its background innumerable controversies over claims, conflicts resulting from the failure to remove the intruded Indians, to bring their lands into the public domain, and to survey them, before the great rush of land-seekers set in. Bickering and violence over claims continued throughout the territorial period but was mitigated in 1856 and 1857 with the approach of the public offering of Indian trust and public lands and the introduction of eastern and southern capital. Increasingly, Kansas demanded the complete removal of the Indians who had been permitted to remain on their diminished reserves surrounded by white settlers, the opening of their lands to development, and the construction of railroads to which the reserves might be made to contribute. To achieve these objectives the proslavery and antislavery interests dissolved and reshuffled into new combinations that were neither the one nor the other but instead consisted of elements from both who were anxiously seeking to give advantage to Wyandotte, to Leavenworth, to Atchison, and to other towns along the eastern border by making them railroad centers.

This mitigation of past hatreds and reshuffling of economic alliances was reflected in the newspapers and writings of the time. A reporter for the *New York Tribune* observed on December 15, 1856: "The love of the almighty dollar had melted away the iron of bitterness and Anti-Slavery and Pro-Slavery men were standing together as a unit on their rights as squatters." Samuel C. Pomeroy, the practical and amoral leader of the antislavery forces, went further in writing to the man who had provided a considerable part of the money that had financed the Emigrant Aid Company activities. On December 19, 1856, Pomeroy said that the future of Kansas never looked so bright, everybody's attention was turned to getting rich, real estate was rising rapidly, railroads and Indian lands were all the rage, and "we don't think or care now whether the laws are 'bogus' or not." Similar views were expressed by John W. Whitfield, Democratic hanger-on and former proslavery delegate to Congress, in a letter to William H. English, Democratic Congressman from Indiana: [1]

All the world and the rest of Mankind are here. Speculations run high. Politics seldom named, *money* now seems to be the question. Stringfellow & Lane good chums, and don't be allarmed when I tell you I live in the same town with *Jim Lane*. Thank God I have a Little too much self respect to make him an associated. I have told him that he must keep at a respectful distance. What will Greely do now that Kansas has ceased to Bleed.

[1] Pomeroy, Lawrence, Dec. 19, 1856, to A. A. Lawrence, Lawrence MSS., Kansas State Historical Society; J. W. Whitfield, Leavenworth, May 9, 1857, to William H. English, English MSS., Indiana Historical Society.

A writer in the *Missouri Republican* expressed sorrow at the decline of aggressiveness on the part of the southern element: [2]

We find Stringfellow, Atchison and Abell and the notorious Lane lying down together, 'hail fellows well met' and partners in trade; growing fat in their purses and persons by speculations in town sites; eating roasted turkeys and drinking champaigne with the very money sent there from Missouri and elsewhere to make Kansas a *slave state;* and refusing to render an account, although demanded, as to how they have disbursed their funds.

Perhaps the best statement of the realignment that appeared in Kansas politics over the question of railroads and lands was written by one who participated in events of the time. R. G. Elliott, in his recollections of Kansas in the fifties, said that it was the influx of gold that brought the proslavery and antislavery groups "in friendly partnership . . . in a revelry of speculation."

"Pomeroy and Stringfellow at Atchison; Lane at Doniphan, in friendly rivalry with General Richardson; 'Jeff' Thompson pushing a railroad from Elwood out into the plains; Lawrence fusing with Delaware, her political antipode, in an attempt to build up a rival to Leavenworth, and hobnobbing over a railroad scheme with Platte City that a year before had sent the battery that destroyed the pride of her city—all a ferment of speculation that lined the western bank of the Missouri with an array of platted cities, rivals in expectancy for the commerce of the plains." [3]

[2] *Missouri Republican,* Aug. 12, 1857, in Kansas State Historical Society, *Collections,* XV, 431. See also the St. Louis *Intelligencer's* views as quoted from the *Herald of Freedom,* May 23, 1857, in James C. Malin, *John Brown and the Legend of Fifty-six,* (Philadelphia, 1942), p. 206.

[3] R. G. Elliott, "The Grasshopper Falls Convention and the Legislature of 1857," Kansas State Historical Society *Collections* (Topeka, 1908), X, 184.

It was at this time that Robert J. Walker wrote to President James Buchanan the discouraging news that a large majority of the squatters who went to Kansas from the slave states favored making Kansas free partly because they felt that would make their claims more valuable. Proslavery men holding town lots and shares in projected railroads were also favorable to making Kansas free. The rage for speculation in Kansas was universal, Walker wrote, but any action denying Kansans the right to determine their own destiny would bring the whole house of cards down in ruin.[4] Caution, benevolence, and understanding were necessary.

Both sides strenuously opposed bringing the public lands on the market in depression- and drought-stricken Kansas in 1858–1860. Both wanted the Indians removed as speedily as possible, and their reserves made subject to pre-emption. Both disliked the public-auction system with its competitive bidding. Both disregarded Indian rights to allotments and favored taxing away Indian equities. In new combinations the leaders lobbied and pulled wires to get land offices located in their communities and to acquire control of reserves to aid in building railroads. Thus Andrew J. Isaacs, favorite of the Pierce administration, and Thomas Ewing, Jr., conservative antislavery leader, joined together to advance Leavenworth in which their investments were centered and to build westward from that community the Leavenworth, Pawnee, and Western Railroad (LP&W). Similarly, Pomeroy joined with the Stringfellows and Peter Abell, vigorous proslavery advocates, to push Atchison and railroads radiating from that ambitious center. Mention might also be made of William W. Corcoran, Washington banker and patron of James Buchanan, who invested in Quindaro where were centered many of the speculative activities of Charles Robinson, rep-

[4] Robert J. Walker, Lecompton, June 28, 1857, to James Buchanan, Walker MSS., Historical Society of Pennsylvania.

resentative of the New England Aid Company and "Free State" governor.[5]

The inrush of more than 100,000 settlers bent on getting ownership of a piece of land led by 1860 to the alienation of more than 4,000,000 acres of trust and public land and the establishment of squatters' rights or claims on a great deal more. With the available lands or at least the more attractive of them thus absorbed, the stage was set for a concerted attack upon the remaining undiminished reserves, the diminished reserves, and the allotments that now were surrounded by settlers making farms for themselves. Because of their location along the Missouri border and elsewhere in eastern Kansas, these Indian lands were potentially valuable for farms, town development, and railroad rights-of-way. Unless they were transferred to private ownership, the future of the territory was dark, for highways and railroads could not be built through them.

Already there were a number of thriving towns on the eastern border which were anxious to make themselves railroad centers by chartering lines to be built westward from them. The next step was to secure land grants, the usual frontier method of financing railroads at the time, or, in the absence of public lands, to get control of the Indian allotments and reserves. If the projected railroads could get ownership of the reserves, even though they had to pay a fair price for them, they could enjoy the full benefit of the enhanced prices which construction would give to the lands, whereas with land grants on the alternate section pattern the railroads received only one-half the benefit. For this reason promoters of the towns of Quindaro, Wyandotte, Leavenworth, Atchison, and Doniphan strained every nerve to acquire the reserves.[6]

[5] Marcus J. Parrott, ardent leader of the antislavery party, was associated with proslavery men in the Missouri River railroad.

[6] Thomas B. Sykes, government agent to the Delawares, maintained

The first reserve to be sold intact was the smallest but it brought the highest yield per acre. The Christian or Munsee Indians had been buffeted from Pennsylvania to Ohio and finally to Kansas, where they hoped to find permanent refuge with their Moravian missionary on a small tract of 2,571 acres which was transferred to them by the Delawares. Unfortunately, the tract was adjacent to Leavenworth, the most rapidly growing city in the territory, which by 1857 had attained an estimated 7,000 population.[7] Squatters seeking the fertile and timbered land of the reserve, town site promoters hopeful of acquiring it to lay out city lots, and a number of combinations of territorial and Missouri capitalists and government officials, all joined in an unseemly scramble to secure this choice bit of land. The Indians were debauched and induced to sign away their rights; but they later protested that they had not known what they had signed in their drunken stupor. Because George W. Manypenny, Commissioner of Indian Affairs, refused to sanction any of the sales, a group of capitalists (headed by Andrew J. Isaacs, recently resigned as attorney general for the territory) who had a contract for the sale allegedly signed by some of the Indians took the matter to Congress and secured in 1858 a special act validating what patently was an illegal transaction. The payment of $43,400 for a tract that had cost the Indians $6,427 in 1854, shows how rapidly land values were working upward. Even this price did not represent the real value, for offers as high as $55,000 were made, and it was intimated

---

that because Kansas had been kept out of the Union in the formative period of its development (1854–1860), so that "there no longer remains any large bodies of arable lands unsettled that can be given her . . . for public improvements, as has been granted to other Territories when they were admitted as States," the reserves should be made available to the railroads. Secretary of the Interior, *Annual Report,* 1860, *Sen. Ex. Doc.,* 36 Cong., 2 Sess., I, no. 1, 328.

[7] Allan Nevins, *The Emergence of Lincoln* (New York, 1950), I, 157.

that at auction the tract might bring as high as $100,000 or more.[8]

The route to ownership of the reserves had now been shown, but without the co-operation of the Office of Indian Affairs little would be achieved. Standing in the path of the spoilsmen who lusted for the reserves was Manypenny, whose probity assured protection of Indian rights so far as possible in a period when public morals were indubitably low.

Manypenny had defended to the utmost the rights of the Indians in their lands, including the right to sell their increasingly valuable tracts at the fair market value when conditions made necessary the removal of the redmen. His insistence on scrutinizing all contracts for the sale of allotments and diminished reserves had brought him into conflict with influential people who saw opportunities of getting rich quick in the rapidly growing section of eastern Kansas, but who were defeated at least temporarily by Manypenny's refusal to approve their deals. Republicans and Democrats, prosavery and antislavery people who were scheming to get their hands on the allotments and reserves, saw that his removal was essential if they were to have their way. When he was replaced by General James Denver, relief was expressed by a group of economic interests then preparing a concerted onslaught on the Indian lands. George W. Ewing, one of the most persistent, shrewdest, and least moral of the traders buying lands of the Kansas Indians and selling goods to them, received the welcome news of Manypenny's removal through Senator Jesse D. Bright, whose public morals were no higher, in a letter which included the following comment: [9] "That 'son a bitch' (as you call him, and he deserves

---

[8] For the competition to purchase this valuable reserve see Paul W. Gates, "A Fragment of Kansas Land History: The Disposal of the Christian Indian Tract," *Kansas Historical Quarterly* (Aug., 1937), VI, 227 ff.

[9] J. D. Bright, Washington, April 17, 1857, to Geo. W. Ewing,

to be called) Manypenny has left this City. Genl Denver has been sworn in as his successor." The *Kansas Weekly Herald* of Leavenworth said (October 3, 1857): "No appointment could have been made, that would have given greater satisfaction to the West. We only wish he had held the office for the last four years, in place of Manypenny."

Now the stage was clear for the drive on reserves and allotments which followed rapidly upon the removal of Manypenny. Between 1859 and 1862 eight new treaties were negotiated with the intruded Indians which opened the way to transfer of the land to private ownership, but not through the democratic process established in the public-land system. Three treaties with the Sac and Fox of Mississippi, the Sac and Fox of Missouri, and the Kansas tribe provided that after allotments had been made to individual members the remaining lands should be "sold . . . to the highest bidder . . . upon sealed proposals. . . ." The Chippewa treaty required that the surplus lands should be sold at auction to the highest bidder but not at less than the appraised price. An effort was made in the Ottawa treaty to protect the right of squatters on the lands but it was so modest an effort that influential persons were certain to have no trouble in freezing out the squatters. A useful reservation specified that unclaimed surplus lands were to be subject to sale under the direction of the Interior officials. Finally, treaties with the Delawares and the Pottawatomie gave the opportunity of purchasing their surplus lands to the powerful group of jobbers, politicians, speculators, and business interests organized in the LP&W Railroad; while a treaty with the Kickapoo assigned their lands to the Atchison and Pikes Peak

---

W. G. & G. W. Ewing MSS., Indiana State Library. Bright was characterized by a contemporary as a "money pimp of Corcoran's," and "a land whore in the Northwest," and by Allan Nevins as the "Midwestern tool of Southern leaders. . . ." Allan Nevins, *op. cit.*, I, 74.

Railroad, in which Senator Pomeroy was deeply interested.[10]

This prosaic enumeration of the treaties and their provisions for the sale of surplus lands does no justice to the struggle for land-ownership which so racked Kansas, the Federal bureaucracy in the territory, and even on occasion the Buchanan and Lincoln administrations. Most ably led and most successful of the groups attempting to get control of the reserves was a Leavenworth combination consisting of William H. Russell, banker, partner in the cross-country trucking industry enjoying large government contracts,[11] and extensive purchaser of Delaware trust lands, and his associates Andrew J. Isaacs, whom we have met as successful purchaser of the Christian Indian tract, Hugh Boyle Ewing and Thomas Ewing, Jr., sons of Thomas Ewing, former Whig Secretary of the Interior and Senator from Ohio and now successful Washington attorney. The vehicle which was planned to make their city pre-eminent—the LP&W Railroad—was projected to run from Leavenworth, already the largest city in Kansas and regarded as the most promising point on the west side of the Missouri River, to Lawrence, and thence to Pawnee, or later Fort Riley by way of the north bank of the Kansas River.[12] A branch to Lecompton and "bearing southwest to Santa Fe" was also contemplated.[13]

[10] Since all treaties mentioned in this study are in Charles J. Kappler, *Indian Affairs, Laws and Indian Treaties*, II, *Senate Documents*, 58 Cong., 2 Sess., no. 319, I have not thought it necessary to make reference for each treaty.

[11] There is much about the trucking and mail business of Russell in Raymond W., and Mary Lund Settle, *Empire on Wheels* (Stanford, 1949), *passim*.

[12] Albert D. Richardson, who visited Leavenworth in 1857 and again in 1866, reported on his first visit that Leavenworth was the largest town in Kansas, having a population of 4,000; in 1866, Leavenworth with 22,000 people was reported to have swept beyond St. Joseph and Kansas City. *Beyond the Mississippi*, pp. 53, 549–550.

[13] As incorporated in 1855 the LP&W Railroad included among its directors William H. Russell, Samuel D. Lecompte, and Amos Rees.

A second group, with Dr. Charles Robinson, noted free-state leader, as the principal promoter, sought aid for a railroad to extend from Quindaro, in which Robinson had invested Emigrant Aid Company money, or from Wyandotte westward to Lawrence and beyond. Robinson's corporate vehicle was the Missouri River and Rocky Mountain Railroad. Robert S. Stevens, one of the most influential Kansas Democrats, worked with Robinson in furthering the interests of a railroad from the mouth of the Kansas River westward.[14] Robinson also was interested in the Parkville and Grand River Railroad to connect St. Joseph, Missouri, the western terminus of the Hannibal and St. Joseph Railroad, with Quindaro. To secure a land grant for this railroad he was asked by the Council of Quindaro to go to Washington and exert his influence.[15]

The third major Kansas group that hoped to build a railroad from the Missouri valley westward to connect with the eastern end of the Pacific Railroad had its principal interests centered in the city of Atchison. Samuel C. Pomeroy was the spark plug of the group. In 1859 it secured charters for three railroads to build west from Atchison to Topeka, Fort Riley, and Pikes Peak.[16]

It was reorganized in 1857 with a combination of proslavery and antislavery men. *Statutes of Kansas Territory,* pp. 914–920; *Kansas Weekly Herald,* Jan. 10, 1857; Hugh Ewing, Leavenworth, Dec. 26, 1856, Jan. 3, 5, 1857, to Thomas Ewing, Ewing MSS., Kansas State Historical Society.

[14] Samuel C. Smith, Lawrence, Dec. 1, 7, 14, 19, 1858, to Dr. Charles Robinson, Robinson MSS., Kansas State Historical Society.

[15] Thaddeus Hyatt and Robinson were both asked to lobby for a land grant for the Parkville and Grand River Railroad and were allowed a per diem of $5 for expenses. Copy of resolution of the Council, March 13, 1860, in *Ibid.*

[16] *Private Laws of Kansas Territory,* 1859, pp. 56–62. For a somewhat different lineup of railroad groups in Kansas see G. Raymond Gaeddert, *The Birth of Kansas,* University of Kansas *Publications, Social Science Studies,* (Lawrence, 1940), pp. 20 ff.

Representatives of these three rival communities and of the railroads they were promoting converged on Washington in 1858 and 1859 to secure land grants, the investment of Indian trust funds in their railroads, and the right to purchase the trust lands.[17] Because there was opposition to granting a railroad the right to purchase solid tracts of Indian lands on which it was known squatters dwelt, as well as because conflicting railroad groups might destroy each other's chances for success, a *modus vivendi* was soon reached whereby all the railroad lobbyists should work together. Robinson had only been a day in Washington, in December, 1858, when he had met with William H. Russell and his banking partner Luther R. Smoot, with W. F. M. Arny, and others who agreed to co-operate for mutual ends.[18] Robinson and doubtless others had previously tried to get the Delawares to agree to sell their diminished reserve, or at least a part of it, to the railroad he was pushing.[19]

Despite Robinson's optimistic statement about the willingness of conflicting groups to work together in behalf of land grants and the right to buy Indian reserves, little progress was made for some time. It became increasingly apparent that the LP&W Railroad had the most solid support among Missouri-valley people and was in a better position for bar-

[17] On Dec. 19, 1856, Charles Robinson wrote Amos A. Lawrence that the Delawares were favorable to investing their money in the bonds of a railroad to be built from Quindaro to Lawrence, and that if the President would approve, the matter would be put through. The proposal was not novel, for $95,000 of funds of the Cherokees, Chippewa, Choctaw, and other Indians were invested in the bonds of the Pacific Railroad of Missouri. *House Ex. Doc.,* 40 Cong., 2 Sess., IX, no. 59, 12.

[18] Robinson, Washington, Dec. 8, 1858, to Alfred Gray, Gray MSS., Kansas State Historical Society.

[19] Power of Attorney of July 2, 1858, given by Charles Robinson to John G. Pratt, Missionary to the Delawares, authorizing Pratt to purchase all or any part of the reserve, Robinson MSS., Kansas State Historical Society.

gaining with Congressmen and other influential people in Washington. Thomas Ewing, Jr., a Leavenworth booster and partner of William T. Sherman in the real estate business, besought John Sherman's aid in keeping William Montgomery off the Committee on Public Lands on the ground that he favored aid to an Atchison railroad. In March, Ewing who was subsequently to become Chief Justice of the Kansas Supreme Court, urged Robinson to make up a purse of $10,-000 to $15,000 in Lawrence property with which to secure aid from "the rapacious lobby," which would never permit the desired land-grant bill to go through "until their hunger is appeased." In April, Ewing wrote to Isaacs, then lobbying in Washington, that he could raise $25,000 to $50,000 in property to aid the move for land grands.[20] Land grants had to wait because there were so many groups maneuvering for preference in the matter of the Pacific Railroad. However, the Delaware lands were a plum that was ripe for a fall and Ewing, Isaacs, Robinson, John P. Usher, and associates moved in to catch it.

On May 30, 1860, a treaty with the Delawares was finally signed, which provided 80-acre allotments to members of the tribe in the southeastern part of the reserve and authorized the sale of the surplus lands—ultimately found to be 223,966 acres—to the LP&W Railroad at their appraised value but not less than $1.25 an acre. Title to one-half the land would pass to the railroad when it had completed construction of twenty-five miles west of Leavenworth and title to the other half would pass when the line was built to the western boundary of the reserve, a distance of fifty miles. No immediate liability in the form of taxes was incurred, and the railroad could anticipate at little cost to itself the full benefit of the

[20] Thomas Ewing, Jr. to John Sherman, Dec. 16, 1859; to Governor Robinson, March 30, 1860; to A. J. Isaacs, April 2, 1860; to G. W. Perkins, June 13, 1860, Ewing letter book, 1860–1861, Ewing MSS., Kansas State Historical Society.

rising land values which construction of its line would assure. The tribal allotments were to be inalienable and "exempt from levy, taxation, sale, or forfeiture, until otherwise provided by Congress." In thus freeing the lands from any obligation, the Federal government was again placing itself in conflict with state law. To make the treaty and cession palatable to the four Delaware chiefs, 1600 acres were to be patented in fee simple to them. Henry Tiblow, the interpreter, was also to have 320 acres.

Ewing, Isaacs, and their Leavenworth associates were elated with their success but soon realized that the preferential right to buy the Delaware lands might be lost unless they could devise some way to get the lands without having to pay for them. Frontier railroads were not attracting eastern financial support in 1861, even with railroad land grants, and the LP&W was no more favored than the rest. At this point Robinson's earlier suggestion that Indian endowment funds might be secured for railroad construction was seized upon in a slightly different way. Instead of paying the Delawares in gold or silver, the associates proposed to pay them in the bonds of the company, bonds secured by a mortgage on 100,000 acres or less than half the lands. President Lincoln was not happy with the proposal to change the terms of the purchase and insisted on submitting it for approval to the Delawares in the form of a supplementary treaty. This treaty was quickly arranged by the Office of Indian Affairs.[21] As a result the LP&W, without putting up a cent for the land, had the right to sell 123,966 acres, provided the construction

[21] Lincoln's struggle with his own conscience in his effort to justify the change in the terms of sale is displayed in his "Order for the Issue of Bonds for Use of Delaware Indians," Roy P. Basler, *Collected Works of Abraham Lincoln* (New Brunswick, 1953), IV, 400–402, and his letter to O. H. Browning, July 20, 1861, *ibid.,* 455; J. H. McDowell, J. C. Stone, and A. J. Isaacs, March, 1861, to C. B. Smith, Sec. of Interior, and note of Lincoln's on letter of Caleb B. Smith, April 30, 1861, to the President, Delaware Files, National Archives.

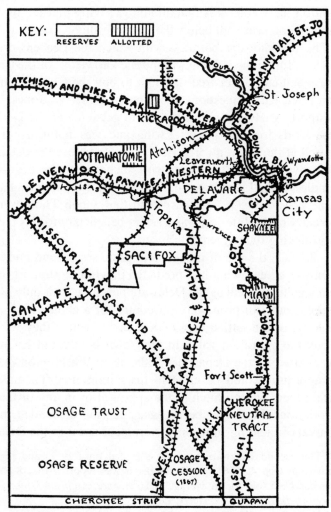

Railroad and Indian reserves in eastern Kansas, 1860–1869.
(Drawn by Mary Young)

schedule was maintained.[22] The second treaty, with its provisions for a mortgage on less than half the land to assure payment on the whole, was tantamount to saying that the price on the whole was well below the market value.

The suspicious smoothness with which the Leavenworth machine functioned, along with public knowledge of the way Isaacs had earlier secured the right to buy the Christian Indian tract, led to questions about methods. H. W. Jones, of Westport, Missouri, who had tried to get some of the Delaware lands for George W. Ewing and was naturally displeased at the Leavenworth victory, wrote before the details were divulged that the treaty was "believed to be a d—d swindle—a Rail Road speculation" and that the Indians had been "driven into it." He suspected that Jacob Thompson, Secretary of the Interior, was a secret beneficiary for his part in producing the agreement.[23]

Influence, the use of money, and promises of land had to be employed as Ewing had predicted in winning support for such a valuable deal as the Delaware purchase. Not only did the Leavenworth promoters get control of a choice tract in the heart of the settled area of Kansas for which they were to pay the appraised value in their own bonds, but Ewing was assured by the Department officials in Washington that the appraisal would be close to the minimum.[24] To make certain there was no hitch in the appraisal or in any further negotiations that might be necessary, Ewing demanded the removal of Fielding Johnson, government agent to the Dela-

[22] The second Delaware treaty was signed on July 2, and proclaimed on Oct. 4, 1861. By December it was reported that 8,000 acres had been sold for an average of $6 an acre. *Atchison Union* in *Leavenworth Daily Conservative,* Dec. 25, 1861.

[23] H. W. Jones, Westport, June 12, July 26, 1860, to G. W. Ewing, W. G. and G. W. Ewing MSS., Indiana State Library.

[24] Thomas Ewing, Jr., Leavenworth, Sept. 8, 1860, to his father, Ewing letter book, 1860–1861, Ewing MSS., Kansas State Historical Society.

wares. The reasons given for removing him were that he had opposed the second treaty, though he apparently signed it, that he had urged a higher price for the land, and also that he was "unpopular." [25] The appraised price was set at $1.28 an acre for land that Ewing somewhat optimistically said was worth at least $10 an acre. For this appraisal too, payment had to be made to the "voracious lobby."

To secure support for the Delaware treaty, Isaacs and Ewing made numerous commitments, some of which were vague and slightly uncertain. Robert G. Corwin, whose services seemed essential for almost any measure involving influence in the Interior Department, was to be paid $10,000. Frederick P. Stanton and J. C. Vaughan were to be paid $500, which may have been for legal services as distinguished from lobbying. J. C. Stone, Isaacs, and Ewing were to share 20,000 acres, Simpson and Stevens were to have 2,133 acres, an unnamed friend of Hamilton G. Fant (Washington banker) was to have 640 acres, another friends of John P. Usher (Federal District Attorney and slightly later Secretary of the Interior) was to have 640 acres, and General James G. Blunt was to have 793 acres, all at the appraised price. [26] In addition Usher, Mark Delahay (Surveyor General in Kansas), and John G. Pratt all received gratuities in

[25] Ewing, Leavenworth, July 2, 1861, to Caleb Smith, Delaware Files, National Archives.

[26] Document in Thomas Ewing, Jr., letter book, 1860–1861, "Financial standing of the Leavenworth, Pawnee & Western Railroad together with debts, gratuities, etc., as of Nov. 1861," Ewing Papers Kansas State Historical Society; "Lands of the Leavenworth, Pawnee & Western Railroad 1863," Leonard Collection, University of Iowa. H. W. Jones, of Westport, Missouri, said it was his understanding that Thomas B. Sykes, government agent to the Delawares, "receives $50,000 from the R.R. Co." for his share in securing the treaty. Jones to Col. G. W. Ewing, W. G. & G. W. Ewing MSS., Indiana State Library. The amount is exaggerated but Sykes probably was taken care of in one of the other payments for he was a key figure in the negotiations.

the form of land grants. Noteworthy were the 2,320 acres that were quitclaimed to Martha Robinson. It was on this land that Charles Robinson built his large estate.[27]

Table 8. LANDS CONVEYED BY LEAVENWORTH, PAWNEE, AND WESTERN "WITHOUT OTHER CONSIDERATIONS THAN FOR SERVICES RENDERED CO." [28]

As given by Thomas Ewing		*As given in document in Leonard Collection*		*Found in deed records of Leavenworth and Jefferson Cos.*	
Robinson	2,560	Simpson &		Martha Robinson	2,320
Fant	320	McBratney	960	Charles W. Adams	1,280
Adams	1,280	Thomas S.		Charles Jonneycake	320
Jonneycake	320	Gladding		William A. Simpson	800
Babcock	640	et al.	2,500	John P. Usher	1,920
Stevens &				Mark Delahay	640
Simpson	1,280			John G. Pratt	320
Usher	1,920			John A. Johnson	640
Delahay	960			Judith C. Rees	240
M.F.C.	320			Gen. James G. Blunt	480
"Robinson's				Robert P. C. Wilson	160
man"	320			Robert McBratney·	1,920
Mr. Robinson	640			Thomas S. Gladding	2,760
Totals	10,560		13,201		13,800

[27] William Elsey Connelley, *An Appeal to the Record* (Topeka, 1903), p. 43; Frank W. Blackmar, *Life of Charles W. Robinson* (Topeka, 1902), p. 293.

[28] Gladding quitclaimed 800 acres to Austin M. Clark and 360 acres to James C. Stone. The Gladding acreage is estimated, as are all the items in column 3 since only the legal descriptions are contained in the deeds. No actual conveyance was found for the McBratney item which is contained in an agreement to convey three sections of land by the Leavenworth, Pawnee, and Western to McBratney. The references for columns one and two are the same as in note 26 preceding. It is worthy of note that Robert S. Stevens, William A. Simpson, and Charles Robinson, who had been influential in the negotiations for the Delaware treaties, succeeded in buying two of the tracts given to the chiefs and located in present North Lawrence, as follows:

305 acres in section 30 for $6,000
294 acres in sections 29 and 32 for $3,000.

It was later charged by former Senator Edmund G. Ross that Pomeroy received three-sixteenths of the Delaware lands for aid in putting the Delaware treaties through the Senate, but whether this applied to the LP&W sale or to the Missouri Valley Railroad sale in 1866 is not clear.[29]

A different note was sounded when Alfred Gray, who was pressing rival claims for the Parkville and Grand River Railroad charged that the treaty had been extorted from the Delawares by "intimidation and misrepresentation" and that liberal supplies of "Fire Water" and "Rot gut" had left the chiefs drunk and powerless in the hands of the agent.[30] Even John P. Usher who aided in arranging the sale of the Delaware lands later protested that the $1.28 price was a gross "fraud" as the land was worth at least $10 per acre.[31]

This purchase was at the rate of $15 an acre for choice locations. Apparently the sales or the payments were not completed, for in 1862 Sidney Clarke bought the same tracts for $5,700 and received patents for them. All these transactions are in Jefferson County Deeds, vol. D.

Many years later James C. Stone, Thomas Ewing, and John P. Usher gave testimony to the United States Pacific Railway Commission concerning the negotiations leading to the purchase by the Leavenworth, Pawnee, & Western Railroad of the Delaware lands and to the treaty authorizing the purchase of the Pottawatomie reserve. The lapse of 27 years had undoubtedly dulled their memory but their evasive answers, their efforts to shift responsibility to others, and their denial that to influence votes they offered stock in the railroad, or lands that might be acquired is disingenuous in view of the clear facts in the case. Their testimony, despite all equivocation, brings out well the way in which railway legislation and Indian treaties were secured. Report of the United States Pacific Railway Commission, *Sen. Ex. Doc.,* 50 Cong., 1 Sess., III, no. 51, part 4, 1595 ff., 1672 ff.; and V, part 8, p. 3849 ff.

[29] Council Grove *Democrat,* April 25, 1872, in Martha B. Caldwell, "Pomeroy's 'Ross Letter'; Genuine or Forgery?" *Kansas Historical Quarterly* (April 13, 1945), XIII, 463.

[30] Draft of letter of Alfred Gray of Quindaro, June 18, 1860, to Geo. W. Patterson, Gray MSS., Kansas State Historical Society.

[31] John P. Usher and J. W. Wright, attorneys for the Delawares,

A. J. Isaacs, who was with Ewing most influential in negotiating the sale of the Delaware lands, had under way in
Washington two other matters involving the Delawares; their
handling throws additional light on the story of the Kansas
difficulties.[32] The first of these matters was a contract with
the Delawares whereby Isaacs was to represent the tribe in
pressing its claims against the government for losses "arising
from depredations of white men." The fee was to be 20 per
cent of everything recovered.[33] At the same time Isaacs contracted to represent a number of traders, including Cyprian
Chouteau of St. Louis and George W. Ewing of Fort Wayne,
for claims against the Delawares. For these services, which
came close to placing Isaacs on both sides of the fence, the
fee was to be $5,000. When the LP&W later found difficulty
in meeting payments on the bonds it had issued to the Indians
an agreement was reached between company officials and the
traders who through Isaacs had successfully prosecuted their
claims against the Delawares that the credit for the amount
allowed them might be exchanged for lands previously sold
to the railroad. Thus, George W. Ewing's claim of $5,000
(for which he was allowed $4,138.96 minus the propor-
tionate fee to Isaacs of $621.30) was exchanged for 560
acres in Leavenworth County. An inveterate land speculator,

Washington, June 4, 1861, to the President, Secretary of the Interior,
and Commissioner of Indian Affairs, Delaware Files, National
Archives.

[32] Thomas Ewing, Leavenworth, Sept. 4, 1860, to C. Robinson,
Ewing MSS., Kansas State Historical Society.

[33] Copy of the Isaacs contract with the Delawares of Dec. 27, 1860,
is in the Pratt MSS., Kansas State Historical Society. The Delaware
treaty of May 30, 1860 had provided for the payment of $30,000 for
depredation on the timber and $9,500 for stolen ponies and cattle.
(Kappler, II, 806) The payments were not made and in a third
treaty with the Delawares in 1866 the payment of $30,000 was again
authorized and it was agreed to examine losses of livestock for later
congressional action. (Kappler, II, 941)

Ewing had been trying to get Delaware land for years, first by employing pre-emptors and now by having his claim against the Indians confirmed and exchanging it for the tract.[34]

Meantime squatters and non-resident claim grabbers had spread by the hundreds hither and yon over the Delaware reserve, as was reported in September, 1857. In October, General Denver, hearing that there were at least a thousand squatters surveying, laying out claims, and preparing for permament settlement, ordered a contingent of troops from Ft. Leavenworth to evict them and destroy their improvements.[35] This may have cleared the tract of claimants for a time, but the following year, on the rumor that a treaty was being negotiated for the opening of the lands to settlers, "several hundred" citizens of Lecompton, Leavenworth, and Missouri again spread over the reserve. A squatters' meeting was held, and an agreement was secured from a major chief permitting settlement.[36] Again the threat of eviction by the army was made, this time through a notice in the Leavenworth *Weekly Kansas Herald,* but to no avail.[37]

In 1861, before the supplementary treaty was drawn and when it was generally believed that the LP&W could not meet the terms of the sale, the Delaware agent reported the

[34] H. W. Jones, Sept. 17, 1862, March 16, 1863, to Geo. W. Ewing; Ewing to Jones, March 26, 1865, and a number of memos of clerks of Ewing relating to this matter, W. G. & G. W. Ewing MSS., Indiana State Library.

[35] B. F. Robinson, Indian Agent, Delaware Agency, Sept. 29, 1857, to Superintendent of Indian Affairs; and J. W. Denver, Commissioner of Indian Affairs, Westport, Mo., Oct. 3, 1857, to B. F. Robinson, Pratt MSS., Kansas State Historical Society; H. W. Jones, Westport, Mo., Nov. 18, 1858, to Geo. W. Ewing, W. G. & G. W. Ewing MSS., Indiana State Library.

[36] H. W. Jones, Westport, Mo., Nov. 19, 1858, to Geo. W. Ewing, W. G. & G. W. Ewing MSS., Indiana State Library; *Wyandotte Argus* in White Cloud *Kansas Chief,* Nov. 18, 1858.

[37] Jan. 8, Feb. 26, 1859.

reserve covered with squatters with scarcely a quarter section not being occupied or claimed. Some settlers had erected "good houses" and had from ten to fifty acres in cultivation, but others were merely holding to resell at a profit. He estimated that no more than one in ten would be able to purchase the land when offered for sale, but all would resist removal. The squatter association promised protection to absentee as well as resident claimants. It would take a full company of troops, he believed, to remove the intruders, who would doubtless return as soon as the troops were withdrawn.[38]

The LP&W found itself faced with the same problem when it assumed control of the Delaware lands in 1862. Many of the nearly 2,000 squatters were refugees fleeing from troubles in Missouri, who had been urged by Senators Lane and Pomeroy to settle upon the tract. They now constituted an important political group whose members were firm in insisting upon their rights as squatters.[39] Not wishing to stir up hostility against itself, the railroad offered squatters the opportunity of earning their land by accepting jobs with construction crews.[40] That many did not respond is shown by the continued controversy with squatters and the decision to evict those who "are obnoxious to the company." In May, 1862 an order was dispatched from the adjutant general's office in Washington commanding Brigadier General Blunt to eject "trespassers" from the Delaware lands.[41] On three successive occasions the troops were called out to dispossess

[38] Copy, Fielding Johnson, Delaware Agency, Kansas, May 4, July 6, 1861, Secretary of Interior, Indian Office Records, National Archives.

[39] P. C. Ferguson, Elwood, Kansas, March 22, 1862, to Lyman Trumbull, Reserve File, Office of Indian Affairs, National Archives.

[40] *Leavenworth Conservative,* April 19, 1862.

[41] *Leavenworth Conservative,* April 23, May 13, 1862; P. C. Ferguson, Elwood, Kansas, March 22, 1862, to Lyman Trumbull, Delaware File, National Archives.

the squatters, who were mostly Northern sympathizers, though it was admitted some copperheads resided on the tract.

Four years later serious trouble still marred the development of the area.[42] The town of Williamsport had been laid out on land which had been bought from the railroad but which was claimed by squatters. On two successive occasions the squatters and their sympathizers destroyed the improvements made by the legitimate owners and threatened further violence if they persisted in violating squatter rights. The town group built a blockhouse to defend its rights. This act of defiance so angered the squatters that forty or more, armed with revolvers, muskets, shotguns, and rifles attacked it; and in the melee one man was killed and four wounded. Finally troops had to be dispatched from Fort Leavenworth to restore order.[43] The squatters spread rumors that the railroad title to the land was invalid, and that the railroad could not meet its obligations, thus trying to induce people not to buy.[44]

Since railroads could not be built through reserves without approval of the Indian owners, building of the LP&W west of Topeka would be held up until the right of way was conceded in treaty negotiations. The speedy engrossment of public lands farther east brought the Pottawatomie reserve

[42] Memorial of 57 settlers on Delaware reserve received Jan. 31, 1863, and letter of John Volk, Delaware reserve, March 16, 1863, to Abraham Lincoln, Delaware File, National Archives.

[43] Atchison *Freedom's Champion,* July 17, 1866, quoting the *Lawrence Tribune.*

[44] Telegram, John D. Perry, President, Union Pacific, Eastern Division, to Secretary of Interior, Aug. 16, 1866, Delaware Files, National Archives. It was not uncommon for economic rivals of land-grant railroads to spread rumors about the nature of the title to their lands. Wall Street opponents of the group controlling the Illinois Central in the fifties, and rival railroad groups in the Pacific Northwest during the seventies and eighties did the same thing.

prominently to the attention of the railroad builders. If they could not secure control of it through the alternate-section method for which they were lobbying, might they not buy the whole reserve as they had already gained ownership of a part of the Delaware lands?

James C. Stone, president and principal stockholder of the LP&W, and Thomas Ewing, Jr., prepared a draft of a proposed treaty to submit to the Pottawatomies that would authorize the purchase of the reserve by the railroad. To smooth their way, they secured the appointment of the friendly Edmund C. Ross as commissioner to conduct the negotiations. Stone and Ross proceeded to St. Marys Mission, where they began negotiations with the Indians.

From Leavenworth Ewing continued to direct activities in behalf of the purchase of the reserve. By way of winning the support of the Catholic missionary to the Pottawatomies, he offered to include a provision reserving a full section of land for the church, and he promised that the Company would give the church another section. He also offered to aid the mission to secure liberal government support for its educational work. Meanwhile he courted trader support by trying to provide for the payment of Indian debts, alleged or actual. Ewing was aware that trader opposition had defeated more than one effort to wrest land cessions from reluctant Indians. During the course of the negotiations, opposition to a sale or cession of the reserve was expressed "by the wildest of the fellows" and "the witch" but this opposition was overcome or shunted aside, and the treaty was signed by some eighty-six Indians, no more than a handful of whom could write their names. Later a council of the dissenting Pottawatomies was held, and a protest against the treaty was signed by forty members—members of no special prominence, according to Ross, who had negotiated the treaty.[45]

[45] Thomas Ewing, Jr., Nov. 9, 1861, to John P. Usher; Nov. 12, Dec. 31, 1861, to Gen. J. C. Stone; to J. S. Chick and Co., Dec. 28,

The Pottawatomie treaty provided for allotments ranging from eighty acres to each child and woman to 640 acres to each chief. Allotments were to be "exempt from levy, taxation, or sale, and shall be alienable in fee or leased or otherwise disposed of only to the United States" or to members of the tribe. "Intelligent" and "prudent" Indians might, according to a supplementary article, be given title in fee. Unallotted lands were to be subject to purchase by the LP&W for $1.25 an acre within six months after the allotments and special grants had been selected and the reserve surveyed. With a friendly surveyor in charge, the deal might be held up; and thus the interest of six per cent would not be assessed for two years or more. It was for this reason that Ewing was anxious to have his business partner, Hampton B. Denman, appointed surveyor. The road was to be built halfway across the reserve in six years and all the way across in nine years. Payment for the land was to be made in gold or silver coin to be held in trust for the Indians.[46]

On learning that the treaty was signed, Ewing telegraphed the Commissioner of Indian Affairs, William P. Dole, urging that he have it submitted to the Senate on the opening day, that he order the agents who had negotiated it to go to Washington to explain the various provisions, and that he appoint Hampton B. Denman to be surveyor for the tract. John P. Usher, who had been helpful in securing ratification of the Delaware treaties, was asked to talk with Dole and see that things were moving properly and to approach Senator Pomeroy to make certain that he and his Kansas friends who "must be provided for" were favorable. Money was to be used where necessary. Ewing also invoked the aid of his

---

1861, Ewing letter books, 1860–1861, Ewing MSS., Kansas State Historical Society.

[46] Thomas Ewing, Jr., Leavenworth, Nov. 20, 1861, to his father, Ewing letter books, 1860–1861, Ewing MSS., Kansas State Historical Society.

influential father in Washington.[47] The LP&W was lobbying at the same time for a land grant and government loan to aid in constructing its line westward and was relying heavily on Frederick P. Stanton and his partner Robert J. Walker for assistance. For their aid in pushing the treaty through the Senate and the land-grant bill through both houses, Stanton alone was to get four sections of average quality from the land grant and Walker and Stanton were to receive one section of Pottawatomie lands.[48]

In the Leonard collection of material relating to Thomas Durant there is an illuminating document that throws further light on the way in which political plums were secured in Washington. The document bears the caption "Leavenworth, Pawnee, and Western Railroad Stock contracts made for the Company by J. C. Stone and Thos. Ewing, Jr. agents for the Company to secure the ratification of the Delaware and Pottowottomie Treaties & the passage of the Pacific Railroad Bill." Here one sees that 4,600 shares of stock listed in the names of McBratney and Gaylord were "supposed to be for S. C. Pomeroy," 1,000 shares in the name of a New Yorker were listed as "mostly blackmail," 20,000 shares were held for J. P. Usher, Caleb B. Smith, and R. W. Thompson, all

[47] Ewing to Dole, Nov. 19, 1861; to John P. Usher, Nov. 19, 1861; and to his father, Nov. 20, 1861, *loc. cit.* Having successfully engineered through Congress the land grant and treaties authorizing the sale of reserves to the Leavenworth, Pawnee, and Western, Thomas Ewing, Jr., sought the post of Assistant Secretary of the Interior. It may be doubted that he could have done anything more for his railroad interests in Kansas than Dole and Usher were willing to do for him. Ewing's father exerted his influence to secure the political plum for him, but Lincoln awarded the position to another candidate while stating that he held Ewing, Jr., "in very high estimation." Basler, *op. cit.*, VI, 67.

[48] The five section conveyances were authorized on a contingent basis by the Board of Trustees on March 10, 1862. See copy of the memorandum of May 22, 1862, in Leonard collection, University of Iowa.

prominent Lincoln appointees, and other shares were awarded "for blackmail." A number of similar lists indicate that Pomeroy and Lane were beneficiaries of much that was being done in Kansas in the matter of Indian reserves. William P. Dole, Commissioner of Indian Affairs, and Charles E. Mix, Chief Clerk in the Office of Indian Affairs, were scheduled to have 1,200 and 640 acres respectively for their co-operation in the negotiations.[49]

After some delay the Pottawatomie treaty was ratified on April 15, 1862; but what had earlier promised to be a bonanza proved less attractive when the allotments had been selected. Between 1862 and 1867, 1,400 Pottawatomies selected 152,128 acres along the streams in almost solid array where the only available timber was located. A representative of the Union Pacific, Eastern Division—successor of the LP&W—expressing doubts about the numerous allotments, complained that they contained the best timbered tracts. This selection, he held, would leave only the poorer land for the settler-customers that the railroad might bring in, would make it difficult to attract any but less desirable settlers, and would assure continued tension between them and the Indians.[50] The allotments also included practically all the land along the railroad's right of way, on which its builders hoped to establish towns and sell lots, as the promoters of all western lines were doing. Furthermore, a diminished reserve of 77,357 acres had been selected in

[49] Report of the United States Pacific Railway Commission, *Sen. Ex. Doc.,* 50 Cong., 1 Sess., III, no. 51, part 4, 1616–1619.

[50] Copy, J. P. Usher, Attorney for the Union Pacific, Eastern Division, Oct. 3, 1866, to O. H. Browning, and J. P. Usher, Washington, D.C., Nov. 9, 1866, to L. V. Bogy, Commissioner of Indian Affairs, Indian Affairs, National Archives. Study of the Pottawatomie allotments in Wabaunsee County indicates that a large part of some 16,000 acres quickly passed by loans on mortgage and outright purchase to O. H. P. Polk and John D. Lasley, of Kansas City. Deed Records, Wabaunsee County.

central Jackson County which a local writer later described as "exceedingly fertile, and highly desirable for settlement. . . ." [51] Despite complaints against the selection of the most wanted land in terms of location, timber, and soil, the selection of allotments proceeded until May, 1867, when the railroad officials were informed that the remaining lands were ready for purchase.

A careful appraisal of the diminished reserve of the Pottawatomies after the selection of the allotments left the railroad officials doubtful of its value to them. Although their line struck squarely across the entire length of the reserve and was the only railroad then planned to touch it, although they would be most interested in developing the tract, President John Perry concluded that "it was not for the interest of the Company to become the purchaser" and forfeited the right.[52]

In anticipation of such a move, the Pottawatomie treaty had provided that the surplus lands should be appraised at not less than $1.25 an acre and sold "in quantities not exceeding one hundred and sixty acres at auction to the highest bidder for cash at not less than such appraised value." This phrasing would seem to require that the lands should be sold as the trust lands of the Delaware, Iowa, and Kaskaskia Indians had been sold in 1856 and 1857; it suggested a public auction where settler associations might dominate the sale, and where individuals could get their claims even though with borrowed capital. Such a policy might have hastened development, met settlers' demands, and perhaps produced a settler pattern that was less burdened with debt than on some other tracts, but it was not to be.

[51] Andreas, A. T., *History of the State of Kansas* (Chicago, 1883), p. 1335. A copy of a map showing the tracts allotted to the Pottawatomies is in the Division of Maps and Charts, National Archives.

[52] W. T. Otto, Acting Secretary of the Interior, May 11, 1867, to Perry; and Sept. 16, 1867, to O. H. Browning, Secretary of the Interior, Indian Affairs, National Archives.

A new railroad enterprise with powerful political support was looming on the horizon, a railroad which was soon to become Kansas' biggest and most important company and a great rival of the UP, Eastern Division. It not only won the right to buy the Pottawatomie lands but was enabled to get early construction under way through the returns it received from the sale of these lands.

Samuel C. Pomeroy divided with James H. Lane the honor of bossing the Republican Party in Kansas and distributing its patronage. Pomeroy looked farther afield than Lane in the use of his political power; he concerned himself with railroads and worked to secure land grants, Indian reserves and both county and Federal bond subscriptions to provide the cost of their construction, or at least to get them under way. In 1857 Pomeroy had joined with previously proslavery Atchison and its chief promoters Peter T. Abell and Benjamin F. Stringfellow to make the town the great commercial center of the Missouri valley. The success of the LP&W in securing the right to buy a part of the Delaware lands and the Pottawatomie reserve, along with a most liberal grant of land and in even getting its line under way, had not daunted Pomeroy. Atchison should have its railroad connections with the East and should be the center from which lines were to radiate out to the North, the West, the Southwest, and the South. To achieve these ends Pomeroy lined up politically with the radical-reconstruction wing of his party, the wing that was devoting its energies to raising tariff rates, providing for the importation of contract labor, assuring highly profitable contracts to industry, chartering transcontinental railroads, and securing land grants and bond subsidies for them. Through close co-operation with groups in and out of Congress that were interested in these matters, Pomeroy acquired friendships and support for measures in which he was deeply concerned and before the denouement which produced his defeat in 1873 he was a powerful senatorial figure who enjoyed a dominant position in determining government economic policy concerning Kansas.

To make Atchison a railroad hub it was necessary to twist, contort, and divert railways from a straight line, to forget that St. Joseph, which was already connected with the East, was better situated on the Missouri and might well be the principal railroad center rather than Atchison, and to neglect—indeed to work actively against—the claims of the more strategically located Leavenworth, Kansas, and Kansas City, Missouri. Pomeroy struck heavy blows at the UP, Eastern Division, in order to assure greater benefits to railroads tributary to Atchison.[53] Repeatedly he came forth in Congress with schemes to grant lands, provide the $16,000-per-mile government subsidy, secure Indian reserves, deflect reasonably straight routes to include Atchison, and extend the routes of projected railroads receiving government subventions.

Table 9. POPULATION OF PRINCIPAL MISSOURI VALLEY TOWNS [54]

	1860	1870
Kansas City, Missouri	4,418	32,260
St. Joseph	8,932	19,565
Leavenworth	7,429	17,873
Atchison	2,616	7,054
Wyandotte (Kansas City, Kansas)	1,920	2,940

His persistence and lack of squeamishness in bargaining for support enabled him to secure the usual land grants for the Atchison, Topeka, and Santa Fe (Santa Fe) and the Atch-

[53] This is the theme of a series of newspaper articles critical of Pomeroy that were published by the *Nemaha Courier,* the *Leavenworth Times* and other papers and brought together in a pamphlet, *The Political Record of Hon. S. C. Pomeroy as Shown by His Own Party Newspaper Press in Kansas* (Seneca, Kansas, 1866), *passim.*

[54] *Census of 1870,* Vol. *Population, passim.*

ison and Pikes Peak Railroads and the generous government bond subsidy for the latter. At the time it was said Pomeroy had a one-sixteenth interest in the Pikes Peak Road.[55] Certainly, he owned a one-sixteenth interest in all the town sites on the line of the road.[56] For the Santa Fe, $950,000 in county bonds were voted by Atchison, Jefferson, Shawnee, Osage, and Lyon Counties in exchange for railroad stock; while for the Atchison and Nebràska Railroad $350,000 in county bonds were voted by Atchison and Doniphan Counties.[57]

Notwithstanding the generous aid thus provided by the Federal and county governments, railroad construction was slow. Since the Delaware reserve had enabled the LP&W Railroad to get under way, might not other reserves, if sold to the Atchison railroads, be beneficial to them? The Kickapoo reserve of 150,000 acres in Brown, Jackson, and Atchison Counties stood in the way of Pomeroy's favorite enterprise, the Pikes Peak Line, of which Pomeroy himself was president. Permission to build through the reserve had to be secured, but if the entire reserve could be bought, so much the better.

Leavenworth interests which were planning a railroad up the Missouri River on the Kansas side and on to Fort Kearney maneuvered in 1860 to secure both the Kickapoo reserve and the Oto reserve, which was on the Kansas-Nebraska border. Blessed as they were with the skilful aid of A. J. Isaacs and Ira McDowell and the favorable attention

---

[55] 12 *Stat.*, 489, 772; 13 *Stat.*, 356. General H. V. Boynton in his effort to "unmask" and bring into the open the boodlers who were dividing up the Kansas reserves between themselves and the railroads attacked Pomeroy as a willing tool and major beneficiary, *Cincinnati Daily Gazette,* Jan. 1, 1869.

[56] This interest was conveyed to Otis B. Gunn on March 1, 1867. E. Nemaha County Deeds, p. 289.

[57] A. T. Andreas, *History of the State of Kansas* (Chicago, 1883), 243, 252.

of some of the Indian agents, they could anticipate success unless they were forestalled by persons advocating railroads centering in Atchison or St. Joseph.[58] A second rival consisted of the the Hannibal & St. Joseph Railroad, which had reached the latter city and was looking westward for a further extension.

While Isaacs was pressing his Washington contacts in behalf of the Leavenworth interests, Senator Pomeroy drew up the terms of a treaty to be submitted to the Kickapoo, and which he induced the Commissioner of Indian Affairs to forward to Charles B. Keith, agent to the Kickapoo, with instructions to negotiate with the Indians for their approval of it. By securing the jump on his two rivals, Pomeroy with the help of Keith, won the approval of the Indians on June 28, 1862, to a treaty which provided for inalienable and untaxable allotments to chiefs, to heads of families and to other members of 320, 160 and 40 acres respectively, and which authorized the Pikes Peak Railroad to buy the remainder of the land (amounting to 123,832 acres), not at appraised value, but at $1.25 an acre. The company was authorized to give its bonds as security for completing the contract and was permitted to sell the land before it had made any payments. Other than 6 per cent interest, no payments were due the Indians until six years after the contract was signed; and as things fell out, this was 1871. If the treaty were ratified, Pomeroy's railroad was thus provided with a possible source of income from sales of the reserve without investing a cent in it or in construction.[59]

[58] H. Miles Moore, Leavenworth, Aug. 6, 1860, to Col. A. J. Isaacs, Washington, Care, Commissioner of Indian Affairs, H. Miles Moore Letter Book, 1859–1871, Kansas State Historical Society.

[59] As president of the Pikes Peak Line, Pomeroy addressed letters concerning the purchase of the reserve from his office in 58 Wall St., New York. See his letter of Jan. 26, 1865 to William P. Dole, Indian Affairs, National Archives.

But Pomeroy had won only the first round in the fight to gain control of the much-sought Kickapoo lands. Promoters of the Kansas extension of the Hannibal & St. Joseph Railroad were distressed at their initial failure. They seem to have joined with other opponents of Pomeroy's project line to defeat ratification of the treaty.[60] They stirred up opposition to the treaty among the Kickapoo, always an easy task; and the Kickapoo brought the usual charges that Keith had threatened to use military force to effect a treaty, had offered $250 to each chief for his signature to the treaty, had withheld the expected annuity until favorable action, had set the Indians against their chiefs, and had permitted whites to intrude in the reserve.[61] Members of the Kansas legislature dispatched a remonstrance against ratification which maintained the treaty had been signed by squaws, boys, and half-breeds and not by the chiefs.[62] The treaty was dubbed the "Kickapoo fraud." Continued criticism led to the holding of a grand council with the Kickapoo, attended by William P. Dole, Commissioner of Indian Affairs, Judge S. W. Johnston, Senator Pomeroy, Keith, and others. Hostile critics called the council a farce and a whitewash, but the defenders contended that the Indians were "well satisfied" with the sale.[63]

Before ratification of the Kickapoo treaty Pomeroy tried to peddle the charter, the land grant and Federal loan, and the right to buy the surplus lands of the Kickapoo to James F.

[60] Albert W. Horton, Atchison, June 20, 1863, to Pomeroy, endorsed by Pomeroy and sent to Dole, Indian Affairs, National Archives.

[61] Affidavit of John C. Anderson, June 13, 1862, and protest signed by five chiefs and a hundred Indians, urging that the treaty be rejected, *loc. cit.*

[62] White Cloud *Kansas Chief,* Sept. 10, 24, 1863; *Sen. Ex. Journal,* Feb. 12, 1863, XIII, 128.

[63] *New York Tribune,* Sept. 23, 1863; Annie Heloise Abel, *American Indian as a Slaveholder and Secessionist* (Cleveland, 1915–1925), II, 230.

137

Joy and the group associated with him in the Hannibal and St. Joseph and the Burlington railroads. Possibly Pomeroy had earlier bought off the opposition of the St. Joseph interests, for there is evidence that the latter had assigned any rights they might have in the reserve to the Pikes Peak Line. In any case, during late 1863 John Murray Forbes, John W. Brooks, and James F. Joy were still dickering with Pomeroy for joint promotion of the Pikes Peak Railroad on the understanding that the Senator would prevent any tampering with the treaty.[64]

On March 13, 1863, the Kickapoo treaty was ratified after long delay and much undercover opposition by a Senate that had neither time nor inclination to investigate complaints of improper negotiations that were directed at one of its chief figures. Search of the deed records of the three counties in which the reserve was located has brought to light information which shows that Sol Miller's denunciation of the treaty was well founded. It should be remembered that the Pikes Peak Railroad came close to being a Pomeroy family concern, for the Senator was president until succeeded by Ralph M. Pomeroy; Daniel C. Pomeroy of Atchison was one director; and Willis E. Gaylord, the Senator's brother-in-law, was another director, as well as contractor on construction. Senator Pomeroy it was said, received for his share in the negotiation and ratification of the treaty 50,000 acres in the Kickapoo Reserve.[65] Charles B. Keith, who negoti-

---

[64] Letters of Sidney Bartlett, Nov. 21, 1863, to J. W. Brooks; J. W. Brooks and J. M. Forbes, Boston, Dec. 9, 1863, to Pomeroy (copy); and telegram of Brooks, Dec. 9, 1863, to Pomeroy, in Joy Manuscripts, University of Michigan.

[65] Senator Ross made this charge in the Council Grove *Democrat*, April 25, 1872, see Martha B. Caldwell, "Pomeroy's 'Ross Letter': Genuine or Forgery?" *Kansas History Quarterly*, XIII, 463. Ross also accused Pomeroy of having stolen a "princely fortune" from the Union Pacific, Central Branch, formerly the Atchison & Pikes Peak Railroad.

ated the treaty or at least secured some signatures to it and who aided in the grand council that later expressed its approval, in 1865 sold 1,300 acres to Senator Pomeroy for $7,000. They were to be used for the raising of goats. More beneficial was the transfer of 1,280 acres of the Kickapoo lands from the railroad to Mary B. Keith in 1866.[66] To Elizabeth Dole, wife of the Commissioner of Indian Affairs, 640 acres were conveyed for one dollar.[67] Sol Miller accused Jim Lane of selling out the Northern Tier for which "he received a handsome 'pile' in cash . . ."[68]

In common with all Indian reserves in Kansas, the Kickapoo lands had been taken up and improved to a considerable degree by squatters prior to the sale to the railroad. These squatters and other settlers in the vicinity of the Kickapoo tract were not happy at the sale. Though the squatters had ultimately to come to terms for the purchase of their claims, they delayed buying as long as possible and undoubtedly took pleasure in plundering the unoccupied railroad lands of their timber.[69]

The Pikes Peak Railroad put the Kickapoo lands on the market as soon as they were surveyed, appraised, and a land office set up; many early sales were reported. Income from these sales and from the 6,400 acres of lands granted for each mile of road, together with the $16,000-per-mile subsidy provided by the Federal government, enabled the railroad to push rapidly westward from Atchison, 90 miles in 1868, giving it rank next to the UP, Eastern Division, as the long-

[66] Atchison *Freedom's Champion,* Oct. 19, 1865.

[67] Brown County Deeds, I, 591 ff. and N, 558. The advertising of the railroad stressed that it was prepared to sell land to settlers only but at least a dozen transactions were found in the Brown County deeds that clearly were not made for settlement.

[68] *Kansas Chief,* May 19, 1864.

[69] Abram Bennett, Indian Agent, Kickapoo Agency, Feb. 6, 1865, to W. P. Dole, Indian Affairs, National Archives.

est railroad in Kansas.[70] In that year the Union Pacific, Central Branch (as the Atchison and Pikes Peak Railroad was now called) was advertising 1,280,000 acres of "Agricultural and Stock Lands" for sale at $1 to $10 an acre, the average price being less than $7, on credit of three to ten years. As an added inducement for the sale of the Kickapoo lands, they were declared to be "not subject to taxation." [71] Construction of the railroad undoubtedly gave these added values to the lands, but the settlers in buying lands at such prices were providing much of the cost. Also, the alternate reserve lands for a distance of 10 miles on each side of the road had been withheld from sale and settlement until 1868, and then were only to be sold to pre-emptors at $2.50 an acre or to be open to homestead in 80-acre lots. As much of the better land had been picked up by speculators prior to the withdrawal, the $2.50 price was not low, and the small homestead unit was inadequate.[72]

The next Indian reserve in Kansas to go under the hammer to a railroad was the segment of Delaware lands in Leavenworth County which had not been allotted. Being considerably improved, enjoying railroad connections, and lying in the heart of the settled region, the tract was in great demand. Estimates of its value ranged as high as $15 an acre, and one offer of $3.50 was actually made. Two groups favored by James Harlan, Secretary of the Interior, were interested in securing this tract. The first, the American Emigrant Company, was a land-jobbing and scab-importing agency consisting of a group of Iowa and Connecticut promoters

[70] *Atchison Champion,* Jan. 16, 1868. *Poor's Manual,* 1868–1869 (p. 297), gives the western terminus at Waterville, 100 miles from Atchison. It was then known as the Union Pacific, Central Branch. It later became part of the Missouri Pacific system.

[71]*Atchison Champion,* March 26, 1868.

[72] Announcement of the reopening of the reserved sections to entry was made in the *Atchison Champion,* April 9, 1868.

who already had acquired through questionable means some of the swamp lands of Iowa.[73] Earlier it had sought to buy one of the railroad land grants in Iowa.[74] On July 30, 1866, the superintendent of its land department wrote Harlan that he intended to submit a bid for the Delaware tract and would offer more than $2.50 an acre. He asked for ten or twelve days in which to prepare an offer, but his request came too late.[75] A rival had forestalled the Emigrant Company but the latter was to have its day in connection with the Cherokee Neutral Tract.

The Missouri River Railroad had the inside track to ownership of the diminished reserve of the Delawares. Rivals such as the American Emigrant Company and the UP, Eastern Division, were beaten down by the smart footwork of Thomas Ewing, Jr., currently an incorporator and lobbyist of the Missouri River Railroad.[76] To forestall opposition and get a sale arranged quickly, a treaty was drawn up in Washington, rushed to Kansas, and shown to three chiefs and four braves who when properly "manipulated" were induced to append their mark. Rushed back to Congress, the treaty was quickly confirmed and proclaimed, and the 92,598 acres of the reserve were assured to the Missouri River Railroad for $2.50 an acre plus the appraised value of any improve-

---

[73] For a detailed examination of the immigration activities of the American Emigrant Company see Charlotte Erickson, "The Recruitment of European Immigrant Labor for American Industry from 1860 to 1885," (Unpublished Ph.D. thesis, Cornell University, 1951), pp. 66 ff.

[74] *Des Moines Register* clipped in *Sioux City Register,* Feb. 8, 1862.

[75] Copy, J. C. Savary, American Emigrant Company, N.Y., July 30, 1866, to James Harlan, Delaware Files, Indian Office Records, National Archives.

[76] Wm. McNeill Clough, of Clough and Wheat, Leavenworth, April 23, 1864, to John G. Pratt, Pratt MSS., Kansas State Historical Society; L. C. Bogy, Commissioner of Indian Affairs, Washington, Nov. 6, 1866, to Jas. D. Perry, National Archives.

ments.[77] Payment could be made or security for payment
provided with the bonds of the company, which could sell
the lands and derive revenue from them without having to
put up the cash price. Already Leavenworth City and County
had voted $500,000 to aid the railroad, and this money
with the income from the Delaware lands, amounting to
"upwards of $1,000,000," contributed much to the comple-
tion of the road from Wyandotte to Leavenworth in 1866
and to Atchison in 1869.[78] The Delaware lands had been
the object of much strife, pillage and timber stealing; and
to reimburse the Indians for their known losses, credit of
$30,000 was allowed on the purchase of a new reserve in
Oklahoma. Even after the sale, there was much dispute over
timber ownership on the reserve, with the Delawares supporting the rights of a lumber company which had acquired
some timbered allotments where it was cutting for the UP,
Eastern Division while the Missouri River Railroad opposed
the cutting.[79]

Most laggard of the railroads in which Pomeroy was interested was the Atchison, Topeka, and Santa Fe. The grant
of ten sections per mile of March 3, 1863, which was mostly
Pomeroy's work, brought no early income, for no lands were
available under such a grant in eastern Kansas where settlement was proceeding.[80] More immediately helpful was the

[77] General H. V. Boynton has a hostile account of the negotiations
that checks with other sources in the *Cincinnati Daily Gazette,* Feb. 5,
Dec. 17, 1869. After appraisal the price of the Delaware lands was
set at $2.96 per acre. Commissioner of Indian Affairs, *Annual Re-
port,* 1867, p. 359.

[78] *Atchison Champion,* Jan. 16, 1868; Andreas, *op. cit.,* 251.

[79] D. N. Cooley, Commissioner of Indian Affairs, Jan. 11, 1866,
to James Harlan, and L. V. Bogy, Commissioner of Indian Affairs,
Nov. 7, 1866, to John G. Pratt, Pratt MSS., Kansas State Historical
Society.

[80] 12 *Stat.,* 772; Atchison *Freedom's Champion,* Aug. 29, 1863.
Pomeroy was elected president of the Santa Fe on Nov. 30, 1863.
Council Grove Press, Nov. 30, 1863.

exchange by the counties of Atchison, Jefferson, Shawnee, Osage, and Lyon of $950,000 of their bonds for stock in the railroad company.[81]

The failure of the LP&W and the UP, Eastern Division, to take up the Pottawatomie tract left this valuable reserve open for jockeying; and the Atchison, Topeka, and Santa Fe soon entered the field. Up to this point reserves had been sold only to railroads being built through them. It was the prospect of making allotments more attractive and hence more valuable by bringing railroads to their vicinity that aided in inducing the Indians to sell.[82] But Pomeroy and others working for the Santa Fe had to cast aside this argument, for their favored line would not even touch the Pottawatomie tract.

"Old Subsidy" was not one to let principle stand in the way of the interests he favored. As president of the Santa Fe and with the aid of Willis Gaylord, his brother-in-law who had strong eastern connections, abetted by Ross and Harlan in the Senate, he succeeded in having a treaty negotiated with the Pottawatomies which gave Pomeroy and the Santa Fe just what they wanted. The new treaty provided for the sale of the 340,180 acres of surplus lands to the Santa Fe at $1.00 per acre instead of the $1.25 which the UP, Eastern Division had been asked to pay. Also, where the first treaty had provided for payment in specie, the second treaty permitted payment in greenbacks, a provision which assured a still further reduction in the real cost per acre.

[81] Andreas, *op. cit.* 243. L. L. Waters, *Steel Trails to Santa Fe* (Lawrence, 1950), p. 34, says Jefferson County did not carry through its exchange of bonds for Santa Fe stock.

[82] Section 5 of the Treaty of Nov. 15, 1861 reads in part: "The Pottawatomies . . . being desirous to have said railroad [the Leavenworth, Pawnee, and Western] extended through their reserve . . . so that the value of the lands retained by them may be enhanced, and the means afforded them of getting the surplus products of their farms to market" agree to sell their surplus lands to the railroad.

Settlers on neighboring land had to pay $1.25 an acre, if they pre-empted their tracts, and were allowed only one year in which to complete their entry and make their payment. To them and to Kansas generally the sale to the Santa Fe was just another instance of the way in which the Pomeroy-Gaylord-Harlan combination was mulcting the Indians and the settlers of their rights. The secrecy which surrounded the whole process of making treaties with the Indians invited inside deals of this character. The Pottawatomie treaty was negotiated on February 27, 1868, amended by the Senate in secret or executive session on June 23, and 30, to provide for the sale to the Santa Fe, and the treaty was ratified on July 25.[83] George W. Julian, land reforming representative from Indiana, who was already deeply involved in efforts to defeat the much bigger sales to railroads dominated by James F. Joy of the Cherokee Neutral Tract and the Osage Reserve, learned of the treaty before its final ratification but after the amendment to provide for the sale to the Santa Fe had been approved. Although he had no copy of the treaty, Julian rushed through the House on July 7 a resolution calling for the facts in the treaty, declaring the Pottawatomie lands to be valuable, and stating that the price of $1.00 an acre was believed to be "in monstrous disproportion" to their actual value.[84] Julian's resolution came too late to halt the sale.

The bargain gained by Pomeroy is best judged by the financial results obtained from it. The Pottawatomie lands came into quick demand as soon as they were surveyed, appraised, and offered for sale. In the *Annual Report* of the Santa Fe for 1873, the cash receipts from the land are given as $646,784 and the remaining lands are valued at $507,-366.[85] As the railroad had to pay only 6 per cent interest

[83] *Sen. Ex. Journal,* XV, part 2, 449; XVI, 225, 287, 381.

[84] *Cong. Globe,* 40 Cong., 2 Sess., IV, 3786.

[85] Atchison, Topeka and Santa Fe Railroad, *Annual Report,* 1873, p. 10. In later reports the meager data given indicate that the estimate

on its obligation until 1873, it is apparent that the lands provided funds for construction at a critical time and at little cost. Also, the unsold Pottawatomie lands provided a basis for a bond issue that assured additional funds. At the time the railroad had no other lands available for sale, since the regular land grant could not be sold until earned. It is understandable that a recent historian of the Santa Fe should say that the acquisition of the Pottawatomie reserve "improved fortuitously" the chances of success of the railroad.[86] In this instance the settlers on a tract not touched by the railroad that acquired their lands were, in effect, to provide through the prices they paid for their land the funds with which construction was begun.

The Pottawatomie lands were not permitted to pass into the hands of the railroad without a struggle. Squatters in considerable numbers had long since settled on the tract, renting the lands from the Indians on shares, or becoming laborers on it for Indians. Their purpose was to acquire a settlement right which might enable them to get the land either as a free homestead or as a pre-emption right for $1.25 an acre when the Indians were removed. The improvements that they made bound them to the land and led them to resist efforts of the agents to remove them.[87] Squatter opposition to the sale of tracts to railroads and popular resentment at the preferential treatment given the railroads in the purchase of the reserves were increasingly marked after news of the Pottawatomie treaty reached Kansas.

of return contained in the *Annual Report* for 1873 was somewhat optimistic. Waters (p. 220) says the company netted a "sizable sum" from the lands. The Santa Fe received 1,454 acres for the right of way through the reserve and bought 338,795 acres at the one-dollar price. These lands brought an average price of $4.41 per acre.

[86] Waters, *op. cit.*, 35, 220.

[87] L. R. Palmer, U.S. Indian agent to Pottawatomies, Dec. 19, 1865, to Thos. Murphy, in Pottawatomie File, 1865, Indian Affairs, National Archives.

Willis Gaylord, brother-in-law of Pomeroy, later claimed 100,000 acres of Pottawatomie land as his fee for securing the tract for the Santa Fe. The amount is large, but Pomeroy and his associates did things in a big way. Ninety thousand acres of this land or the equivalent, there is evidence to believe, went to the Senator.[88] Sidney Clarke, Kansas Representative, maintained that he had been promised two sections of land for his aid in securing ratification of the treaty.[89] Thomas Ewing, Jr., who had undoubtedly been disappointed that the LP&W had not managed to buy the tract, was solaced by the conveyance of 4,141 acres at the price the railroad paid for them. William P. Borland of Leavenworth also acquired 4,049 acres at the same price. In addition five eastern financiers were privileged to buy from 1,920 to 20,703 acres at one dollar an acre.[90]

The railroad attack upon the Kansas reserves was not always successful. The Sac and Fox lands of some 453,000 acres in Osage and neighboring counties were partly ceded

[88] The Gaylord claim was resisted by the Santa Fe, but a cryptic statement in the *Annual Report* for 1874 (p. 49), lends substance to it. See *Emporia News,* July 9, 1869. Former Senator Ross charged Pomeroy with having received 90,000 acres of Pottawatomie lands for his share in arranging the purchase. Council Grove *Democrat,* April 25, 1872, in Martha B. Caldwell, *op. cit.,* p. 463.

[89] James Craig, Washington, May 3, 5, 1870, to Joy.

[90] These transactions were made in 1873 and are recorded in the Jackson County Deeds. Following are the purchases by the eastern capitalists:

Buyer	Residence	Acres
Lewis Haight	New York City	3,389
Lewis May	New York City	1,920
George Opdyke	New York City	4,000
Charles W. Pierce	Boston	11,952
John Swinburne	Albany, N.Y.	20,703

A more comprehensive study of conveyances of the Pottawatomie lands by the Santa Fe, after allowing for almost certain duplications, shows the following purchases by directors of the railroad:

in trust by a treaty of 1860 which specified that they should be sold on sealed bids. The Burlington & Topeka Railroad, then being projected through the tract, naturally sought to get control and in 1862 induced the Indian Office to negotiate a treaty with the Indians which would authorize sale of 200,000 acres for $1.12½ per acre. Ratification was denied by the Senate, and the plan fell through.[91] Two years later the trust lands were offered on sealed bids which, it was charged, permitted insiders to slip in offers on the best lands slightly above the highest bids. Whatever the collusion, the bulk of the land went in 1870 either directly or indirectly through dummy bidders to five parties or groups, chief of which was John McManus, of Reading, Pennsylvania, who was a director of the Kansas Pacific Railroad (KP) (the old Leavenworth, Pawnee, and Western). McManus conveyed the 142,929 acres he had acquired at various prices but mostly at less than the Burlington & Topeka Railroad had offered, to Seyfert, McManus & Co., an iron manufacturing company, which had secured amendments to its charter, permitting it to colonize and hold land in other states; [92] 27,677 acres at least went to the UP, Eastern Division, at a cost of $1 an acre; 39,414 acres were acquired by various buyers and transferred to Northrup and Chick, a real estate

---

	Acres
Charles W. Pierce	23,349
George Opdyke	20,946
Alden Speare	2,720 (part forfeited)
E. Raymond	1,584

These data were compiled from a brief of W. D. Davis submitted in support of the Pottawatomie claim for additional compensation for the sale of their Kansas lands, United States Department of Justice.

[91] *Kansas State Record* (Topeka), Aug. 27, 1862.

[92] United States to W. J. Keeler and Lucien Scott, Oct. 6, 1865; Keeler and Scott to William R. McKeen, and McKeen to John D. Perry, Pres. Union Pacific, Eastern Division, Dec. 1, 1865, in Franklin County Deeds, Vol. H, 230–235.

and banking group of Kansas City and Brooklyn. In this
and in other deals relating to the Sac and Fox lands, Hugh
McCulloch and J. P. Usher, respectively Comptroller of
the Currency and Secretary of the Interior, and Stephen A.
Dole were major participants.

The Kansas Indian tract, in present Morris, Lyon, and
Chase Counties, for years was sought, in whole or in part,
by squatters, land speculators, and railroads. By error of the
Indian Office, a portion of the tract was declared open to settlement in early territorial days, and settlers flocked to it and
established their homes. Subsequently, when the survey lines
were run, they were found to be within the reserve and were
listed as trespassers. In 1859 a treaty with the Kaws provided
for a diminished reserve to be retained by the Indians and
allotted to individual members of the tribe, while the surplus lands were ceded in trust to be sold on "sealed proposals"
to the highest bidder. Settlers who were on the ceded lands
prior to the survey were to be permitted to buy at the high
price of $1.75 an acre, and settlers on the diminished reserve
were to be given "fair compensation for their improvements."
Squatters who had moved to the tract after December 2, 1856
would have to bid for their land against competitors whom
they could not know or intimidate through squatter associations.

Announcement of the treaty was followed by the usual
violent denunciation from local residents who had come to
fear the management of lands by the Indian Office and the
"Land jobbing Administration" of James Buchanan. The
sealed proposal method forces settlers into competition with
"heartless speculators" who, if permitted, will utterly "blast
and ruin" the citizens, said a petition signed by 200 legal
voters.[93] It is a "foul wrong concocted by a corrupt Administration," said the *Kansas Press* of Council Grove; the people will not "permit a set of land jobbers and speculators to

[93] *Kansas Press* (Council Grove), Dec. 12, 1859.

rob us." [94] The squatters were urged to organize a claim association and to make certain that "no speculator will interfere with the rights of the settlers unless he expects to run his head into a halter . . ." "Resist to the death," was the cry.[95] Despite local opposition, the treaty was ratified, but its confirmation boded no good to the Buchanan administration. Local feeling was being turned by this and numerous other incidents which all seemed to show that the Indian reserves and public lands were being used for the benefit of speculator groups rather than to make possible easy access to ownership for settlers. It was to be disillusioning to Kansans that when the Lincoln administration came into power its officials in the Indian Office seemed no more sensitive to settler interests than their predecessors had been.

In 1863 "sealed proposals" were invited for 160,000 acres of the Kansas trust lands and when they were opened it was found that on some 75 of the best claims Robert Corwin, Washington contact man and one of the top ranking lobbyists and attorneys working on Indian claims and lands, had bid just slightly above competitors. The protest against this evidence of unfairness in the "secret" bids was so great that the Indian Office rushed to cover. All bids were cancelled.[96] Small lots were, however, sold thereafter without arousing as violent opposition.

In 1866, it was proposed to sell 80,000 acres of the much fought-over reserve to the UP, Southern Branch, later the Missouri, Kansas, and Texas Railroad (Katy). An estimated 500 squatters on the land raised a storm of opposition to this proposed sale, a storm which swiftly reverberated

[94] *Ibid.*

[95] *Council Grove Press,* June 22, July 30, 1860; *Emporia News,* Sept. 3, Nov. 5, 1859; *Leavenworth Times* in White Cloud *Kansas Chief,* Sept. 8, 1859. A protest against ratification signed by "sundry citizens" was presented in the Senate, *Sen. Ex. Journal,* June 1, 1860, XI, 200.

[96] *Council Grove Press,* April 13, June 8, Sept. 14, 1863.

through Kansas and led the Senate to hold in abeyance for six months the treaty authorizing the sale, and then to reject it. One objection was that the price of 87½ cents an acre was too low. In 1867 still another effort was made to purchase the tract by the same railroad, this time for $1.50 an acre.[97]

This second effort of the Katy Railroad to obtain the Kansas lands was likewise a failure.[98] Concern about settler interests doubtless had some part in the defeat of the two Kansas Indian treaties, but a more important factor was that other speculative groups and individuals who had claims against the Kaws were pulling at cross purposes and for a time prevented any action involving disposal.[99] The remaining unsold and unallotted lands—181,212 acres—were offered for sale on sealed bids in 1871. Numerous bids were received, one of which called for the entire amount at $2.42 an acre, but all were rejected on technicalities.[100] As late as 1873 one or more railroads were lobbying to get control of the Kansas lands, but by this time the treaty-making power was abolished, and the uprising against sales to speculators and railroads had reached such a proportion that it was no longer feasible to sell to other than actual settlers.[101]

[97] *Sen. Ex. Journal,* May 10, 1866, XIV, 781; Anna H. Abel, "Indian Reservations in Kansas and the Extinguishment of their Title," *Kansas Historical Collections,* VIII, 99.

[98] Commissioner of Indian Affairs, *Annual Report,* 1869, p. 511.

[99] Wm. A. Ewing, Washington, D.C., Feb. 20, 1867, to B. D. Miner, Executor; A. N. Blackledge to B. D. Miner, March 4, 10, 1867; W. G. & G. W. Ewing MSS., Indiana State Library.

[100] Leonard T. Smith and W. S. Van Doren, representing the Kansas Immigration Society, which was nothing more than a land-speculating company, presented this bid. The bids are in the Kansas Indian Land File, National Archives. See also the Commissioner of Indian Affairs, *Annual Report,* 1871, p. 681.

[101] Report of T. C. Jones, Special Commissioner, to the Commissioner of Indian Affairs, Sept. 16, 1863, in Commissioner of Indian Affairs, *Annual Report,* 1873, p. 168.

Four other Kansas reserves come in for some consideration. Kersey Coates, of the Missouri River, Fort Scott, and Gulf Railroad (the Fort Scott Line) tried to purchase the small Quapaw tract, amounting to some 30,000 acres, of which 7,680 acres were in Kansas. He also sought the remaining Ottawa and Miami lands but was being hindered in his efforts, as he reported, by "designing men." [102] An offer of 50 cents an acre for the 2½-mile-wide strip of Cherokee land stretching for a distance of 276 miles along the southern border of Kansas failed to attract support in 1870, and the tract was subsequently thrown open to pre-emption but not to homestead. [103]

Thus far there had been no very effective opposition to the sale of the reserves to railroads, except among squatters; and their views were not always convincingly expressed nor presented early enough to stop the purchase. Furthermore, the railroads that had been privileged to buy reserves were more or less of a native brand, and Kansans were so desperately anxious to bring in railroads that they were, seemingly, willing to promise anything to get them. When, however, a group of rich eastern capitalists, who were on the way toward creating the first great railroad combination in the Missouri Valley, attempted to get control of the Cherokee Neutral Tract of 800,000 acres and the Osage tract of 8,000-000 acres, an explosion occurred. While failing to stop the Cherokee sale, the thunderous outburst did prevent ratification of the Osage treaty. More important, it brought to a halt the treaty-making power which had permitted a group of influential lobbyists, working closely with the Indian Office, to acquire the reserves at prices highly advantageous, to

[102] Kersey Coates, Dec. 15, 1869, Feb. 26, 1870, to James F. Joy; Joy to Coates, March 1, 1869. Joy MSS., Burton Historical Collections, Detroit Public Library.

[103] George H. Vickery, Washington, Feb. 23, 1870, to Cherokee Delegates, Cherokee File, National Archives.

151

Crisis

Fifty Million Acres

them. The story of the Cherokee "steal" and of the attempt to buy the Osage tract as a unit therefore has significance not only for Kansas but also for the history of public land policy on a national scale.

them. The story of the Cherokee "steal" and of the attempt to buy the Osage tract as a unit therefore has significance not only for Kansas but also for the history of public land policy on a national scale.

CHAPTER V

Settler-Railroad War
on the Neutral Tract

THE LARGEST Indian reserves in Kansas were those of the
Cherokees and the Osages, which stretched westward from
the Missouri line along the southern border for a distance
of 300 miles. The Cherokee holdings of 1,234,000 acres
consisted of the Neutral Tract, a region in the southeast
corner of the state measuring 50 miles from north to south
and 25 miles from east to west; and the Strip, a narrow tract
two and one-half miles in depth and 276 miles long just north
of the boundary of Indian Territory. The Osage reserve of
8,841,927 acres lay west of the Neutral Tract and north of
the Strip. Both reserves were in the path of railroads projected south from the growing centers of Kansas City and
Topeka. Any railroad planning to build to or through the
Indian country needed, it was thought, either grants of rights-
of-way and of alternate sections of land or, in lieu of the lat-

ter, the right to buy the entire reserves at the government minimum price. Railroad promoters were not alone in eyeing enviously these great reserves. Land speculating groups and squatters were also deeply interested.

Like the other reserves on the eastern border of Kansas, the Cherokee Neutral Tract was well taken up by squatters prior to the outbreak of the Civil War. This occupation was made easier by the fact that the Cherokees never had established themselves on it. By 1859 there were said to be between 600 and 700 settlers and in 1860 2,025 on the tract.[1] Some squatters seem to have thought that they were on the New York Indian reserve, which, while not officially opened to settlement prior to 1860, was not so clearly closed as was the Neutral Tract. Others hoped either that the tract would become part of the public domain and that the Pre-emption Law would be applied to it or that it would be sold in small units to squatters as the Delaware, Iowa, and Confederated Peoria lands had been. Inevitably the area was wracked by disputes over claims and by conflicts between the bushwhackers and jayhawkers. Some of the bitterest battles of the territorial period were fought in the vicinity of Fort Scott, just north of the tract. Although the Pierce and Buchanan administrations had at no time followed a clear line of policy concerning intruders on the reserves, local officials determined to oust the squatters on the Neutral Tract. The fact that the squatters were antislavery and were accused of planning to free slaves in the neighboring Missouri counties doubtless had some part in the decision. In 1860 the Indian agent, with fifty dragoons, swept through the tract burning houses and improvements and driving out the settlers. In three days 74 houses were destroyed and 100 families made homeless; but swift newspaper denunciation and organized opposition to further destruction stopped action for a time.[2]

[1] *Fort Scott Democrat,* Oct. 20, 1859, Sept. 22, 1860.
[2] *Kansas Chief,* (White Cloud) Nov. 29, 1860; *Fort Scott Demo-*

Early in 1861 the Kansas legislature memorialized Congress asking that a strip of land eight or nine miles wide on the north side of the Neutral Tract and the Osage lands, on which settlers had unknowingly taken up land, be acquired from the Indians and surveyed and sold as public lands.[3] Then came the Civil War and succeeding invasions of secessionists and Cherokees who drove off the settlers, burned and pillaged their homes, and carried away the livestock.[4]

After the restoration of peace, it was rumored that the Cherokee lands were to be opened to settlement, and 2,000 families rushed in expecting either to pre-empt the lands at $1.25 an acre or to acquire them as free homesteads.[5] They were quickly disillusioned, however, for the two Kansas Senators and the Indian Office were more concerned with land speculation and railroad development than with the welfare of settlers. On July 19, 1866, a treaty was signed with the Cherokees by which the Neutral Tract was ceded "in trust" to the United States, which was either to sell on sealed bids to the highest bidder for cash at not less than $1.25 an acre all lands not occupied by squatters and not having improvements valued at $50, or was to sell the entire tract without regard to settlement rights for cash to "any responsible party" for $1 an acre. Under the first method the land was

---

crat, Feb. 23, Oct. 27, Nov. 15, Dec. 1, 1860; *Kansas National Democrat* (Lecompton), Nov. 1, 1860; *Lawrence Republican,* Nov. 8, 1860, quoting the *Mound City Report; Commercial Gazette* (Wyandotte), Nov. 3, 1860; Secretary of the Interior, *Annual Report, Sen. Ex. Doc.,* 36 Cong., 2 Sess., 1860–1861, I, no. 1, 444–451. Annie Heloise Abel, *American Indian as a Slaveholder and Secessionist* (Cleveland, 1915–1925), I, 46 ff., has some information concerning the alleged abolitionist tendencies of missionaries on the Tract.

[3] *Fort Scott Democrat,* Feb. 9, 1861.

[4] *Kansas Chief,* Aug. 15, 1861; *Leavenworth Conservative,* May 10, 1862.

[5] Petition of 36 individuals to President Andrew Johnson, Shawnee Ford, Cherokee File, 1866, National Archives.

to be sold in quarter-sections, and squatters were to be privileged to buy their claims provided they had improvements
on them to the value of $50 at the time of the treaty. The
treaty was rushed to ratification within 12 days after being
signed, but only after Senator Edmund G. Ross of Kansas
had succeeded in amending it to assure squatters the right to
buy their claims no matter how the unoccupied lands were
sold.[6]

Nine days after the Cherokee treaty was officially proclaimed, a deal was made with the American Emigrant Company for the purchase of the tract. In the treaty negotiations
James Harlan, Secretary of the Interior, had insisted on including a provision that would permit selling the entire tract
to a single party without regard to squatters' rights. This
provision was included, so many critics charged, to make
possible sale to the Emigrant Company. At the time of the
treaty negotiation Harlan was on the point of breaking
with President Andrew Johnson, and in fact his successor
had already been picked, but Harlan insisted on retaining
office until he could "close some business in the Department. . . ." [7] The business was the sale of the Neutral
Tract, and when the contract was signed, Harlan resigned
and took his seat in the Senate where he joined the opposition to the President.

When the sale of the Neutral Tract to the American
Emigrant Company was made public, a storm of criticism
was directed against it. Harlan was called a "pious swindler,"
and the Indian Office was described as "the seat of enormous
corruption, the fruitful source of Indian wars, the scandal of
the government." [8] The *Fort Scott Monitor* said of Harlan

[6] *Sen. Ex. Journal,* July 27, 1866, XIV, 1171–1172.

[7] James G. Randall, *The Diary of Orville Hickman Browning* (Illinois State Historical Library, *Collections,* XXII; Springfield, 1933),
II, 86.

[8] *New York Herald* in *Iowa City State Press,* Oct. 10, 1866; *New
York Evening Post* (semi-weekly) Oct. 9, Nov. 6, 1866. A letter of

in 1872 there was "no end to his public stealings," that he "preached, prayed, and blundered," and held that Iowa, like Kansas, was cursed "with pickpockets for Senators." [9] A later characterization of the sale by Eugene F. Ware, notable Kansas editor, is strong but not entirely unjustified: [10]

It was a great and dishonest act. It was done by Secretary Harlan just as he was to retire from office, and newspapers were full of complaint against it as being a dishonest, corrupt, boodling transaction, and it, among other things, assisted in retiring Mr. Harlan from the United States Senate, and raising a great outcry against him as a dishonest man. There were some who stated that he did it at the instigation of Mr. Pomeroy, the Senator from Kansas. Such charge was probably true. Pomeroy and Harlan enjoyed, in the newspapers of that time, a similar notoriety. Both of them were intentionally devout. Both of them worked under ministerial influence to the fullest extent, and both of them were charged with bribe taking and bribe giving, and both of them went out of office under the same kind of a cloud.

President Andrew Johnson was naturally distressed at the condemnations of the sale that came from so many sides, and his distrust of Harlan made him question it the more. With the aid of Thomas Ewing, Jr., who had been influential in negotiations leading to the purchase of two Delaware tracts and the Pottawatomie reserves in Kansas, and who, as legal representative of the Cherokees had been present and participated in the writing of the Cherokee treaty of 1866, the President found solid reason to cancel the sale. Thomas Ewing, Jr., his father, and his brother Hugh were close personal friends of Orville H. Browning, who succeeded Harlan

---

Thomas Ewing, Jr., Washington, Aug. 29, 1866, to James Harlan, protesting the sale, was published in the *National Intelligencer* and the *New York Evening Post*.

[9] *Fort Scott Monitor,* Jan. 12, 1872.

[10] Eugene W. Ware, "The Neutral Lands," Kansas State Historical Society *Collections* (1900), VI, 154–155.

as Secretary of the Interior. Before his appointment to the Department, Browning had been associated with the Ewings in prosecuting claims against the government. The Cherokees, it is worthy of note, were among their principal clients.[11] As Secretary, Browning took Thomas Ewing, Jr., to talk with the President on a number of occasions. So influential had he become that in Kansas it was said of Ewing: "a good fee, and Thomas Ewing Jr., on one's side, is all that is necessary to secure almost anything in the line of Indian contracts or government lands from the Department of the Interior." [12] Now as attorney for the Cherokee Indians who wished to get as much for their abandoned reserve as possible, and at the same time as legal representative of a group of creditors who were pressing the Cherokees for payment of claims against them, Ewing brought the weight of his influence against the sale to the American Emigrant Company. He pointed out that it was in direct violation of the treaty which required appraisal of the lands before sale, and sale only for cash, not on nine years' credit at 5 per cent interest. Attorney General Henry Stanbery, an earlier law partner of Ewing, Sr., borrowed the son's argument *in toto,* embedded it in a maze of legal verbiage, and declared the sale invalid.[13]

Four railroad groups immediately jumped into the picture

[11] Abel, *American Indian as a Slaveholder and Secessionist,* III, 70, footnote.

[12] Correspondent of the *Cincinnati Gazette,* Lawrence, Kansas, Nov. 25, 1868, in *ibid.,* Nov. 30, 1868. I have relied on Browning's diary and the introduction by James G. Randall, for the Browning-Ewing relations. Theodore C. Pease and James G. Randall, *The Diary of Orville Hickman Browning* (Illinois State Historical Library, *Collections,* XX, XXII, Springfield, 1925, 1933).

[13] Thomas Ewing, Jr., and John W. Wright, Washington, Aug. 29, 1866, to James Harlan; and Ewing, Washington, Nov. 3, 1866, to Harlan, Thomas Ewing MSS., Kansas State Historical Society. Attorney General Stanbery's statement is in the *National Intelligencer* (Washington), Oct. 10, 1866.

in the hope of acquiring the Cherokee lands. The Tebo and Neosho Railroad offered $1.12 an acre for the entire 800,000 acres, the payments to include $45,000 on execution of the sale, $45,000 in a year and the balance in nine annual installments. On the letter containing this offer Browning wrote: "No bid for lands other than for cash can be considered." [14] The second proposal which won the approval of the Commissioner of Indian Affairs, provided for sale to the Southern Branch, Union Pacific, in exchange for stock.[15] The third deal reached the treaty stage. John C. Fremont, president of the Atlantic and Pacific Railroad, offered to buy the tract for $1,000,000 and to pay $150,000 cash upon the signing of the contract, $150,000 in two years and the balance in payments to extend five years more. Despite its credit provision and Browning's specific statement that only a cash sale would be considered, the offer was incorporated in a treaty which was approved by the Secretary and President and transmitted to the Senate for approval. The fourth proposal was submitted by James F. Joy for the Missouri River, Fort Scott, and Gulf Railroad (the Fort Scott Line). Still another speculative group, perhaps comparable to the American Emigrant Company, called the Robert H. Gibbons & Co., Real Estate and Insurance Agents, of New York, expressed the wish to make an offer for the lands but was not encouraged.[16]

Rumors of dickering over the Cherokee Tract reached Kansas, and petitions and letters descended upon the Indian Office, the Secretary of the Interior, and the President de-

[14] P. A. LaDue, St. Louis, Mo., to L. V. Bogy, Jan. 19, 1867, in file: "Material on Indian Land Sales," National Archives; P. A. LaDue, *An Argument in Favor of a Land Grant to the Tebo and Neosho Railroad Company* (Washington, 1867), pp. 5–6.

[15] N. S. Gass, President, Southern Branch, Union Pacific, Washington, Jan. 5, 1867, to Browning; and draft of letter of L. V. Bogy to Browning, Jan. 23, 1867, Cherokee File, National Archives.

[16] Gibbons, April 5, 1867, to Browning, Indian Land Sales File, National Archives.

159

nouncing the "soulless railroads," "land sharks," and "swindling land companies" that were trying to keep the land from the "thousands of landless poor here" and urging the officials not to "crush our hopes or blight our reasonable expectations" by turning settlers over to the tender mercies of a railroad company.[17] A flood of protests against selling the land to any but squatters and immigrants who came in seeking free homesteads swept over Kansas; the governor, the legislature, many newspapers, and prominent individuals all urged that no hasty action be taken.[18] The ease with which speculators and railroad men had acquired the best of the Sac and Fox lands, the Pottawatomie, Delaware, and Kickapoo reserves, combined with the near misses of other special groups who had secretly sought to get control of large segments of Kansas lands, had excited suspicion. Now the mystery surrounding the action of Harlan in selling and Browning in voiding the sale of the Neutral Tract particularly inclined many to be deeply suspicious of the Indian Office and the Interior Department. Senator Samuel C. Pomeroy especially was coming under suspicion by many who had not

[17] Robert Y. Glenn, Lawrence, Sept. 10, 1867, and Elihu E. Coppinger, Pleasant View, Aug. 18, 1867, to President A. Johnson; Isaac F. Mead, Drywood, March 26, 1867, to Sec. of Interior; John D. Cargill, Hamilton, March 24, 1867, to Browning; L. C. Wheeler, Arcadia, undated but 1867, to S. Chase, and others in Indian Land Sales File, National Archives.

[18] Circular of Cherokee Co. Board of Immigration, May 20, 1867, Indian land sales, National Archives; W. M. Matheny, Secretary, Cherokee Co. Board of Immigration, Aug. 13, 1867, to Gov. S. J. Crawford, *loc. cit.;* S. J. Crawford, Topeka, Aug. 19, 1867, to O. H. Browning, *loc. cit.; Olathe Mirror,* June 4, 1868; Kansas Legislature, *Special Laws,* 1868, pp. 67–68. There was also some newspaper support for a sale of the Neutral Tract to Joy. The *Miami County Republican* (Nov. 23, Dec. 21, 1867; April 25, 1868) of Paola through which the "Border Tier" or Fort Scott Railroad was projected, favored the sale as it would aid in hastening construction.

profited from the numerous deals he had engineered. The presence upon the Neutral Tract of an estimated 2,000 families comprising 10,000 or 12,000 people made the problem of sale and management not only delicate but politically dangerous.[19]

Of all the groups that were dickering for the Neutral Tract, James F. Joy and his Boston associates were the best able to swing the purchase and to build a railroad through the tract that would hasten its development. Joy was president of the Chicago, Burlington, and Quincy (CB&Q) and of the Burlington and Missouri River Railroads; he was pushing the St. Joseph and Council Bluff Railroad as well as the Fort Scott Line. This group of railroads, together with the Hannibal and St. Joseph, would make the strongest railroad combination in the Missouri Valley. With two lieutenants, James Craig, president of both the Hannibal and St. Joseph and of the St. Joseph and Council Bluffs lines, and Kersey Coates, president of the Fort Scott Line, Joy worked the local county and city governments for loans; and together they secured $750,000 for the Fort Scott Railroad. In addition, the state of Kansas was induced to grant the same railroad 125,000 acres of its internal improvement lands.[20] The next step was to gain control of the Neutral Tract, through the center of which the Fort Scott road was to be built. This control would give to that road much of the advantage which land-grant railroads elsewhere were receiving from the increased value which construction gave to their lands. For the entire 800,000 acres the Joy men were willing to pay as

[19] Petition of 36 individuals, Shawnee Ford, Dec. 2, 1865, to Andrew Johnson, Indian Land Sales, National Archives; the Kansas legislature stated the number of residents on the tract to be not less than 20,000 in 1868. Resolution of Feb. 3, 1868, in *Laws of Kansas, 1868*, p. 68.

[20] *Olathe Mirror,* Oct. 26, 1866; Nov. 12, 1868.

high as $1,000,000, but they hoped to get the tract for less.[21]

Coates, Craig, Joy, and William Sturges, president of the Leavenworth, Lawrence, and Galveston Railroad (LL&G), began the campaign to secure the Neutral Tract in January, 1867, first by approaching the Emigrant Company, which had not accepted the finality of the cancellation. Both groups seemed to agree on mutual interests, and the groundwork was laid for the assignment of the original sale that was later to be made.[22] At the time Coates was in Washington urging the Cherokee chiefs gathered there to sell at the minimum price authorized in the treaty and pressing a bill upon Congress to permit the government to buy the land, the alternate sections of which he hoped to get for the Fort Scott Railroad. He preferred to buy the entire tract at $1 an acre rather than have one half given free and the other half lost to other interests.[23] Clearly he felt that control of a solid tract, such as had already been gained by the LP&W Railroad on the Delaware lands, was more valuable than an alternate-section grant.

Coates, Craig, Joy, and Sturges had first to defeat the treaty which Thomas Ewing, Jr., counsel for the Cherokees and, it was said, for Fremont, had drawn for the sale of the Neutral Tract to the Atlantic and Pacific Railroad. With Ewing as their opponent, this was no easy task. They worked on Browning, on a dissenting group of Cherokees who were induced to oppose ratification, on the Senate Committee on Indian Affairs and on other members of the Senate, combating "the large sums of money" that Fremont and his supporters were said to be using to influence senators. They

[21] K. Coates, Kansas City, July 15, 1867, to Joy, Joy MSS. All letters to Joy, hereafter cited, are in the Joy MSS. at the Detroit Public Library.

[22] William Sturges, January 16, 17, 1867, to Joy.

[23] Coates, Washington, Jan. 16, 1867, to Joy.

argued that the Fremont road was not projected through
the tract, nor even through any part of Kansas, and would
not benefit it in any way; that the treaty was illegal, as the
Indians who signed it were not the properly constituted
chiefs; and that it was against public policy to permit "speculators" to purchase Indian lands in large quantities. The argument that the Fremont line was a speculative company
because it was buying for a price-advance to which it would
contribute nothing may sound like sophistry, coming as it
did from the Joy group, but it undoubtedly aided in defeat-
ing the treaty.[24] On April 17 the Senate refused ratification
by a vote of 4 yeas and 29 nays. That Harlan and Pomeroy
opposed ratification may indicate that the Joy interests were
able to outbid Fremont.[25]

There followed six months of hectic lobbying by Coates,
Craig, Joy, Robert T. Van Horn, a Kansas City Congressman, and Nehemiah Bushnell, a Quincy, Illinois, law partner
of Browning and attorney for the Burlington Railroad. In
the correspondence of these skilled attorneys and railroad
men Browning appears vacillating, timid, anxious to favor
the Joy group, but fearful what public opinion would be, and
inclined to maintain that no sale could be made except for
cash. Coates described the Secretary's uncertainty and vacillation: [26] "Mr. Browning in his timidity flew the track, not
having the nerve to take the requisite final action. The fear
of public clamor, & possibility of a Congressional investigat-
ing Committee, I think haunts him like a spectre." Meantime,
a report of a reconnaissance of the Fort Scott Line had been
submitted to Joy; it confirmed his views about the high quality of the land, the deep, rich prairie soil, the absence of waste

[24] Coates, Washington, March 11, 21, 26, 1867, to Joy; James
Craig, Washington, March 17, 18, 27, 1867.
[25] *Sen. Ex. Journal,* 1867, XV, part 2, 749.
[26] Coates, New York, Aug. 5, 1867, to Joy.

land, the belts of timber along the streams, and the coal deposits. No better wheat country existed in the United States, reported one of the surveyors.[27]

It was embarrassing to Joy as well as to Browning that Fremont had offered $1,000,000 for the land, though in credit rather than cash. No one disputed that this price was justified, but Joy was anxious to get the tract for less. Furthermore, despite the failure of the two previous offers on credit, he hoped to get the land without any substantial cash payment. To help Browning decide the matter favorably, Bushnell proposed to get a letter from leading Cherokees expressing their desire that the Fort Scott Line be built and that the lands be sold to it at $1 an acre.[28] Finally, on October 9, 1867, Browning bucked up enough courage to make the sale, as he had wanted to do all along.[29] The contract with Joy provided that all lands not occupied by settlers were to be sold at $1 an acre in cash.

No one seemed satisfied with the second sale of the Neutral Tract, Joy had obviously not made as good a bargain as had the American Emigrant Company, since he had to put up cash, and the cash price was commonly regarded as higher than the same figure on a credit basis. As Joy said, money was worth 8 or 10 per cent, and the 5 per cent interest charged in the contract of the Emigrant Company looked good to him.[30] The Emigrant Company had never conceded the right of Attorney General Stanbery to cancel its original contract, which it held to be valid; and it now threatened suit to up-

[27] J. M. Walker, Aug. 12, 1867, to Joy; A. P. Clark, Civil Engineer, Chicago, Aug. 13, 1867, to Joy.

[28] N. Bushnell, Quincy, Aug. 10, 1867, to Joy.

[29] Coates, Washington, April 10, May 19, 1867 to Joy; Kansas City, July 15, to Joy; New York, July 27, Aug. 5, 1867, to Joy; N. Bushnell, Quincy, June 10, July 23, Aug. 9, 10, 1867 to Joy; Washington, Sept. 28, 1867, to Joy; Joy to Bushnell, Sept. 21, 1867.

[30] Argument of James F. Joy in *House Reports,* 41 Cong., 2 Sess., II, no. 53, 2.

hold its right. Public opinion in Kansas was strongly hostile. The Kansas Republican State Convention condemned "the policy of disposing of Indian reservations to railroads, or land monopolies" and demanded that they should be open to settlement at $1.25 an acre. Sidney Clarke of Kansas, George W. Julian, and William S. Holman of Indiana, Benjamin F. Butler of Massachusetts, and William Lawrence of Ohio, all of the House of Representatives, joined in an effective campaign against the Cherokee sale that was not to kill it but did prevent a much larger sale of the Osage tract to the same interests.[31]

James F. Joy was a man of great influence when it came to pushing his interests in Washington and state capitals. For years he had lobbied for and secured charters, rights-of-way, land grants, local government aid, and other special privileges for a powerful group of capitalists who were building railroads from Michigan through Indiana, Illinois, Iowa, Nebraska, Missouri, and Kansas, constructing the Soo Canal in Michigan, and dealing largely in timber lands in the Lake states. His visits to Iowa, where he had sought to induce, if not to coerce, cities to vote bond subsidies to the Burlington Railroad, had brought the complaint that he and his associates made it a "practice (warrior-like) of demanding tribute money every time they visit us, and threaten us if we do not comply with their request, with total annihilation." [32] To say that he was a practical man who knew he had to deal with congressmen who were debased and could only be influenced by corrupt means is not to say that he lacked business morals. The fact is that in the Gilded Age, as Mark Twain showed, public morals had so declined that it was difficult to get adopted any measures dealing with large business enter-

[31] *Cong. Globe,* 40 Cong., 1 Sess., I, 13, 58; *Ibid.,* 40 Cong., 2 Sess., I, 90, 134; 40 Cong., 3 Sess., I, 343–347.

[32] *Burlington Hawk-Eye* in Richard C. Overton, *Burlington West* (Cambridge, 1941), p. 101.

prises without employing means that today would be regarded as questionable.

Joy was thoroughly familiar with the practices of the lobbyist, had intimate contacts with influential people, and knew how to secure the necessary political aid. To solve the controversy over the purchase of the Neutral Tract he agreed to meet with Josiah B. Grinnell, an Iowa congressman who had a one-tenth interest in the Emigrant Company. Grinnell was characterized by a hostile writer in much the same way as Harlan and Pomeroy were: [33] "A blustering, beefy, corrupt, Pharasaical foo-foo, he is as much out of place in congress as a bull in a China shop." After some negotiations, Grinnell, Bushnell, and Joy came up with an agreement that was acceptable to the two groups who were trying to get their hands on the Neutral Tract. For $25,000 plus any payments already made on the contract the Emigrant Company agreed to convey to Joy its rights to purchase the land on credit.[34]

[33] *Iowa City State Press,* Feb. 24, 1866.

[34] Joy's story of the transaction is in *House Reports,* 41 Cong., 2 Sess., no. 53, p. 2; Grinnell's side is found in *Men and Events of Forty Years, Autobiographical Reminiscences of an Active Career from 1850 to 1890* (Boston, 1891), p. 378 ff. Grinnell allowed his own hatred of President Johnson and his anxiety "to cover up" so to color his account as to make it wholly unacceptable. He neglects the story of the rival groups, except the American Emigrant Company and Joy, does not mention the contract he received for his part in the deal, and glosses over the affair with the sanctimonious air that characterized everything he did and said publicly. Joy was straightforward and clear in his analysis of the negotiations leading to the second treaty, but was careful not to discuss the efforts to gain ratification. William Sturges, representing Joy in negotiating with the American Emigrant Company in January, 1867, reported that the officials of the latter company feared Joy would get the Neutral Tract by direct purchase from the government and were anxious for an agreement between the two groups, being willing to take perhaps as much as $400,000 in stock of the Joy road. Sturges, New York, Jan. 16, 17, 1867, to Joy.

The new deal, as slightly modified later, provided for the purchase at $1 an acre of all lands not occupied by settlers and not improved as of June 8, 1866. Within ten days of ratification (by June 16, 1868), $75,000 was to be paid, and the balance was to be spread over seven years with interest at 5 per cent.[35]

In this welter of negotiations and contracts for the sale of the Neutral Tract, the government position was anything but clear. Browning had voided the first sale to the Emigrant Company because it was not for cash, but he then recommended a sale for credit to Fremont. The Senate refused its consent, and then Joy agreed to buy for cash, but later regretted his action, took over the Emigrant Company contract, and induced Browning to favor it. Still, Browning as a lawyer could scarcely hold that a sale made by his predecessor and political enemy was invalid, while the same contract when assigned to business associates of his own was valid. In this impasse, it was decided to borrow a leaf from a previous sale of a Kansas reserve, the Christian Indian tract. A purchase of this four-section reserve by political insiders, which was patently a violation of the Intercourse Act, was made legal by a simple act of Congress. Browning found an easier solution. Since the House was opposing sales of reserves to railroads, he had a supplementary treaty negotiated with the Cherokees that "reaffirmed and declared valid" the sale to the Emigrant Company, confirmed the assignment of the contract to Joy, and cancelled the earlier Joy purchase. The supplementary treaty went further in making the new contract desirable to Joy by including a provision that forgave accrued interest of $71,660. By this device the matter

[35] The agreement for the original sale to the Emigrant Company is in *Report of the Cherokee Delegation of Their Mission to Washington in 1868 and 1869,* pp. xii–xiv. The final payment on the Joy purchase was made on Aug. 20, 1870. Statement accompanying letter of J. D. Cox, Secretary of the Interior, Aug. 13, 1870, to R. S. Watson, Treasurer of the Fort Scott Railroad, National Archives.

was arranged to require only Senate approval, and House opposition was effectively avoided. Grinnell, now well established in the Joy camp, undertook to "pull every string and have my personal friends well advised" in securing ratification.[36]

Mention should also be made of the close relationship between Senator James W. Grimes of Iowa and Joy, for it may have neutralized any possible opposition, if it did not gain outright support for the purchase of the Neutral Tract. In 1857, as governor of Iowa, Grimes had been anxious to borrow $15,000 to aid in liquidating other debts. He approached persons close to Joy and John Murray Forbes, who, as officials and promoters of the Burlington Railroad, were seeking legislation at Iowa City that would exempt the Burlington lands from taxation and make easier the floating of bond issues. Being assured that the loan might aid the Burlington interests, Joy, his brother, and Forbes supplied the governor with funds.[37] In March, 1858, Grimes solicited a further loan of $5,000 in a letter which described the work he was doing before the legislature in support of bills that Joy fathered.[38] Funds provided by Joy's brother made possible the additional loan.[39] Thereafter Grimes invested heavily in Burlington securities, taking advantage of his friendship with Joy to gain tips about the market and to secure preferential treatment.[40]

[36] J. B. Grinnell, House of Representatives, May 22, 1868, to Joy. On Jan. 13, 1870, James Craig wrote Joy: "Ross & Pomeroy both seem willing to do anything either by Bill or Treaty to facilitate the building of Rail Road. Thayer also. Tipton is always liberal to Roads."

[37] John G. Read, Burlington, Dec. 7, 1857, to Joy; note of Grimes, Dec. 7, 1857; and letters of Grimes to Joy, March 13, 18, 1858.

[38] Grimes to Joy, March 11, 1858.

[39] H. P. Joy, Sept. 4, 1861, to James F. Joy. John Murray Forbes provided the original $15,000. Memo of Jan. 23, 1864, and Grimes to Joy, Feb. 7, 1864.

[40] Grimes to Joy, Sept. 24, 1864; April 14, 1866; and May 4, 1868; and Joy to Grimes, May 11, 1868.

Before proceeding with the resulting conflict between Joy and the settlers on the Neutral Tract, we should give attention to the final payoff. Grinnell received contracts for providing ties and constructing part of the Fort Scott Line; he was anxious to keep from the public information about these contracts.[41] John T. Cox, who had been Browning's assistant in the Department of the Interior, became General Agent of the Fort Scott Railroad and Joy's first lieutenant in the fight against the settlers.[42] Browning accepted railroad passes from Joy in the same letter in which he confirmed the contract of sale.[43] Bushnell, who resumed active partnership with Browning in railroad legal practice (especially for the Joy lines) when the Secretary of the Interior quit his position in 1869, was allowed a $20,000 fee for his service in arranging the purchase of the Neutral Tract. Most of this sum was paid after the partnership was resumed.[44] Kersey Coates later asked Joy for reimbursement of $14,000 for "legislative expenses" incurred in the purchase of the Neutral Tract. Included in this amount were the cost of bringing General James Blunt to Washington for almost a year and expenses involved in entertaining the Cherokee chiefs, visiting them in their homes, and keeping them in Washington.[45] A Washington lobbyist for Joy reported to him on October 29, 1869: "Many intelligent men think you got the land of Mr. Browning by a corrupt arrangement and that he received a large reward for selling it to you." [46] The suspicion was natural, given the way influence was exerted upon government bureaus and members of Congress, but no evidence of improper action other than what has been described has been found.

[41] J. T. Cox, Jan. 11, 1869, to Grinnell; and to Joy, Jan. 23, 1869.
[42] Cox's letter book for 1868–69 is in the Joy MSS.
[43] Browning, Washington, June 23, 1868, to Joy.
[44] N. Bushnell, Quincy, Sept. 9, 1871, to Joy; and K. Coates, Kansas City, Missouri, April 16, 1872, to Joy.
[45] Kersey Coates, Kansas City, July 8, 1868, to Joy.
[46] I. N. Morris, Washington, Oct. 29, 1869, to Joy.

Kansas had been racked by conflicts between squatters, railroads, and speculators since the first opening of the territory in 1854; but the fight which now got under way between the settlers on the Cherokee Tract and James F. Joy's Fort Scott Line surpassed them all in duration and probably in violence. The squatters were angry at a number of the ways in which the Cherokee lands were being handled. In the first place, the right of pre-emption was to be given only to those who were on the tract at the time the first treaty was negotiated, and they were to pay not the usual price of $1.25 an acre but the appraised price, which proved to be close to $2 an acre. In the second place, settlers who had moved upon the tract in good faith between the date when the first sale had been declared invalid and the date when the second treaty made valid the first sale had no right to their land and had to bargain with Joy on his terms. It was, of course, true that Browning's action in voiding the original sale had not returned the Neutral Tract to the public domain but had left it as trust lands from which settlement was excluded. Yet experience elsewhere on the Kansas reserves had shown settlers that if they moved upon reserves early and fought aggressively for squatter's rights they might be successful in gaining them. Settlers took the calculated risk in this two-year period in which the lands seemed to them open to settlement; and when Joy succeeded in having the Emigrant Company purchase assigned to him and validated, they were astonished and angered to find that they had lost. Since Joy had purchased the tract to enable the Fort Scott Railroad to secure the profit which its construction would provide in the form of rising land values, it was certain that settlers would have to pay to him a price much higher either than the pre-emption figure or the government-appraised price. To people who believed that improvements personally put on the land gave it the value it attained, the prospect of having to pay Joy $4 to $10 an acre was intolerable. Better, it was felt, to challenge his title before Congress, the courts, and the bar of public opinion. If arguments did not promise results, many favored carrying on open warfare with Joy and with the railroad. They desperately wanted the railroad for their community, but not at the expense of high land-prices and heavy mortgage indebtedness.

From their first settlement on the Neutral Tract the settlers had been in jeopardy from bushwhacking Missourians, southern rebels, and Cherokees, as well as from Federal troops. Time and again enemy raids had destroyed homes and other improvements and driven off occupants. Inured to fighting and pillage as they were, and accustomed to taking the law into their own hands to defend their rights, the embattled settlers now used all their tactics to prevent the building of the Fort Scott Line and to keep their own members from buying claims from the railroad or taking any action that would acknowledge its title. In true frontier style the Cherokee Neutral Land League was organized to protect the settlers in their rights. Fifteen hundred men in the League drilled in regiments, battalions, and companies, in preparation for resisting the Joy forces that might seek to evict them. Mass meetings were held at which inflammatory and indeed incendiary words were used. At one such meeting it was estimated perhaps optimistically, that 4,000 people were present, some having come in covered wagons as much as 20 and 30 miles. After listening to prolonged speeches by League orators, the mob resolved to defy Joy who was threatening ejectment of settlers, to request the resignation of Senators Pomeroy and Ross for their action in favoring the sale to Joy, to oppose all land grants (a position increasingly being taken by settler groups) and to commend the *Kansas Tribune* of Lawrence, the *Missouri Democrat* of St. Louis, the *Cincinnati Times,* and the *Workingman's Advocate* of Chicago for their support.[47]

[47] *Workingman's Advocate* (Chicago), June 12, July 31, Aug. 7,

Angry feelings aroused at such meetings induced the Leaguers to take the offensive. They raided the land office in Baxter Springs and attempted to destroy the records, they attacked and captured a surveying party, burned their wagons, tents, surveying instruments, and commissary stores, confiscated their blankets, drove off the subordinates, and put to the lash the officers in charge. A construction crew was attacked and driven off and their wheelbarrows, picks, shanties, and tents destroyed. Great piles of ties were burned, all workingmen in the tract were driven off and finally, the *Girard Weekly Press* which was heavily subsidized by Joy to defend its interests and combat the efforts of the League was attacked and gutted by a gang of incendiaries. All work on the railroad south of Fort Scott was thus effectively stopped.[48] Threats were made against persons buying land from Joy, two men were actually murdered for paying for their claims, and others, many others the *Fort Scott Monitor* said, were driven off.[49] A sheriff who tried to resist the Leaguers in their destruction was arrested for insanity; he was tried and convicted, and a guardian appointed; a candidate for the legislature who attempted to defend Joy was stoned, and Pomeroy was burned in effigy.[50] Pitched battles between

14, 1869; *Miami County Republican* (Paola), May 1, 8, 29, 1869; *Fort Scott Monitor,* June 9, 23, 1869; the League published in the summer of 1870 a *Manifesto of the People of the Cherokee Neutral Lands, Kansas,* in which Pomeroy was called a tool of the monopolists, the "big Injin" of the "ring" that had benefitted so largely from the disposal of the Indian reserves in Kansas.

[48] Letters of O. Chanute, Feb. 4, 1869; of J. T. Cox, Feb. 16, May 13, 15, 22, June 14; of K. Coates, July 8, 1868; of T. H. Annable, July 15, 1869; of Israel W. Davis, Aug. 8, Nov. 10, 1869, to Joy. Paola *Miami Republican,* May 1, 8, 29, Aug. 15, 1869; *New York Herald,* April 11, 1870; *House Reports,* 41 Cong., 2 Sess., no. 53, pp. 27–28.

[49] *Fort Scott Monitor,* June 9, 23, 1869.

[50] *Miami County Republican,* May 1, 8, 29, Aug. 14, 1869; *Workingman's Advocate* (Chicago), July 31, 1869. A useful if sympathetic

Leaguers and anti-Leaguers further enlivened the scene.

All this violence was quite in the American tradition. As prototypes of the League one need only recall the anti-renters on the Livingston and Van Rensselaer estates in the Hudson Valley and the extreme measures to which they resorted to prevent the collection of rents they regarded as excessive. Or the desperate settlers on the Holland Land Company tract in western New York come to mind, with their destruction of the land office at Mayville. Numerous more immediate precedents were to be found in Kansas where settlers on the Delaware tract united to protect their equity against the LP&W Railroad; others on the Pottawatomie tract united for common defence against the Santa Fe and against miscellaneous speculators on the Kansas, Wyandot, and Sac and Fox tracts.

The Land Leaguers, like their fellow sufferers, took the issue into politics, into the courts, into Congress, and to the public. They gained political control of Crawford and Cherokee Counties, had strong influence at Topeka, and able friends in Washington. An effective *Manifesto of the People of the Cherokee Neutral Lands, Kansas,* was issued to rally sentiment inside and outside the tract against the sale to Joy and at the same time to strike a blow at the growing railroad influence in political activities. The *Manifesto* sought to play upon the sentiment of its readers by picturing the settlers as innocents seeking their rights who had been "stigmatized

account of the Neutral land controversy by a participant is Eugene F. Ware, "The Neutral Lands," Kansas State Historical Society, *Transactions,* VI, 147–169. Lula Lemmon Brown, *Cherokee Neutral Controversy* (Pittsburg, Kansas, 1931), tells in a more critical vein the story of the revolt of the League and of its efforts to upset the Joy title to the tract. It draws heavily upon the *Fort Scott Monitor,* and *Girard Press.* For a detailed statement of the position of the League see *Manifesto of the People of the Cherokee Neutral Lands,* Kansas, 1870, signed by C. C. McDowell and W. R. Laughlin of Cherokee County and A. Perry and C. Dana Sayre of Crawford County.

through subsidized newspapers . . . as trespassers, outlaws, murderers. . . . Hired emissaries have been, and still are being, sent among us to create division and confusion . . ." Money was being lavishly spent to influence opinion, settlers were being harassed, malicious arrests were being made, members of the League were being shot at and one was murdered by a "hired assassin . . ." The honest settler was engaged here, the *Manifesto* stated, in a crucial war with a monopoly: "the West is being smothered by land monopoly." [51]

In an argument before the House Committee on Indian Affairs, W. R. Laughlin, representative of the Neutral Land League, resorted to every trick of the agitator and rabble rouser to indict Joy and the railroads he represented. Joy was insolently pitting his "prospective plunder against the rights of thousands of soldiers of the Union army to soil enough to build them homes upon" and was cracking the "whip over the lower house of Congress for having dared to recognize the settlers' rights." For what reason, he asked, "should the people of the neutral land be given over to the tender mercies of the railroad king?" Was it "to divide our newer States and Territories into dukedoms and baronies, tenanted by serfs?" He maintained that among the 20,000 persons living on the Tract three-fourths of the men were Union soldiers. Nowhere, he said, was there a "more loyal, moral and substantial, or a better behaved people of equal numbers . . . the vile slanders of our enemies to the contrary notwithstanding." What the people wanted was the right to "enjoy the benefits of our labor, instead of sending it east to gorge the coffers of pampered aristocrats." [52]

Another aspect of the Land-League fight against Joy and

---

[51] C. C. McDowell, W. R. Laughlin, *et al., Manifesto of the People of the Cherokee Neutral Lands, Kansas* (no date, no place), pp. 1, 2, 22.

[52] *House Reports,* 41 Cong., 2 Sess., II, no. 53, 10–27.

the Fort Scott Railroad's management and sale of the Neutral Tract may be seen in the rivalry between the Katy and the Fort Scott Railroads over the right to build through Indian Territory and to win the promised land grant for construction. Since only one railroad could have the land grant and so build to the Gulf where through traffic might be secured, the struggle to get to the border first was vital. V. V. Masterson has described this dramatic conflict—its tensions, intrigues, fist fights between work gangs, and Indian difficulties. He intimates that the Katy officials by furtive visits to Land Leaguers did their best to stimulate them to make raids, burn ties and trestles, and tear up rails of the Fort Scott Railroad, thereby slowing down its construction progress.[53] Kansas squatters, threatened with the loss of their homes, did not need artificial stimulation of this kind but doubtless it had the effect of impelling them to more drastic action. There was considerable risk in arousing squatter resentment against a rival railroad, for the Katy itself was troubled with squatter opposition to its land-sale policy; and it was notorious that land leagues on various tracts borrowed from each other and worked together for mutual advantage.

The conservative defense against the attack by the Neutral Land League in Kansas and the land reformers in Congress was well-financed and ably led. A venal press was secured by subsidies in the form of direct payments, advertising patronage, and railroad passes. Even the leader of the Neutral Land League and editor of the *Workingman's Journal* accepted a trip pass and asked for annual passes for himself and his wife, declaring that he was not opposed to railroads but fought Joy on the land question.[54] Special favors

[53] V. V. Masterson, *The Katy Railroad and the Last Frontier* (Norman, Oklahoma, 1952), pp. 32–35.

[54] Amos Sandford, Columbus, Kansas, March 10, 1870, to Col. B. S. Henning, Joy MSS. The *Girard Press* drew $100 a month from 1868 to 1874, and for two years its editor received an additional $150

were granted settlers who would support Joy and fight the League; in one case a loan of $3,000 was made to an influential settler who agreed to work in Joy's behalf. Passes that were good during the session were distributed to members of the state legislature and were renewed for those who were friendly to the railroad. Members of Congress were similarly treated.[55] Detectives were employed to insinuate themselves into the inner circle of the League and secure information that might lead to prosecution or publicity harmful to members. Their reports told of the bitter feeling and frequently reiterated threats of violence and murder that were directed against the railroad officials.[56]

Mob violence, including the destruction of railroad property, the sacking of a Joy-subsidized newspaper, the intimidation of engineering and construction parties, and threats of drastic action against persons buying land from Joy, reached such proportions on the Neutral Tract that sheriffs were powerless to maintain order, and the League was in control. Construction and land purchasing stopped. The railroad officials induced law-abiding citizens to petition the governor for intervention on the grounds that property and life were unprotected, and the law-enforcing agents were powerless in the face of such concerted opposition. As a result of these petitions Governor James Harvey called upon the President for military aid, and in the summer of 1869

---

monthly for services as land agent. K. Coates, Kansas City, April 8, 1874, to Joy. Consideration was given to a plan to purchase an interest in the *Leavenworth Times* for which $7,000 or $8,000 was considered essential. Coates, Kansas City, April 25, 1870, to Joy.

[55] B. S. Henning, Superintendent of the Fort Scott Railroad, Kansas City, Missouri, Jan. 14, 1870, to Joy; Craig, Washington, May 4, 1870, to Joy.

[56] J. T. Cox, May 13, 1869, to Joy, Impression letter book, 1868–69; copy, John A. J. Chapman, Engineers Camp, Head of Richland, Aug. 12, 1869, to O. Chanute; K. Coates, Kansas City, Aug. 12, 1869, to Joy.

four companies marched into the tract to re-establish order.[57] Quiet was restored for a time, to such a degree that the chief engineer of the Fort Scott Railroad urged the withdrawal of the troops. But when suits of ejectment were brought against those settlers not willing to meet the railroad terms, tremendous excitement was again aroused, only to be heightened by the speeches of William Lawrence, vigorous congressional advocate of land reform and opponent of the Joy purchase. W. R. Laughlin and other League leaders also did their best to incite the settlers. Again violence broke out, this time against the *Girard Press,* the principal Joy newspaper, which was destroyed.[58] A reward of $500 was promptly offered for the apprehension of persons guilty of arson, the troops were re-activated, and order of a kind was restored; but sullen discontent continued.[59] The *Columbus Journal* called for the end of all land-purchasing by the settlers and urged them to use force, if necessary, to close the land office until the courts had determined the legal rights

[57] *House Reports,* 41 Cong., 2 Sess., II, no. 53, 22–23; K. Coates, Kansas City, Jan. 14, July 25, Dec. 31, 1869 to Joy; *Miami County Republican,* June 5, 1869. Agitation for the removal of the troops was begun at once, but the Joy lobbyist, after talking with Grant, was able to say that there would be no early withdrawal. The railroad would, however, have to pay for stabling the horses. I. N. Morris, Washington, Nov. 16, 1869, to Joy.

[58] Joshua V. Himes, preacher of the gospel who had undertaken to carry Joy's case to the people, reported on April 26, 1871, that most people questioned the validity of Joy's title, that the Kansas legislature and the Democratic Party favored the settlers against Joy, and that the sympathies of Kansans outside the tract were so definitely favorable to the settlers that any attempt to eject them would produce further violence. Himes, Columbus, April 9, April 26, 1871, to Joy; John A. Clark, Land Commissioner, Missouri River, Fort Scott, and Gulf Railroad, Fort Scott, May 23, 1871, to Joy.

[59] The proclamation of Governor Harvey was dated July 31, 1871. K. Coates, Fort Scott, Aug. 4, 1871, to Joy; James Craig, Washington, Jan. 16, 1872, to Joy.

in the matter.[60] Threats of ejectment and the presence of troops could not compel the people to pay for their land, and sales and collections came to a complete stop while both sides waited for the Supreme Court to speak.[61]

Meantime, Joy maintained a battery of lobbyists at Topeka and Washington to guard against and prevent the adoption of legislation favorable to the .Leaguers.[62] In addition to Craig, Coates, Joy, Van Horn, and Bushnell, who served to protect railroad interests in Washington, Isaac N. Morris, a former congressman and lobbyist from Illinois, and Benjamin R. Curtis, formerly of the United States Supreme Court were employed.[63] Also Austin Blair, representative from Michigan, Thomas Ewing, Jr., and Peter T. Abell, of Atchison, were added to this group.

In a pinch, Joy was fairly certain to receive support from the two Kansas senators and one representative. Pomeroy was characterized by James Craig, President of the Fort Scott Railroad as a "Blow-gun and Blatherskite" because he always demanded boodle; but he was certain to come to

[60] Quoted in *Fort Scott Monitor,* July 16, 1871.

[61] The settlers and the League made every effort in Washington and in Topeka to have the troops withdrawn, but President Grant and Governor Harvey were reluctant to give way. In 1873 Governor Osborn, who was apparently more sympathetic to the settlers, asked the President to withdraw the troops. Letters of P. T. Abell, March 1, 1872; C. W. Blair, Fort Scott, Dec. 17, 1872; and James Craig, Washington, Jan. 20, 1873, to Joy.

[62] J. T. Cox, May 18, 1869, to Coates, Impression letter book, 1868–69, Joy MSS.

[63] After his retirement from Congress in 1861 Morris took charge on a contingent-fee basis of efforts to recover from the United States additional sums for Illinois for lands entered with military warrants for which the 2 per cent for internal improvements had not been allowed. Disliking Morris' politics as well as his badgering, Lincoln displayed his annoyance, though he conceded that the claim was probably sound. Basler, *Collected Works of Abraham Lincoln,* VI, 403–412.

terms. Ross was less subject to influence but equally desirous of promoting railroads and not particularly sensitive to interests of settlers.

Clarke was the least dependable of the three, for he made political capital from the opposition of his Kansas constituents to the Joy group and to the sale of the Neutral and Osage Tracts. Time and again at meetings of the Neutral Land League he urged the members to fight to the last ditch against Joy, to prevent construction, and to evict purchasers who bought from him. Yet when the chips were down Clarke was secretly in the Joy camp; and with all his rodomontade, it was clear that he had not affected the validity of the Joy purchase. In 1870 and 1871 Craig and Abell directed their energies to elect Clarke to the Senate in place of Ross; but they found that the $10,000 the Kansas Pacific Railroad was willing to spend to elect Caldwell was too much for them.[64]

Kansans had good reasons to be disturbed at the way "land monopoly" was being rapidly extended to the disadvantage of settler interests. Reserve after reserve on which were established, illegally it is true, many thousands of people

[64] James Craig, Washington, April 10, 1868; May 5, 1870, to Joy; P. T. Abell, Topeka, Jan. 13, 25, 1871; and Washington, April 7, 1871, to Joy. On January 25, 1871 Abell wrote that despite all the hard work he had done in behalf of Clarke, Alexander Caldwell had been elected to the Senate by the Kansas legislature after the Kansas Pacific had contributed $10,000 to his "corruption fund." The interesting feature of the election is that both the Joy partisans and the Neutral Land League supported Clarke. For some time Clarke had been able to play both sides of the question. In the midst of the hottest part of the controversy over the Neutral land sale, when Clarke was attacking the treaty-making policy and the sales under it, Craig wrote: "I think him still favorable to us." Craig to Joy, May 5, 1870. For a devastating exposé of Clarke see *Political Affairs in Kansas. A Review of Official Acts of Our Delegation in Congress. Shall Inefficiency and Corruption be Sustained? The Issues of the Coming Political Campaign. A New Deal and Less Steal*, no place, no date, but 1870 or 1871.

attempting to erect homes
for themselves, had passed
into the hands of specu-
lators, land companies, and
railroads to whom the settlers had to pay a pre-
mium for their land. If the
Cherokee and Osage sales
were confirmed to the railroads some 9,500,000 acres
would have fallen to their
lot. But this was only half
their bag, for just as large
an acreage went to railroads
through land grants. Meantime, the state had received
3,100,000 acres as a sub-
sidy for education, which
it was expected to sell for
the highest possible price.
Moreover, great inroads
were being made on the
public domain in Kansas
by eastern institutions and
capitalists seeking to profit
from the expected rise in
land values and the demand

A land advertisement by the Missouri, Kansas and Texas Railway,
1877.

for land that continued
immigration would assure.

Among the absentee in-
vestors in Kansas at this time were Brown University, Ezra
Cornell for Cornell University, Amos Lawrence, and Alvah
Buckingham. Large absentee ownership in eastern Kansas
had left numerous areas undeveloped, since immigrants
sought the cheap government land farther west; now, with

speculative intrusion in the central third of the state, the same situation was developing there.

Table 10. SOME LARGE LAND ACQUISITIONS IN KANSAS, 1865–1871 [65]

	Acres		*Acres*
Walter B. Beebe	15,000	Amos Lawrence	58,000
Brown University	46,000	John Niccols	18,000
Alvah Buckingham	12,000	T. J. Peter	13,000
Stebbins and Porter	25,000		

Through Indian treaties and land grants 42 per cent of the area of Kansas was taken out of the public domain and denied to settlers as free grants. In no other state was the public-land system so restricted. On an additional two or three million acres within the primary-grant area of the railroads, free homesteads were limited to an inadequate eighty acres. The sale of the reserves and the pricing policy of the railroads brought to the fore in Kansas the land-reform movement. Leaders seized upon the Cherokee Neutral sale and that of the Osage lands, and, borrowing from the ideas of George Henry Evans and Horace Greeley, and anticipating Henry George, began a campaign with two broad objectives. They aimed to stop all further land grants and all further sales of Indian reserves to railroads and to effect the withdrawal of all public lands from every use except that of homestead making. The reformers sharpened their teeth on the sales of the Cherokee Neutral Tract by developing their

[65] Compiled from abstracts of scrip, cash, and warrant entries for the different Kansas land offices, National Archives. Ezra Cornell would have liked to invest heavily in Kansas, had conditions been right, but was advised that the best land had already been taken up when he was ready to move. His total investment in Kansas for Cornell University was 3,960 acres. Paul Wallace Gates, *The Wisconsin Pine Lands of Cornell University* (Ithaca, 1943), p. 62.

philosophical position, erecting strong support for it in Kansas and joining with similar groups from other areas to push common objectives in the national capital. For a time Kansas provided much of the fireworks and a considerable part of the leadership in the move to reform government.

Mr. C.—I am devoted to business, gentlemen, business—*never idle— "money makes the mare go." No bills go through or stop without the cash.*

A cartoon censuring Sidney Clarke's part in the Indian land steals, from *Political Affairs in Kansas: A Review of Official Acts of Our Delegation in Congress.*

Among the most effective leaders of the land-reform movement in Kansas while the conflict raged over the Neutral Tract was Amos Sandford, organizer of the Neutral Land League and editor of the *Workingman's Journal,* the chief newspaper spokesman of the anti-Joy forces. Octave Chanute, chief engineer of the Fort Scott Railroad, called Sandford a "monomaniac" on the land question because he made it the principal theme of his paper and went to the extreme

182

of advocating the abolition of private ownership in land and the substitution of life tenure.[66]

A four-pronged attack was directed at the title of the Fort Scott Railroad to the Neutral Tract. The first onslaught originated in the House of Representatives, where George W. Julian and other land reformers attempted to void the sale by legislation. This move was an element of the campaign being conducted by land reformers to end the treaty-making process by which the House was excluded from any share in determining policy relating to Indian lands. The second move was through litigation to test the validity of the action of the Secretary of the Interior in selling the Neutral Tract to Joy. The third device was a remonstrance to the President, in which the representatives of the settlers pointed out the hardships and difficulties of meeting the exacting demands of the Fort Scott Railroad. The fourth attack was an occupying claimants' measure being pushed in the Kansas legislature to recognize the right of the occupant to land which he had held and improved for a stipulated number of years.

Most easily handled of these attacks was the remonstrance to the President. In view of Johnson's past sympathetic attitude toward pioneers seeking farms on the public lands and his advocacy of free homesteads, it was natural to expect that he might view with concern the sale to Joy and the stiff prices the Fort Scott Railroad proposed to charge for the land. But Johnson had long since become surrounded by the most conservative and property-conscious leaders in the Republican Party—by such men as Orville H. Browning, Thomas Ewing, Sr., Jeremiah Black, James R. Doolittle, and William M. Evarts, who had no interest in the rag-tag of squatters. Nehemiah Bushnell who had come to Washington,

[66] At least two subscriptions were made to this paper by the Fort Scott Railroad. O. Chanute, Kansas City, Dec. 8, 1870; Jan. 2, 1871, to Joy; Craig, Washington, May 19, 1872, to Joy.

183

doubtless to defend the Joy title, and also to secure a major privilege for the successor to the Atchison and Pikes Peak Railroad, was entertained by Browning who would recommend action to the President on both matters. Browning mentions in his diary the discussions with the President and his cabinet as a result of which all action on the settlers' remonstrance was postponed indefinitely, but does not say what action, if any, was authorized on the other question raised by Bushnell.[67]

It was not difficult for Joy to secure from the courts favorable decisions respecting the title he had acquired to the Neutral Tract. The principal attorney for Joy was one of the great figures of the American bar, Benjamin R. Curtis, a former member of the United States Supreme Court, whose fee in the case was $7,000. Aiding him at various stages of the trial were William P. Hale of Washington, Sidney Bartlett of Boston, and Charles W. Blair.[68] The League case was put in the hands of William Lawrence and Benjamin F. Butler, Representatives from Ohio and Massachusetts respectively, and leaders in the fight to end the treaty-making power. So strongly favorable to the League case was feeling in Kansas that the state legislature appropriated $2,000 to carry the suit to the highest court.[69] All the contentions of the League —that the Cherokees never had had ownership of the tract and therefore could not sell it, that Indian lands could not be conveyed by treaty, that the Neutral lands were actually public lands and hence subject to pre-emption—were easily brushed aside by the United States circuit and Supreme

[67] Randall, *Diary of Orville Hickman Browning,* II, 238–243.

[68] B. F. Simpson, Paola, June 7, 1870, to Joy; John A. Clark, Ft. Scott, April 24, 1871, to Joy; K. Coates, Kansas City, May 31, 1871, to Joy; Charles W. Blair, Topeka, June 1, 1871, to Joy; William P. Hale, Washington, D.C., Jan. 11, 1872, to Sidney Bartlett; B. R. Curtis, Washington, March 19, 1872, to Bartlett; Bartlett, Boston, Dec. 7, 1872, to Joy.

[69] Joshua V. Himes, Columbus, Kansas, April 9, 1871, to Joy.

Courts. On November 19, 1872 in Holden vs. Joy, the validity of the sale of the Neutral Tract was upheld on every contested point.[70]

Joy's agents had also to watch the Kansas legislature carefully to make certain that no measure harmful to the Joy purchase was adopted. They gave railroad passes to those members whose record was "friendly to Rail Roads," and spent money freely to influence opinion.[71] P. T. Abell, president of the Atchison and Nebraska Railroad, who was co-operating closely with the Joy group, spent a good deal of time in Topeka buttonholing legislators. He argued with them, he entertained them, and one suspects from his letters that he influenced or attempted to influence their votes through the use of money.[72] But the tide of opinion in Kansas was running so strongly against the Joy group that much of his effort was in vain. In 1868 and again in 1869 the legislature condemned any sale that would prevent the 20,000 inhabitants on the tract, most of whom had settled after the treaty of 1866, from getting their land at pre-emption prices.[73] In 1872 Abell failed to stop a joint resolution calling for the withdrawal of the troops from the Tract.[74] Craig, who was trying to prevent the withdrawal of the troops, reported that President Grant and his Secretary of War were unfavorable to removal, but the pressures were heavy on Congress and the order for withdrawal might have to go

[70] Telegram, James Craig, Washington, Nov. 19, 1872, to Joy; B. R. Curtis, Dec. 7, 1872, to Joy; 17 *Wallace*, 211 ff. For the legal questions involved in the Joy title see Brown, *The Cherokee Neutral Lands Controversy,* pp. 35 ff.

[71] B. S. Henning, Superintendent, Fort Scott Railroad, Kansas City, Mo., Jan. 14, 1870, to Joy.

[72] P. T. Abell, Aug. 22, 1870; Jan. 13, 25, April 7, 1871; March 1, 1872, to Joy.

[73] *Laws of Kansas, 1868,* Feb. 3, 1868, (Topeka, 1868), p. 68; J. T. Cox, Feb. 4, 1869, to Joy.

[74] Abell, March 1, 1872, to Joy.

185

through. To combat the move he asked for passes to be distributed among cabinet officers and Senators.[75]

The proposal to amend the occupying claimant's act of 1868 brought much anguish to Abell, who stalled off action until 1873. As then passed, the measure provided, among other things, that settlers who had occupied and made improvements upon Indian or trust lands on which there was no other claim at the time of their settlement should not be "evicted or thrown out of possession" without being paid the "full value of all lasting and valuable improvements made" on their claims. The law came late so far as the settlers on the Cherokee Tract were concerned, for many of them had long since become discouraged in their fight with Joy and the Fort Scott Railroad and had thrown up their rights or contracted to buy. Kersey Coates, president of the Fort Scott Line, was displeased that the measure got through the legislature; but he had little reason to fear its effect, as it was primarily sought by the Osage settlers. Furthermore there were grave doubts of its constitutionality.[76]

In Washington the fight to revoke the sale of the Neutral Tract was vigorously pushed by Julian, Butler, and Lawrence and equally vigorously opposed by Craig, Coates, Morris, Grinnell, and Joy. To prevent the reformers from getting unanimous consent to introduce legislation inimical to the railroad, Craig and Grinnell arranged to have Anderson, Van Horn, or Newcomb, Representatives from Missouri, present to object.[77] Grinnell, who as a former Representative had the run of the House floor where he did effective work,

[75] James Craig, Washington, Jan. 16, 17, 1872; Jan. 20, 1873, to Joy.

[76] K. Coates, Kansas City, Mo., March 16, 1873, to Joy; P. T. Abell, Feb. 5, 18, 19, 21, to Joy; *Laws of Kansas, 1873,* March 6, 1873, (Topeka, 1873), pp. 203–205.

[77] Craig, Washington, Feb. 14, 19, 1869, to Joy; *Cong. Globe,* 40 Cong., 3 Sess., Feb. 5, 1869, I, 914–915.

was confident that the Senate was dependable, in view of the fact that his friend Harlan who had made the sale to the Emigrant Company held a seat there and was chairman of the Committee on Indian Affairs.[78] He was much less confident of the House, for there were centered the movements for land reform and for ending the land-grant and Indian-reserve policy. Craig penned a real tribute to the effectiveness of Julian, Butler, and Lawrence against the Cherokee sale when he wrote Joy from Washington, on Feb. 14, 1869: [79] "The House is awfully demoralized on Indian Treaties, but we will give him [Julian] a good fight in the House, and certainly kill him in the Senate."

I. N. Morris worked on Grant to assure favorable presidential action—no very difficult task—and prepared two "long articles" on the Neutral-Tract controversy which appeared in the *National Intelligencer* and the *Baltimore Gazette*.[80] Peter Abell, who was in Washington to aid Craig and Morris in 1871, sought to influence James G. Blaine, Speaker of the House, to have a "decent, honest, intelligent Indian Committee" from which should be excluded those who sympathized with the Leaguers.[81] Craig, who had the run of the House floor, found Blaine responsive to his suggestions but not to the point of removing John P. C. Shanks of Indiana who was now the principal thorn in the flesh of the Joy group.[82] Shanks, like Julian and Holman, was active in the

---

[78] *Cincinnati Gazette,* Feb. 13, 1869; J. B. Grinnell, Washington, Feb. 9, 1869, to Joy. Commenting on Grinnell's lobbying, Craig said he worked "too publicly," that it was getting into the newspapers that he was Joy's representative, and suggested that he should "still hunt." Craig, Washington, Feb. 14, 1869, to Joy.

[79] *Ibid.*

[80] Morris, Washington, Nov. 16, 1869, with clippings of articles, to Joy.

[81] Abell, Washington, March 20, 1870, to Joy.

[82] Craig, Washington, March 31, 1871, to Joy.

move for land reform and was championing the cause of the settlers on the Neutral Tract. Craig sought to have friends on guard against Shanks and Butler.

In this welter of controversy over the sale of the Neutral Tract to Joy, settlers were not encouraged to buy, partly as a result of the intimidation of the Leaguers who threatened drastic action to those who came to terms with the railroad, and partly because of the hope that they could secure the pre-emption right upon the land. Why, they argued, should settlers upon the Neutral Tract, which essentially was no different from any other part of the public-domain area of Kansas, be required to buy from a railroad the land they were improving when the railroad in turn had secured it at less than the government minimum? Consequently, sales lagged for years.

Persons who had settled upon and improved claims prior to the ratification of the first treaty of 1866 also had grievances, as they had to pay the appraised price, not the usual $1.25. Some 1,004 claimants were privileged to buy at the appraised price, but many were unable to meet the cost. It was no small task to raise from $200 to $400 when settlers were making their farms and putting everything they had into improvements. Yet to fail to complete the purchase at the time prescribed by the government would throw their claims open to selection by anyone, whether a prospective settler or speculator. As the other lands in the tract were to be priced by the Fort Scott Railroad at much higher minimums, there was a strong incentive to buy. In the midst of the turmoil about purchasing land from the government which could not grant credit, the proposal was advanced by Joy that he might buy the lands thus claimed and resell on credit at low prices to the settlers.[83] Nothing came of the proposal, but Joy probably had some responsibility for inducing

[83] Letters of John T. Cox, of Jan. 9, 1869, to D. P. Bullock; of Jan. 15, 1869, to O. C. True; and of Feb. 4, 1869, to Joy.

the government to follow an easy policy in selling the land to the claimants. Because credit could not be given, settlers were allowed a considerable time in which to make their purchases—as Table 11 indicates.

Table 11. PAYMENT ON LANDS AWARDED TO SETTLERS ON
CHEROKEE TRACT [84]

Total area awarded to settlers	154,395 acres	
Appraised valuation	$296,851	
Paid from Nov. 1, 1868 to Nov. 1, 1869	81,442 acres	$156,097
Paid from Nov. 1, 1869 to Nov. 1, 1870	68,201	130,851
Paid from Nov. 1, 1870 to May 1, 1871	1,519	2,858
Total	151,162	$289,806
Balance not taken by claimants	3,231 acres	
Offered to highest bidder, receipts	$8,966.	

Notwithstanding the bitterness of feeling against Joy and the Fort Scott Railroad that was shown by the settlers on the Neutral Tract, there seems to have been no recrimination. In fact, as one reads the Joy correspondence, one is impressed with the generally conciliatory tone of the railroad people, their desire to end ill feeling and to hasten the development of the area. That is not to say that the railroad officials were prepared to give way to the settlers or to concede in any way

[84] Commissioner of Indian Affairs, *Annual Report,* 1871, p. 671; W. F. Cody, Sept. 9, 1870 to Aaron Decker, Cherokee File, National Archives. When the 3,231 acres not taken by original claimants were offered on sealed bids, a favorite device of the Indian Office to avoid the squatter intimidation against anyone bidding competitively, 720 acres were acquired by Thomas A. Cunningham of Baltimore, Maryland, for $2,040, and 1,831 acres were acquired by Walter H. Smith of Mt. Vernon, Ohio, for $4,926. In newly surveyed areas in Kansas the maximum individuals could acquire at this time was 320 acres under the pre-emption and homestead laws, but in areas offered at public sale at an earlier time there was no limit on the amount individuals could buy. Schedule of Cherokee Neutral Lands disposed of under treaty of July 18, 1866, Land Office Papers, Kansas State Historical Society.

189

Table 12. SALES OF LAND, MISSOURI RIVER, FORT SCOTT, AND GULF RAILROAD [85]

	Acres	Price Ave.	Total	Cancellations			Total Sales (Minus cancellations)	
				Acres	Ave. Price	Amount	Acres	Amount
Privileged settlers	117,752	$4.04	$518,634					
Non-privileged settlers								
June 23–Dec. 31, 1870	165,260	7.18	1,186,763					
1871								
1872								
1873								
1874	17,736	9.15	162,399	17,794	11.61	$206,664	420,735	$2,385,211
1875								
1876	59,324	6.59	391,175	25,733	7.28	187,602	404,281	2,152,578
1877	33,853	6.73	228,176	16,292	6.70	109,200	420,303	2,265,656
1878	29,170	5.45	158,987	14,503	6.75	97,946	434,970	2,326,697

[85] Compiled from *Annual Reports*, Fort Scott Railroad, 1871–1878.

that the railroad's action in purchasing and maintaining right to the land was improper. Aside from the price, and of course that was the fundamental cause of conflict, the settlers had little reason to complain.

Those persons who had moved upon the tract after the negotiation of the first sale to the Emigrant Company and before the proclamation of the second treaty with the Cherokee (between July 27, 1866 and June 10, 1868) were permitted to buy the land on which they had made improvements at prices ranging from three to five dollars an acre, or as things turned out, at an average of $4.40 per acre. The price seems high and certainly appeared high to the beleaguered settlers, who were fighting for the privilege of buying at the pre-emption price of $1.25 an acre, but it was substantially less than the current market value, as shown by the sales of the remainder of the railroad lands. The preferred buyers, who had settled between July 27, 1866 and June 10, 1868, bought 117,752 acres. As for the lands not settled upon prior to June 10, 1868, which presumably were less attractive, during the first year of sales to non-privileged settlers 165,260 acres were sold for $1,186,763, or at an average price of $7.18 an acre. From these and later sales there were to be many cancellations, especially of the higher-priced land, a fact which indicates the extreme difficulties that farmers had in completing payments on sales contracts entered into in the seventies. The Company sugared the pill by granting a rate of interest that was sharply lower than that prevailing on farm mortgages, and also by giving one year's free use of the land. Furthermore, no payment on the principal was required until two years after the signing of the contract.[86]

In 1873 economic conditions on the tract were quite un-

[86] Circular of Jan. 1, 1871, of John A. Clark, Land Commissioner of the Fort Scott Railroad.

favorable, and the trustees of the railroad voted to lower the price of land by $1 an acre. They also agreed to grant a reduction on existing contracts of 20 per cent for cash. This was common practice for land-grant railroads and was of little aid to settlers at the time because money was so difficult to raise.[87]

This leniency brought the Fort Scott Line little relief from anti-railroad attacks, for the Grange in 1874 joined in the onslaught against the railroad. In resolutions directed at the Fort Scott Line, the Grange denounced the "insatiate greed of Railroad Monopoly," the "grasping avarice of this monstrous monopoly," and the encroachments of "soulless corporations sustained by the decisions of corrupt government officials." [88] Further legal controversies over the title to part of its land leading to two unfavorable Circuit-Court decisions brought distress to the railroad officials.[89] Heavy tax-assessments against railroad property, which officials regarded as "enormously high" and patently discriminatory, heightened tension.[90] In 1878 when the Fort Scott Railroad was in receivership after years of failure to meet its fixed charges, another wave of anti-railroad feeling swept over the Neutral Tract. As the railroad officials reported, the disaffected sought to prejudice the people by making them believe that the title the railroad gave was not sound. The League came back into existence, the friends of the railroad were threatened with violence, and purchasing and payment on all contracts stopped. The after-effects of the panic of 1873 were largely responsible for the plight of the Fort Scott Railroad,

[87] Charles Merriam, Boston, April 24, 1873, to Joy.

[88] R. A. Williams, Secretary, Plymouth Grange, Glendale, May 7, 1874, to Joy.

[89] Stroud vs. Missouri River, Fort Scott, and Gulf Railroad, 23 *Federal Cases*, 261 ff., and Langdon vs. Joy, 14 *Federal Cases*, 1109 ff.

[90] *Railroad Gazette* (May 15, 1875), VII, 201.

but settler resistance to its sales and collection policy also contributed to it.[91] Truly, the way of the railroad was hard in Kansas.

[91] Missouri River, Fort Scott, and Gulf Railroad, *Annual Reports,* 1874, 1875, 1878; *Railroad Gazette* (Dec. 27, 1873), V, 516.

CHAPTER VI

Struggle over the Osage Reserve: The End of Treaty Making

THE GREATEST uprising against the use of the treaty-making power to dispose of Indian reserves outside the public domain resulted from the management of the Osage Reserve of 8,841,927 acres stretching westward 276 miles in southern Kansas. This was the largest, and, barring the Cherokee Strip, the last of the major reserves in the state. It contained a considerable part of the good-to-better land extending from today's area of mixed farming through the Flint Hills pasture region and the wheat belt slightly beyond the 100th meridian.[1]

[1] Compare map on plate 134 in Charles Royce, *Indian Land Cessions in the United States* with that opposite p. 1, in James C. Malin, *Winter Wheat in the Golden Belt of Kansas* (Lawrence, 1944).

The great grants of land to the Santa Fe and the Union Pacific, Eastern Division, in addition to the large acreage acquired by speculators, limited the amount of desirable land accessible to transportation facilities; and settlers hungry for farm ownership were intruding upon the Osage reserve by the thousands after the Civil War, though it was legally closed to them. Farther west lay the buffalo country where the Osages went for their annual hunt, and their reserve was but slightly used, save for winter residence. The Osages did not altogether resent intrusions by whites, provided they would pay some rent; but white settlers, once they had taken up and improved land, wanted to own it.

The coming of the settlers to the Osage reserve and the approach of four railroads to it brought to the promoters of these lines a realization of the prospective value of this vast area that was still held by the Indians and not subject to the usual land grants. These promoters added their voices to the demands of other real-estate interests, intruders on the reserve, and politicians that the Osages should be removed and their lands opened to settlement. Persons desiring to settle upon the reserve and to take up land naturally hoped that it would become a part of the public domain and be subject to its liberal policies of land distribution; but the elements concerned with railroads and speculation could see more advantage to themselves in having the tract managed by the Office of Indian Affairs through the treaty-making power.

In response to the demand for the removal of the Osages and the opening of their lands to settlement, an effort was made in 1863 by Senator Samuel C. Pomeroy and William P. Dole to divest a part of the reserve of its Indian title. The Osages were persuaded to accept a treaty that provided for the sale of 1,500 square miles of the eastern portion at a price of $300,000. These lands were not to be subject to settlement, occupation, or pre-emption unless or until the Presi-

dent reversed this position. The Osages also agreed to cede
in trust a tract twenty miles deep and extending on the north
side for the entire distance of their diminished reserve. The
usual school sections were to be reserved within the trust area,
for which the Osages were to be paid twenty-five cents an
acre. When the treaty was resubmitted to the Osages for
amendment, however, the Indians refused their assent, and
the treaty died.[2]

In 1865 a second effort to cut down the Osage reserve and
open its land to settlement was more successful, though also
more fraught with trouble because of the differences between
it and the first treaty. By the treaty of September 29, 1865
the Osages agreed to cede the 1,500 square miles on the
eastern end of their tract, containing 843,927 acres for $300,-
000. The cession was not an outright unconditional sale, but
rather was a sale with conditions that required the land to be
sold at $1.25 or more an acre, barred pre-emption and home-
stead claims on the tract, and provided that after the United
States had recovered from sales the full cost of the cession
and of surveying and selling it, the "remaining proceeds"
should go into the "civilization fund" for Indian welfare.
The other cession was a twenty-mile-deep tract on the northern side, containing some 3,200,000 acres. This tract was
ceded in trust to be sold at a minimum of $1.25 or more, as
had been provided by the abortive treaty of 1863. Nothing
was said in the treaty about school lands.

Despite the fact that the treaty of 1865 barred forever
4,041,937 acres [3] from becoming a part of the public domain, denied the usual rights allowed squatters, prevented
free homesteads from being acquired, and made no provision for the usual land-subsidy for common schools within

[2] Copy of treaty with the Osages of Aug. 29, 1863, in Reserve File,
Indian Affairs, National Archives.

[3] This is the acreage given in the Commissioner of the General Land
Office, *Annual Report,* 1869, p. 44.

the two ceded areas, it seems not to have raised a ripple on the Kansas sea at the time, though it ultimately set in motion one of the sharpest land wars in the history of the state. The treaty was ratified by the Senate without a roll call on June 26, 1866, and proclaimed on January 21, 1867.[4]

Before the Osage treaty was proclaimed, William Sturges, president of the Leavenworth, Lawrence, and Galveston Railroad, (the LL&G, formerly the Leavenworth, Lawrence, and Fort Gibson) made efforts to purchase the whole of the reserve, not just the two ceded portions. He also attempted to acquire the remaining Sac and Fox lands. Although his railroads was not as yet in the rapidly expanding Joy system, there was close community of interest between Sturges and the Joy representatives, and in early 1868 the two groups were working together to bring about the purchase of the Osage lands.[5] Coates, Grinnell, Craig, Sturges, Bushnell, and Ewing made a formidable lobby; with the aid of Senators Ross, Pomeroy, and Harlan, who was chairman of the Committee on Indian Affairs, and Interior Secretary Browning, they seemed almost irresistible.[6]

The lobby clothed its negotiations in the closest of secrecy, for premature announcement might bring down upon the administration such an attack as was being directed against it for the sale of the Neutral Tract to Joy, and might make difficult further proceedings. Because of its direct access to officials, the group may well have been aware of the warning of Sidney Clarke, Kansas representative, that the reserve, however acquired, should be "opened up to actual settlers,

[4] *Sen. Ex. Journal,* June 27, 1866, XIV, 874; Charles J. Kappler, *Indian Affairs. Laws and Treaties,* II, 878.

[5] For the early history of the Leavenworth, Lawrence, and Galveston Railroad see Harold J. Henderson, "The Building of the First Kansas Railroad South of the Kaw River," *Kansas Historical Quarterly* (Aug., 1947), XV, 225 ff.

[6] Coates, Washington, Jan. 18, 1867; undated letter of William Sturges, around Nov. 17–20, 1867; and also April 10, 1868, to Joy.

free from all schemes of speculation and monopoly so disastrous to the prosperity of the new States." While Clarke was quite willing to permit a railroad that should build through the reserve to buy the land at 20 or 25 cents an acre and to retail it at $1.25, he declared he would insist that it should charge no more.[7]

Well before June, 1868, the lobby had established a favorable attitude among Washington officials so that a commission was appointed to secure a treaty and to effect sale of the Osage lands to the LL&G, although this latter transaction was not specifically mentioned in instructions.[8] After the commission reached the Osage country and began negotiations, it showed its hand by rejecting proposals submitted by a rival railroad to participate in the purchase or to buy the entire tract at a better price than was offered by the LL&G. The commission may have been somewhat embarrassed by the more liberal features of the rival offer, which included the following provisions: [9]

1. $2,000,000 instead of $1,600,000 for the ceded and diminished reserves.

2. The right of pre-empting 160 acres at $1.25 an acre to every settler on the tract.

3. The 16th section in each township to be donated to the State for common schools.

[7] Clarke, Washington, April 13, 1868, to N. G. Taylor, Commissioner of Indian Affairs, and chairman of the commission to negotiate the treaty, *House Ex. Doc.,* 40 Cong., 2 Sess., no. 310, part 3, pp. 27–28.

[8] Sturges was in touch with the Commissioner of Indian Affairs in November, 1867. With the aid of other members of the lobby he felt sufficiently confident to write Joy on April 10, 1868, that matters connected with the proposed Osage purchase looked better than ever before. See telegrams of Senator Ross to Joy, May 25, 1868, Sept. 24, 1868; and of Joy to Ross, June 1, 1868.

[9] *House Ex. Doc.,* 40 Cong., 2 Sess., XIX, no. 310, part 3, p. 24.

But the commission had come to Kansas to arrange for the sales of the tract to the Sturges-Joy interests and was not to be deterred by other and more generous proposals, which it treated contemptuously.[10]

The advantages of the Sturges-Joy offer were, first, that it was made by a well-established group of capitalists led by one of America's most astute railroad promoters and having adequate resources and skill to assure construction; second, that its line would not only pass directly through the eastern part of the reserves but also was projected through the Indian Territory to the Gulf; and, third, that a part of the road was already completed and in operation.[11] The commission demanded of the Osages their removal to Indian Territory, the cession of all their lands, and their consent to the sale of 8,000,000 acres to the LL&G. According to testimony later given by chiefs of the Osages, rations were withheld, presents and bribery were employed, and other pressures were used to get the Indians to accept the treaty which had been brought from Washington.[12] Opposition was overcome and the principal chiefs were induced to sign the treaty.

No concession won by speculators and land grabbers in Kansas could compare with the rich bargain Sturges seemed

[10] *Ibid.,* pp. 6 ff.

[11] *Ibid.,* p. 11.

[12] Sidney Clarke, Washington, Aug. 10, 1869, to E. S. Parker, Commissioner of Indian Affairs, and accompanying clipping from the *Lawrence Tribune,* Aug. 5, 1869, Indian Affairs, National Archives. Since it was Clarke who was interpreting the attitude of the chiefs in opposition to the treaty which some had been forced to sign, one might well question the evidence, but Clarke was supported by Enoch Hoag, Superintendent of Indian Affairs, who visited the Osages in September, 1869. Hoag, Oct. 11, 1869, to E. S. Parker, *loc. cit.* Later opposition by the Indians was stirred up by the hope of getting a higher price for the land. On the other hand settlers and immigrants looking for free land were convinced the price paid the Indians was adequate.

in the way of securing. The right to purchase the 8,000,000 acres in the Osage diminished reserve and trust lands for 20 cents an acre was a bonanza. The treaty disregarded the interests of squatters on the tracts, required no cash until three months after ratification, and then required only that $100,000 be paid. The only guarantee for payment of the remainder was the bonds of the company. Payments were to be extended over fifteen years, during which time the part not paid for was to be exempt from taxes. Not only were settlers' improvements to give value to the railroad lands, but the settlers alone were to provide taxes for roads and local government, which in turn would make the railroad lands more attractive. These and other objections to a sale of land at near give-away prices to a railroad as a means of aiding in its construction were sufficient to arouse opposition, but more dangerous was the fact that the Indian Office seemed determined to destroy the statutory land system and to replace it with a policy of land sales that subordinated settler interests to railroads and other speculator groups. This sale of land, if completed, would be the biggest made at any time by the Federal government, and, aside from the disposal of refuse tracts under the Graduation Act, was at the lowest price. Pre-emption, homestead, the 16th and 36th school sections, the 5 per cent of net proceeds of land sales which was paid to the states, these and all other basic features of the public land system were made null and void, so far as this tract was concerned. What Congress had taken three-quarters of a century to create was now threatened with destruction by the Indian Office.

It was customary for the Indian Office and the Secretary of the Interior to keep secret news of treaties, and of course the Senate dealt with executive matters behind closed doors, so that the public usually did not learn of Indian land sales until the deed was done. News of the Osage negotiations had been bruited around, however, and opponents of any

sale to a railroad were prepared for a big fight on ratification if they could not prevent the signing of a treaty. Four
days after the treaty was signed—June 1, 1868—but nine
days before it was submitted to the Senate, George W. Julian
introduced into the House a joint resolution which stated
that a treaty was being negotiated with the Osages for the
sale of 8,000,000 acres to the LL&G "in contravention of
the laws and policy of the United States affecting the public
domain," and while further maintaining that Indian tribes
had no power to dispose of their lands except by ceding to
the United States, requested the President to inform the
House "by what authority and for what reason" the lands
were to be sold and not ceded to the government.[13] This
resolution was quickly adopted by a House which was thoroughly angry at the way the Indian Office was using the
treaty-making power to prevent the Representatives from
having any voice in land policies affecting the reserves. Two
days later the House approved another joint resolution direct-
ing the President to issue no patents for Cherokee or Osage
lands.[14]

A third and sharper attack upon the Osage land sale was
made by the House on June 13 when it adopted a resolution
of Sidney Clarke accusing the Indian Office of "grossly and
fraudulently" neglecting the interests of the Indians and of
the people and of using "improper influence" in securing the
treaty. The resolution requested the President to transmit
all documents concerning the treaty and to withhold the
treaty from the Senate until a full investigation had been
made by the House.[15] On July 13, the House went even further, when it accused the Commissioner of Indian Affairs of

---

[13] *Cong. Globe,* 40 Cong., 2 Sess., part 3, p. 2753.
[14] This resolution was fought by Van Horn but was vigorously supported by Lawrence and Washburn of Wisconsin. *Ibid.,* pp. 2814–
2816.
[15] *Ibid.,* part 4, p. 3132.

suppressing certain documents bearing on the Osage treaty, notably those relating to offers from rival railroads and individuals for the Osage lands.[16]

If Browning was not guilty of suppressing information through failure to transmit documents to the House, he clearly was dissembling when he denied on June 15 that he had knowledge of offers by railroad corporations for the purchase of the Osage tract. As early as April 10 Sturges had been in Washington lobbying with Craig and Coates for the Osage lands.[17] Joy's representatives were in the midst of the fight to secure the Senate's approval of that Cherokee treaty which sanctioned the transfer of the contract for the Neutral Lands to Joy; but the move for the Osage lands was not permitted to suffer. Early in June Joy himself was in Washington to marshal the forces in behalf of the two reserves he so much wanted for his railroads. He was in direct communication with Browning, to whom he gave passes some time before June 23.[18] While the lobby was functioning, Browning was seeing Thomas Ewing, Jr., frequently and spending much time with him. Also I. N. Morris, another member of the lobby, was a visitor in Browning's home at this time.[19] The cavalier way in which the commission rejected the offer of the rival Missouri, Fort Scott, and Santa Fe Railroad as well as the fact that it was committed to accept the offer of the LL&G nineteen days before the President submitted to the House information concerning the negotiations all lent strength to the House accusation.[20]

[16] *Ibid.*, p. 4001. The documents for which the House asked are in *House Ex. Doc.*, 40 Cong., 2 Sess., XIX, no. 310.

[17] W. Sturges, Washington, April 10, 1868, to Joy.

[18] Telegram, E. G. Ross, Senate Chamber, June 1, 1868; O. H. Browning, Washington, June 23, 1868, to Joy.

[19] Thomas Ewing, Jr., dined with Browning on April 4, 26, May 1, and June 11; and Browning dined at the Ewing home on May 6. Morris visited the Brownings on April 6, 1868. Randall, *Diary of Orville Hickman Browning*, II, 190–195.

[20] *House Ex. Doc.*, 40 Cong., 2 Sess., XIX, no. 310, part 3, 11.

The House demands for the Osage treaty forced the Indian Office to transmit it in a precedent-shattering move that brought it out in the open before the Senate could act.[21] The uproar over the two sales of the Neutral Tract prepared the way for the wave of angry protest and violent denunciation that swept over Kansas with the publication of the Osage treaty. From the Kansas governor, the other principal state officers, the legislature, newspapers, and individuals came wrathful arraignments and irate condemnations of the treaty. Governor Samuel J. Crawford denounced it as an "audacious attempt on the part of the Secretary of the Interior and his confederates to transfer to a railroad company by unheard-of methods seven million acres of land for a mere bagatelle in comparison to their real value." The Indians were driven into signing the treaty, which he declared was "full of wrong and outrage" and will "prove a lasting disgrace to the Government." [22]

Paul McVicar, Superintendent of Public Instruction, was particularly effective in organizing protest movements to denounce the treaty and sale. As one responsible for the planning and financing of the school system, he was shocked that the Cherokee Neutral Tract had been sold to Joy without the usual reservations of the 16th and 36th sections for common schools. Learning that a commission was on the way to treat with the Osages for their reserve, he hastened to the treaty ground in Indian Territory to set forth the claims of Kansas to school lands in the reserve. To his dismay, he found it was "the settled policy of the Government to dispose of these domains to capitalists and railway companies." After failing at the treaty ground, McVicar circularized county superintendents and other leading citizens "urging them to

[21] The President submitted the treaty with its accompanying documents to the House on June 15, two days after it had been sent to the Senate. *Cong. Globe,* 40 Cong., 2 Sess., part 4, p. 3171.

[22] Samuel J. Crawford, *Kansas in the Sixties* (Chicago, 1911), pp. 300, 304.

call public meetings and send remonstrances" to Washington against "the great public wrong sought to be perpetrated." He opposed the treaty not only because of the loss of the land subsidy for schools but because it would add heavily to the burden of farm makers. "Landed monopolies are a great curse" he held. Not content with opposing the treaty in Kansas, McVicar journeyed to Washington to throw his influence in opposition to a policy that was "wresting the public domain from the settler and creating a gigantic landed monopoly on Kansas soil, regardless of the rights of the people. . . ." [23]

Newspaper opinion in Kansas and elsewhere was sharp in its denunciation of the Osage treaty. Writing of it, the *Marysville Enterprise* said: "It has never been thoroughly tested how nasty a pool of fraud and corruption an Indian agent could swim through to gobble a fat thing." The *Emporia News* called it "another wholesale swindle." Other papers spoke of the Osage treaty as a "nefarious transaction," a "foul iniquity," "swindling land grants," a "manifest swindle," and the "rascality of late officials." [24] A Catholic priest assigned to the Osages spoke of the "many speculators and land sharks" who were present at the negotiation.[25]

The state officers of Kansas in June, 1868 memorialized the United States Senate urging that the Osage treaty be rejected. A resolution condemning "the policy of disposing of Indian reservations to railroad or land monopolies" and insisting that ceded lands be opened to actual settlers at the lowest government price was approved by the Republican

[23] Paul McVicar, Superintendent of Public Instruction, *Eighth Annual Report*, 1868, pp. 10–15 and *Ninth Annual Report*, 1869, p. 34.

[24] *Emporia News*, June 12, 1828; *Marysville Enterprise*, July 4, 1868; *St. Louis Democrat* in *Emporia News*, June 19, 1868; *New York Tribune*, June 10, 16, 23, 1868; *Cincinnati Gazette*, Aug. 14, 1869.

[25] *New York Tribune*, June 16, 1868.

State Convention in July. While the Kansas Republicans were distressed at Republican responsibility for selling the Neutral Tract and for making the treaty to sell the Osage lands, they could point with pride to their authorship of the Homestead Act. The Democrats were more realistic, as it paid them to be in view of their earlier attitude on Homestead. They were aware that the Homestead Act—if it was not being made a dead letter by the government's action in pushing additional lands into the market, enlarging the grants to railroads, and selling the Indian reserves of Kansas instead of permitting homesteading upon them—was not displacing other methods of land disposal. They were also aware that land-reformers like Julian, Holman, and others in Congress had pushed measures to end cash—hence speculative —purchases but were defeated by a combination of conservative Republicans and Democrats. In their Kansas convention the Democrats took the logical step of demanding that the ceded lands be opened to pre-emption and homestead, free homesteads being the ultimate objective of all land reformers especially in conjunction with Julian's move to end cash sales. Both parties thus expressed opposition to the Osage treaty.[26]

The House Committee on Indian Affairs, on which one Joy man sat, brought in a report on the treaty (despite the fact that treaties were not a function of the House to consider) which called the Osage treaty "an outrage . . . that . . . builds up a frightful land monopoly in defiance of the just rights of the settlers" and "assumes the authority, repeatedly denied by this House, to dispose of those lands by treaty otherwise than by absolute cession to the United States, and for purposes for which Congress is alone competent to provide." The House solemnly condemned the "pretended treaty" and "earnestly but respectfully" requested the Senate

[26] Daniel W. Wilder, *Annals of Kansas* (Topeka, 1875), pp. 483, 486, 489.

not to ratify it. In an earlier version the resolution had stated
that the House would refuse to make any appropriation to
carry it out or to "recognize its validity in any form." [27]

Settlers on the Osage-ceded lands which had been sold to
the government by the treaty of 1865 were already in conflict with two railroads over the question of their rights in
the tract. Indignation flamed throughout the tract when efforts were made to evict settlers from their claims, or to compel them to buy at the railroad price. The Settlers' Protective Association of the Osage-ceded lands was organized on
the model of the Cherokee Neutral Land League, and fought
the issue through the press, the courts, and in politics, unit-
ing at the same time with the opposition to the ratification
of the second Osage treaty.[28]

This concerted and well-organized onslaught upon the
treaty caught the Joy lobbyists at a time when, because of
troubles over the Neutral Tract, they were somewhat demoralized. Impeachment proceedings against President Johnson
and subsequent investigation of alleged bribery to influence
votes kept the administration group on the defence and absorbed its attention. Perhaps hoping to let opposition die
down before pushing for ratification they left the treaty to
slumber for a time.

In 1869 efforts were made to revive the Osage treaty.
Under the pressure of lobbyists for rival railroads which had
been defeated in the original negotiations, a total of six Kansas railroads proposed a drastic revision of the treaty. As
reported by the Senate Committee on Indian Affairs, they
were to be permitted to share in the purchase of the reserve
and trust lands in the following proportions:

[27] *Cong. Globe*, 40 Cong., 2 Sess., part 4, pp. 3257, 3265.
[28] Anna H. Abel, "Indian Reservations in Kansas and the Extinguishment of their Title," Kansas State Historical Society, *Collections*,
VIII, 107–109; C. E. Coty, "The Osage Ceded Lands," *ibid.*, p. 196.

Leavenworth, Lawrence and Galveston	5/16
Atchison, Topeka and Santa Fe	5/16
Missouri, Fort Scott and Santa Fe	2/16
Lawrence and Neosho	2/16
Union Pacific, Southern Branch (Katy)	1/16
Leavenworth and Topeka	1/16

Settlers already on the trust lands were to have their claims at $1.25 an acre. The diminished-reserve lands were to be appraised and sold at not over $7.50 an acre for timber tracts, not over $5.00 an acre for prairie within 10 miles of any of the six railroads, and not over $2.50 an acre for prairie more than 10 miles from railroads.[29]

Thomas Ewing, Jr., attempted to counteract the opposition to the Osage treaty expressed by land-reformers and anti-monopolists; his first step was reorganizing the lobby in Washington. He thought I. N. Morris, who had taken an active part in Cherokee matters, was too impetuous, too well-known for his ties with Joy, and urged that in his place General Fitz Henry Warner be employed with an expense account of $200 to $300 a month and a liberal contingent fee. Warner, it was pointed out, knew many Senators and was on particularly close terms with Harlan who was chairman of the Committee on Indian Affairs.[30] From the outset Senator Ross was in the Joy camp and could be counted on to favor ratification.[31] Austin Blair, representative from Michigan, likewise was helpful.[32]

[29] The revised treaty is found in *Sen. Ex. Doc.,* 43 Cong., 2 Sess., no. 29, pp. 11–17.

[30] Thomas Ewing, Jr., Washington, Oct. 20, 1869, to Joy.

[31] Telegrams, Joy to Ross, June 1, 1868; Ross to Joy, May 25, Sept. 25, 1868; and letters of I. S. Kalloch, Lawrence, Nov. 9, 1869, to Joy; and Ross to Joy, Nov. 1, 1869. In this letter Ross expressed optimism about prospects of ratification, adding that he thought there would be "no organized opposition from Kansas."

[32] Austin Blair, House of Representatives, Jan. 11, 1870, to Joy.

207

Revival of efforts to induce the Senate to ratify the Osage treaty produced anew the journalistic attack upon it and its sponsors and authors. The *Emporia News* gave some of the background of the negotiations, doubtless with exaggeration, but, one must suspect, with a kernel of truth; for its alleged facts are similar to the definite information available concerning rewards given sponsors of earlier Kansas treaties. Thomas Ewing was said to have been promised a fee of $250,000, which he was to share with Secretary Browning. The Commissioner of Indian Affairs, N. G. Taylor, was to have twelve sections of land for his share in the enterprise. Sidney Clarke was said to have demanded $20,000 in United States bonds and 25,000 acres for his support. Pomeroy's brother-in-law, presumably the same Gaylord we have met before, was to have $240,000.[33]

But though railroad opposition to the original treaty with the LL&G as its sole beneficiary was dissipated by the revisions that opened its benefits to five rivals, the change was not sufficient to counteract the general condemnation the treaty elicited in Kansas and elsewhere. To the Kansas-settler and land-reform opposition elsewhere were added attorneys for the Osages, who worked against the treaty on grounds of inadequate compensation for the land and because false representations, threats, and duress had been made by the government representatives in the midst of the negotiations. Furthermore, as Austin Blair informed Joy, the Osage treaty had become so mixed up in the contest between the two houses over the practice of selling lands, providing for the payments of debts, and making allotments through treaty-making with the Indians, that the House was opposed to any further treaties.[34]

Despairing of success in the Senate, the Interior Department recommended to President Grant in February, 1870,

[33] *Emporia News,* June 25, 1869.
[34] Austin Blair, Jackson, Dec. 28, 1869, to Joy.

that he withdraw the Osage treaty from further consideration. But the railroads were not willing to give up the battle.
In May, when the Senate was considering a bill to authorize
the government to buy the Osage land for $1,600,000, the
same price at which the railroads were authorized to buy it
in both versions of the treaty, Senator Ross proposed an
amendment that would allow the same six railroads to buy
in the same proportions and at the same price as the revised
treaty had provided. Ross frankly stated that his intention
was to permit the railroads to profit from the increasing value
their lands would gain through development and settlement.[35]
The plan, which would have cancelled all that the land-
reformers had tried to accomplish, found little support in
Congress or in Kansas and got nowhere.

Table 13. SALE OF KANSAS INDIAN RESERVES

Tribe	Acres	Railroad	Present Railroad System
Delaware	223,966	Leavenworth, Pawnee & Western	Union Pacific
Pottawatomie	(not completed)	Leavenworth, Pawnee & Western	
Kickapoo	123,832	Atchison & Pikes Peak	Missouri Pacific
Delaware	92,598	Missouri River	Missouri Pacific
Pottawatomie	340,180	Santa Fe	Santa Fe
Cherokee	640,199	Mo. River, Ft. Scott & Gulf	Frisco

The Osage treaty marked the high-water mark set by the
Indian Office in treating for the sale of Indian reserves to
railroad and other speculative groups. It was a logical successor to the two Delaware, two Pottawatomie, Kickapoo,
and Cherokee treaties, by which 1,420,775 acres in solid
areas had been sold on credit at $1 to $2.96 an acre to railroads now a part of the Santa Fe, Missouri Pacific, Frisco,

[35] *Cong. Globe,* May 4, 1870, 41 Cong., 2 Sess., part 4, pp. 3219,
3743.

and Union Pacific systems. The Osage sale of 8,000,000 acres for 20 cents an acre marked another step in the breakdown of the public-land system. It aroused the land-reformers to a concerted attack, not only to prevent ratification of the treaty, but finally to bring to a halt the treaty-making power of the Senate and thus end forever the power the Indian Office had arrogated to itself in disposing of the reserves.

Congressional opponents of the treaty-making power to sell Indian lands used the Osage treaty as a horrible example of the danger that the entire public-land system might be prostituted or even discarded by the new method of disposal. Their continued attacks upon the treaty-making power were pushed to the point where they wore down its defenders. In 1870 the House of Representatives adopted an amendment to an Indian appropriation bill that would end the treaty-making power, but it was lost in conference. In 1871, the House had its way in the Act of March 3. After five or six years of defending its special prerogative or at times blandly ignoring attacks upon it, the Senate finally surrendered. Henceforth, it was no longer possible for administrative officers secretly to secure Indian approval of "treaties" which, with numerous important and highly significant provisions concerning land policy, became the law of the land when ratified in executive session by the Senate.[36]

Defeat of the second Osage treaty and end of the treaty-making method of selling reserves did not by any means halt the bickering and conflict over the Osage lands. The ratified treaty of 1865 precipitated another clash with the LL&G and the Missouri, Kansas, and Texas Railroad (Katy) that was longer than and as sharp as that over the second and unratified treaty. The issue concerned the ceded tract on the eastern end of the great reserve, a tract that was 30 miles from east to west and 50 miles from north to south, and

[36] *Cong. Globe*, 41 Cong., 3 Sess., I, 765; II, 1811, and Appendix, p. 389.

contained 843,927 acres. Included in the area were practically all of Labette and Neosho Counties and parts of four adjacent counties. The sale of the ceded tract was conditional, for the land was not to become a part of the public domain, nor were the Pre-emption and Homestead laws to apply to it. Also, the net proceeds were neither to go into the Treasury nor to be set aside for the Osages, but were to be placed in the civilization fund. Up to this point the treaty put the tract in a special category that was much the same as trust lands; but the Senate added an amendment which was difficult to reconcile with other features of the treaty and made for much difficulty in interpretation and litigation. This can only be shown by giving the portion of the treaty in which the amendment, here italicized, is embedded.

Said lands shall be surveyed and sold, under the direction of the Secretary of the Interior, on the most advantageous terms, for cash, as public lands are surveyed and sold under existing laws, *including any act granting lands to the State of Kansas in aid of construction of a railroad through said lands;* but no preemption claim or homestead settlement shall be recognized. . . .

There can be little doubt that the amendment was inserted to make it possible for the railroads which had land grants for construction of lines up to the Osage boundary now to have their grants extended into the cession. Two railroads were concerned: the LL&G was building south from Lawrence to the Kansas boundary, and the Katy was building from Junction City in a southeasterly direction. Both followed routes which would take them across almost the entire distance of the Osage cession on their way through the Indian Territory to the Gulf. Congress in 1863 and 1866 had given both railroads grants of land on the alternate-section pattern for a distance of ten miles on each side of their line, and had authorized them to select lieu lands in place of the odd sections already in process of alienation in an area ten miles beyond the primary grant. The grant to the Katy actually permitted the railroad to select both odd and even sections between ten and twenty miles from the road in lieu of what it did not secure within the primary area.[37]

Following the signing of the first Osage treaty, settlers rushed into the eastern portion of the reserve which had been sold to the government, thinking or hoping that they would be allowed at the most homestead rights and at the least pre-emption rights. They were first upheld in their hopes by Joseph S. Wilson, Commissioner of the General Land Office, who decided that the railroads had no right to any part of the tract. Joy and Sturges, and perhaps the representatives of the Katy Railroad, were not so easily defeated in their claim to a large part of the land they deemed theirs by virtue of the treaty of 1865.[38] They carried the issue on appeal to Secretary Browning, who was more sensitive than Wilson to railroad interests and especially those relating to James F. Joy. Browning reversed the decision of his subordinate by declaring that the grants extended throughout the ceded tract.[39] When an indignant House of Representatives tried to reverse Browning by adopting a joint resolution opening all odd and even sections within the tract to actual

[37] Acts of March 3, 1863, and July 26, 1866, 12 *Stat.*, 772 and 14 *Stat.*, 289. A most unusual and doubtfully constitutional provision was included in the Act of July 26, 1866, which authorized the Pacific Railroad, Southern Branch (present Katy) to negotiate directly with the Indians and to arrange to buy from them the right of way for the line and additional lands. Practically, this is what representatives of the LL&G did in negotiating the second and unratified Osage treaty.

[38] Joseph S. Wilson, Washington, May 17, 1867, to Henry C. Whitney, Attorney for the Leavenworth, Lawrence, and Galveston Railroad. Joy MSS.

[39] Commissioner of the General Land Office, *Annual Report,* 1869 (Washington, 1870), p. 44.

settlers, the leaders were frustrated by the action of Senators Harlan and Pomeroy, conferees on a committee to iron out differences between the two houses.[40] Harlan and Pomeroy insisted on including a proviso that saved existing interests and made it possible for Browning's successor again to decide that the grants applied throughout the ceded lands.[41]

With these two favorable decisions, which clearly were against the will of the House but equally clearly were acceptable to the Senate, the railroads proceeded to make their selections. They claimed all but one section of the 843,927-acre reserve, and had 457,907 acres confirmed to them.[42]

Between the date of the treaty of 1865 and the decision of Jacob Cox confirming the land to the railroads, 2,295 claimants settled upon the Osage-ceded tract and paid the United States $297,545, according to the provisions of the treaty and the joint resolution of 1869.[43] Some settlers had been on the land several years, had made substantial improvements, and with the purchase money had important capital investments which they were prepared to defend. Fearing conflict with the settlers if it tried to sell at the usual railroad prices, the Katy contemplated letting settlers have the land they had improved for $1.25 an acre.[44] The plan was not adopted but instead the Katy offered its land at $2 to $15.[45] The LL&G, whose officers had reason to question

[40] *Cong. Globe,* 41 Cong., 1 Sess., p. 683.

[41] 16 *Stat.,* p. 55; *House Reports,* 45 Cong., 2 Sess., II, no. 377, p. 2.

[42] *House Reports,* 45 Cong., 2 Sess., II, no. 377, p. 1. The *Annual Report* of the Commissioner of the General Land Office, 1932, p. 44, footnote, shows that the LL&G lost 186,936 acres and the Katy 270,090 acres by the decisions of the Supreme Court holding that railroads were not entitled to land within the ceded reserve.

[43] *House Reports,* 45 Cong., 2 Sess., II, no. 377, p. 1.

[44] O. Chanute, Supt., Leavenworth, Lawrence, and Galveston Railroad, Lawrence, July 8, 1872, to Joy.

[45] *Kansas Farmer* (Nov. 1869), VI, 192. *Sen. Ex. Doc.,* 44 Cong., 2 Sess., II, no. 35, pp. 2–7.

their wisdom in handling the Neutral-Tract controversy, rushed into another. They advertised that they would sell their land at $4 to $10 an acre with credit of seven years at 7 per cent interest.[46] Later, prices of $3.50 to $8.00 were quoted with credit of seven to ten years. Concerning the settlers who had already bought their claims and received their patents, only now to be told by the railroad that their patents were of no value, the advertisement stated: [47]

Owing to a misapprehension in regard to the status of these lands, a large number of hardy pioneers settled upon them under the impression that they were or would be subject to preemption. Disappointed in this, many of them are willing to sell their improvements and seek new locations further west on lands yet held by the Government.

To the wealthier and more conservative class of immigrants who follow in the wake of adventurous pioneers, who value railroad facilities and the advantages of a comparatively well settled country, and are willing to pay something for them, no better opportunity can be found than is here afforded to buy land on which a commencement has already been made.

The improvements are of all sorts, from the most primitive shanty with a few acres broke, to farms well inclosed and in a good state of cultivation, and can generally be bought for a slight advance over the cost of making them, to say nothing of the expense of living while the land is being reduced to a condition fit for cultivation.

Elsewhere in the same advertisement the railroad officials said: [48]

A considerable portion of the land is occupied by squatters, who settled on it under the impression that it was government

[46] Advertising circular of John W. Scott, Land Commissioner, Joy MSS.

[47] *Homes for All, and How to Secure Them. A Guide to the Leavenworth, Lawrence & Galveston Railroad and Its Lands in Southern Kansas* (Lawrence, n.d.), pp. 16–17.

[48] *Ibid.*, p. 47.

$200,000!

LOST! LOST.

☞LOST—A carpet bag, containing $200,000 in Government vouchers belonging to the Soldiers of Kansas, their Widows and Orphans. Apply to SIDNEY CLARKE.

LOST—26 tons of Government hay, which SIDNEY CLARKE sold to the Government at $20 per ton. Said hay was supposed to be in front of Sid. Clarke's residence, but Government could never find it.

LOST—The Representative in Congress from Kansas. When last heard from he was on the BORDER TIER RAILROAD, traveling in the direction of Kansas City, making occasional inquiries for Government vouchers—lost in a carpet bag. One Van Horn is supposed to know something about him. He was supposed to have a large sum of money, which was paid him for working on the Border Tier Railroad,

WANTED!

A Congressman who has some faith in the future of Lawrence.

WANTED—A Congressman who can do the Soldiers justice, without increasing his own pay Twenty-Five Hundred Dollars a year at the same time.

WANTED—A Congressman who won't sell out his own town, county and state.

WANTED—A Congressman who prefers bridging the Missouri river at Leavenworth, *Kansas*, instead of *Kansas City, Missouri.*

WANTED—A man to take charge of two hundred acres of very valuable land near Fort Scott, which was given to *Sidney Clarke* as part pay for services rendered the *Kansas City Border Tier Railroad.*

STRAYED.
200 HEAD OF GOVERNMENT CATTLE!

That were taken from a man who was supposed to have stolen them from the Cherokee Nation while *Sidney Clarke* was Provost Marshal of the State of Kansas.

A handbill attacking the activities of Congressman Sidney Clarke. (Courtesy, Kansas State Historical Society)

land, and although they have no legal rights, the Company is disposed to deal leniently with them, and expects that purchasers will satisfy them for their improvements. These can generally be bought for less than it would take to make them, and the purchaser saves the expense and loss of time incident to a beginning on the new prairie.

The sales experience of the LL&G reveals how well worth defending was the right to acquire the Osage-ceded lands. Although it is impossible to distinguish the railroad's sales of its Osage lands from those of its grant outside the reserve, we may safely conclude that most of the lands sold in 1871 and 1872 were Osage tracts. Between June, 1871 and April, 1872 the net sales were 42,539 acres, which brought an average price of $8.15 an acre.[49] Only by giving long credit could buyers take land at such prices, and it may be hazarded on the basis of the experience of other Kansas railroads that a substantial portion of these purchases would be forfeited.[50]

[49] *Annual Report,* Leavenworth, Lawrence, and Galveston Railroad Company, June 3, 1872, p. 21. By February, 1874, it was reported that the two railroads had sold over 40,000 acres of their disputed land to 340 individuals or partnerships, on which about one-tenth of the consideration was paid. The names of the purchasers of the Leavenworth, Lawrence, and Galveston and the Katy, the description of the land they bought, the consideration, and the amount they had paid are given in *Sen. Ex. Doc.,* 44 Cong., 2 Sess., no. 35. The sales were mostly in quarter-section tracts. One intriguing buyer is La Rue Smith, who appears on the Katy list as the purchaser of 1,279 acres for $3.50 each, or fifty cents an acre less than the minimum for all other tracts. He also appears on the Leavenworth, Lawrence, and Galveston list as the purchaser of two adjacent sections and with a footnote statement: "No records of consideration or payments."

[50] In 1878, after the Leavenworth, Lawrence, and Galveston had lost its Osage lands, it reported net sales of land as 165,074 acres which brought an average of $2.91 an acre. The sale of 1878 amounted to 22,645 acres at an average of $3.83 an acre. *Annual Report,* Leavenworth, Lawrence, and Galveston Railroad, 1878, p. 23.

Questions concerning the title to the lands and wrangling with the Company brought sales nearly to a halt in 1872.[51]

Table 14. LAND SALES, LEAVENWORTH, LAWRENCE AND GALVESTON RAILROAD CO., FROM JUNE 16, 1871 TO APRIL 30, 1872

Month	No. of Acres	Average Price	Amount of Sales	Advance Payment
1871				
June	5,104.96	8.46½	43,208.63	1,573.92
July	7,970.86	8.20	65,349.20	2,164.55
August	2,023.75	8.02½	16,698.55	458.63
September	12,965.46	8.61½	111,704.66	2,365.70
October	3,483.92	8.55	29,813.10	731.99
November	1,615.41	7.90	12,766.40	215.16
December	1,159.32	7.58	8,795.92	64.45
1872				
January	1,866.15	7.97	14,889.20	1,064.10
February	880.00	7.82	6,880.00	426.59
March	1,284.05	8.07¼	10,374.80	1,600.40
April	5,999.73	7.00	41,996.39	1,298.14
Less by	44,353.61		362,476.85	
can. sales	1,814.19		15,752.06	
	42,539.42	8.15	346,724.79	
Town lots	158.05	90.82	14,354.50	
Total			361,079.29	

Kansans were not easily intimidated on land matters and particularly when absentee-owned railroads challenged their rights. Squatters' conflicts with railroads and speculators on the Delaware lands and on the Cherokee Neutral Tract had shown that compromise and more generous treatment could be secured by vigorous and forthright opposition. They had also shown that squatters' rights could be maintained for years

[51] *Annual Report,* Leavenworth, Lawrence, and Galveston, 1872, pp. 10–11.

by the widespread opposition of all interested people. Borrowing from the experience of the embattled squatters on the Neutral Tract, the Osage squatters determined to fight for their rights as long as humanly possible.

A Settlers' Protective Association was organized to represent the Osage residents and to safeguard members in the enjoyment of their land claims against claim jumpers or others who purchased from the railroads. A participant in the Association later described its activities:[52] "The association was practically 'the government' in the region. It had supreme control. It had the mass of the people with it and no one to dispute its rights who had any force. As an organized society, it had almost every settler back of it." At its open-air meetings as many as 4,000 and 5,000 people listened to the oratory of its leaders denouncing the railroads and their grasp for lands. One great meeting at Parsons brought together 4,000 people who filled the streets with their 560 wagons on parade, their banners carrying flaming inscriptions:

We fought for our Union, We will fight for our Homes
Our homes at all hazzards
We will save our homes, in peace if we can, by war if we must
Our cause is just
God speed the right
Justice to the settlers
In God we trust, no Rail Road title unless we must

Addresses by the Governor, by Sidney Clarke, and by Senator Preston B. Plumb stirred the crowd to wrathful indignation.[53] The aid of leading land reformers like Julian and Lawrence was invoked, and the House moved to assure settlers' pre-emption rights, as stipulated in the treaty of 1867.

[52] C. E. Cory, "The Osage Ceded Lands," Kansas State Historical Society, *Transactions*, VIII, 197.

[53] "Rick," writing from Mound Valley, Kansas, May 30, 1874, in *Piatt Republican* (Monticello, Illinois), June 11, 1877; Wilder, *Annals of Kansas*, p. 616.

Though the joint resolution was emasculated by Harlan and Pomeroy, as has been seen, the move had the effect of further delaying any efforts the railroads might make to dispossess squatters.

Failing in Congress, the Settlers' Protective Association levied assessments upon members to finance litigation to test the railroad title to the ceded lands. At the request of the Association, William Lawrence prepared a brief in which he set forth for public consideration the grounds for believing that the railroads had no rights in the ceded lands other than the right of way. His letter of June 5, 1871 to the leaders of the Association was an effective argument that cast discredit on the decisions of Browning and Cox.[54] The Association also secured an appropriation from the Kansas legislature to aid the fight against the railroads.[55] Lawrence's brief, the action of the Kansas legislature, and continued agitation on the tract brought the issue so forcibly to the attention of the Federal officials, especially the Department of Justice, that they reversed their previous judgment and joined with the settlers in efforts to test the validity of the decisions of Browning and Cox.

Several hundred ejectment suits and other legal actions had already been brought in the local courts by the railroads and the settlers. After considerable maneuvering, a case embodying the basic issues was framed and carried up to the Supreme Court. A battery of extraordinarily able legal talent was brought together in its support, including Jeremiah Black, former cabinet officer; Lawrence, whose brief of 1871 contained the principal grounds on which the settler's case rested; and Wilson Shannon, former territorial governor of Kansas. After dreary years of wrangling, which engendered

[54] *The Osage Ceded Lands. Who Owns Them? The Settler vs. the Railroads. Views of Judge Lawrence of Ohio* (n.d., n.p.). A copy of this pamphlet is in the Newberry Library.

[55] *Wilder, op. cit.,* pp. 638–642.

deep hatred against the two railroads, kept the people in continued tension and worry about the question of ownership, and retarded the development of the disputed area, the attorneys succeeded in getting the issue before the Supreme Court in 1875. The legal questions involved in the Osage case were quite different from those in the case of Holden vs. Joy which determined ownership of the Cherokee Neutral Tract, though both concerned the right of the government or the Indians to provide for the sale or donation to railroads of Indian reserves. In Holden vs. Joy the Court decided that the Cherokees could sell their Neutral Tract to a private individual through the treaty process. The issue in the Osage case was whether or not the grants of land of 1863 and 1866 to the Katy and LL&G Railroads extended through the ceded lands.

David Davis, a liberal land reformer and anti-monopolist despite his ownership of many prairie farms in Illinois which put him with William Scully among America's richest landlords, carried a majority of the judges with him in upholding the settlers' contention that the railroads had no right to the land in the Osage cession. He declared that the interpretation of the treaty must rest on the words used, "nothing adding thereto, nothing diminishing." He thereby reversed the earlier decision of the Secretary of the Interior and assured the settlers of their land under the joint resolution of 1869. Justice Stephen Field, who was becoming the great protector of property rights, handed down a sharply-worded dissenting opinion, in which he held that the amendment to the treaty extended to the railroads the right to odd sections within the primary grant area of the Osage cession. Two other judges joined him in maintaining the right of the railroads to the land.[56]

In 1876 Congress again enacted, and for the third time,

[56] 92 *U.S.* 733 ff., for the Leavenworth, Lawrence, and Galveston decision and p. 760 for the Katy decision.

that settlers on the Osage-ceded tract should have the privilege of buying the land on which they had established themselves for the basic government price of $1.25 an acre.[57]
A year's time was given them to raise the cost. Victory was
thus finally achieved, for with the legislation described below,
all the Osage tract, consisting of the ceded lands, the trust
lands, and the diminished reserve was now open to the
equivalent of pre-emption. The victory was by no means
complete, however. Where free land adjacent to the reserve
was available under the Homestead Act, Osage lands could
be acquired only by purchase. Furthermore, the settlers on
the ceded lands had to meet a heavy bill for legal services
in defending their rights to homes which successive Secretaries of the Interior had declared to be railroad property.[58]
For their difficulties the settlers had to thank the Indian policy
of the government, which had evolved without rhyme or
reason so far as the surrender of Indian rights to land was
concerned, and had become in Kansas a nightmare to persons
seeking to establish themselves as farmers.

Land-seekers did not wait for the official opening of the
trust and diminished reserve lands or in fact for the divest-
ment of Osage rights, but rushed into the eastern portion
of the Osage tract as early as 1867. On February 28, 1870
Isaac T. Gibson, government agent to the Osages, reported
that a number of thousand settlers had moved to the lands
in the past three years, where they had taken over Indian

[57] 19 *Stat.*, 127. This privilege had previously been given in the
treaty of 1867 and the joint resolution of 1869.

[58] Wilson Shannon and McComas and McKeighan, attorneys for
the settlers, prepared a statement with the caption "The Osage Ceded
Lands in Kansas. In the Matter of the Bill now pending in the Senate
to Amend a Bill providing for the Sale of said lands" in an effort to get
officials to permit the payment of their fees and other legal costs from
funds derived from the sale of the lands they had recovered from the
railroads. A copy of this two-page document is in the Library of
Congress.

cabins, cut timber, and begun farming operations.[59] There was some friction between Osages and whites, but commonly the Indians accepted the intruders provided they would pay small sums in goods or money as rent for the land. In Montgomery County settlers on prairie claims were dunned $5 and those on timber claims, $10.[60] These "sooners," to borrow the expression from later Oklahoma history, were found on every reservation in Kansas before the Indian lands were officially sold or open to settlement. They gambled that the lands would not be sold to speculators or railroads; they had lost on the Delaware, Pottawatomie, Kickapoo, and in part on the Cherokee Neutral lands, but they won on the Osage lands.

When it appeared that the lands in the Osage trust and diminished reserve were not to be sold to railroads, Congress enacted on July 15, 1870, that the trust lands were to be opened to settlement and sale, after survey, and subject to the withdrawal of the 16th and 36th sections for common schools. Only actual settlers, that is the squatters who had moved to the lands before the adoption of the Act, and new immigrants who came in the role of pre-emptors were permitted to buy, as was the case on the unoffered lands of central and western Kansas. New settlers were allowed a year to pay for their land from the time they took up their tracts or from the time the township plats were available at the land office; and the "sooners" were given a year from the adoption of the act if the lands were already surveyed.[61] With the approval of the Osages, the diminished reserve was to be surveyed and sold on the same conditions. Approval was received on October 22, 1870, thereby completing the

[59] Isaac T. Gibson, Osage Agency, Feb. 28, Nov. 8, 10, 1870, to Enoch Hoag, Indian Affairs, National Archives.

[60] Andreas, *History of the State of Kansas,* pp. 1564, 1588. Andreas mentions the frequency of such rental agreements between whites and Osages in Montgomery and Cowley Counties.

[61] 16 *Stat.,* 362.

surrender of the Osage right of occupancy of all their Kansas lands except for a few allotments. The lands in the trust and diminished reserve were to be sold, and the receipts therefrom were to become a part of the endowment funds of the Osages.[62]

Settlers on the Osage lands were hard put to make their payments within the required year. Farm making called for considerable capital investment other than the purchase money for the land, and to have to put up $200 for a quarter-section when the settler needed all his capital for other things added greatly to his burden. The advertisements of the land-grant railroads of Kansas emphasized the need for pioneers to bring capital with them for buying and developing their land. Said the LL&G in its promotion literature: [63] "The new settler here ought to have means enough to buy a good span of horses or yoke of cattle, and a plow; to build some kind of comfortable house, and enough left to subsist his family for a year. . . ." The Santa Fe literature advised people who could not "command capital enough to equip or stock a small farm" not to move to Kansas.[64] The Kansas Pacific counseled immigrants not to bring heavy or bulky material such as farm implements, household goods, or livestock but to bring sufficient capital to buy them.[65]

[62] Commissioner of the General Land Office, *Annual Report*, p. 24. For an account of the removal of the Osages to the Indian country see Berlin B. Chapman, "Removal of the Osages from Kansas," *Kansas Historical Quarterly* (Aug. and Nov., 1938), VII, 287–305, 399–410.

[63] *Homes for All, and How to Secure Them. A Guide to the Leavenworth, Lawrence and Galveston Railroad and Its Lands in Southern Kansas,* pp. 10–11.

[64] *How and Where to Get a Living. A Sketch of "The Garden of the West." Presenting Facts Worth Knowing Concerning the Lands of the Atchison, Topeka, and Santa Fe Railroad Co. in Southwestern Kansas* (Boston, 1876), p. 46.

[65] *Emigrants' Guide to the Kansas Pacific Railway Lands* (Lawrence, 1871), p. 23. Allan Bogue has brought together a good deal of information concerning the cost of farm making in Kansas in the

Settler difficulties were made the more serious by scant rainfall, a serious drought in 1880, the grasshopper plague in 1874 and 1875, and low prices from the panic of 1873 until the turn came in the early eighties.[66]

Settlers on the Osage trust lands and diminished reserve were in serious difficulties in 1872, when many failed to make their payments as the Act of 1870 required. Congress came to their relief on May 9, 1872 by extending credit until January 1, 1873 but required interest of 5 per cent on the delayed payments.[67] In the bad year 1874 few settlers could meet their obligations, and an additional extension of one year was granted.[68] Three years later a discouraged settler on the Osage lands near Winfield, who was having a hard time meeting the 36 per cent interest on his debt, declared that three-fourths of the farms in southern Kansas were mortgaged; and he expressed doubts that more than a half of the owners had any hope of ridding themselves of debt.[69] The accumulation of ill fortune which resulted from a series of calamities, especially on the western portion of the Osage lands, induced Congress in 1880 to grant a further extension of three years to the delinquents.[70] Even in the eastern portion the Osage lands were going begging, for with such trying times land-lookers were extremely hesitant to undertake to buy land when more remote tracts might be acquired free. Consequently in 1881 Congress undertook to apply the principle of graduation to the remaining unsold lands east of the

---

introduction to his unpublished doctoral dissertation, "Farm Land Credit in Kansas and Nebraska, 1854–1900," Cornell University Library.

[66] James C. Malin, *Winter Wheat in the Golden Belt of Kansas* (Lawrence, 1944), pp. 40–45.

[67] 17 *Stat.*, 90.

[68] 18 *Stat.*, 283.

[69] Walter Denning in *Iroquois County Times* (Watseka, Illinois), Nov. 24, 1877.

[70] 21 *Stat.*, 144.

second tier of townships in Sumner County, in order to make them more palatable. Lands unsold on June 30, 1881 were to be priced at seventy-five cents, those unsold on June 30, 1882 were to be priced at fifty cents and those unsold on June 30, 1883 and thereafter were to be priced at twenty-five cents an acre.[71] The measure was made subject to the approval of the Osages, and that approval was denied, thereby making graduation "inoperative" in the words of the Commissioner of the General Land Office.[72] After 1882 conditions on the Osage lands improved, hordes of new settlers came there in search of lands, and the bulk of the remaining tracts were entered in 1883–1888. In the single year 1886 no less then 1,033,825 acres were sold to settlers. After 1890 the few tracts still held by the government were scattered, small pieces, having little to interest settlers.

Representatives of Joy were not content with their acquisition of the Neutral Tract and their negotiation for the rich prize in the Osage lands. When some forty-three Miami headrights of 200 acres each were being patented in 1869, the Joy representatives were on hand to acquire these lands, which were adjacent to their Fort Scott Line.[73] At the same time their yearning for land turned their eyes to the Cherokee Strip.

Stretching for a distance of 276 miles between the Osage reserve and the boundary of the Indian Territory and 2½ miles deep, the Cherokee Strip contained some 434,679 acres. Representatives of the LL&G accompanied by Senator Ross, went into the Cherokee country in November, 1869, to arrange for a sale by treaty of the Strip. They found agents of three other railroads ahead of them and could do

[71] 21 *Stat.*, 510.

[72] Commissioner of the General Land Office, *Annual Report,* 1882, *House Ex. Doc.,* I, no. 1, part 5, 37.

[73] *Miami County Republican* (Paola), April 10, 17, 1869; J. F. Joy, March 1, 1869, to K. Coates, Joy MSS.

no more than gain a promise that none of their rivals should get the tract.[74] A little later one George H. Vickery submitted a bid of fifty cents an acre for the tract. He agreed to sell lands on which settlers were already established at the basic $1.25 an acre, as the Cherokee treaty of 1866 provided. The offer was approved by a man who claimed to represent the settlers on the Strip but was rejected by Jacob Cox, Secretary of the Interior, because it did not conform to the government policy of disposing of Indian trust lands.[75]

In 1871 and 1872 the Cherokees and settlers on the Strip joined together in urging Congress to make provision for the sale of the land to occupants. The first price proposed was $1.25 an acre, but insistence of the Cherokees on a higher figure led to a concession; lands east of the Arkansas River were to be sold for $2.00, and those west of the river were to be sold for $1.50. Persons already on the Strip and those moving to it within a year after the passage of the measure were to have a pre-emption right with these prices and a year to pay. Land unsold at the end of a year was to be offered on sealed bids—an ominous feature when one considers the use to which this device had earlier been put in Kansas.[76]

In 1877, with depression, low commodity prices, and diminishing demand for the Cherokee Strip, it became apparent that the base price of the lands had been set at "too high" a figure. Congress in conceding its error lowered the price of all the Strip to $1.25 an acre for an additional year, and thereafter it was to stand at $1.[77] This reduction did not satisfy prospective purchasers, and efforts were made there-

[74] Commissioner of the General Land Office, *Annual Report*, 1872, p. 16; I. S. Kalloch, Superintendent, LL&G, Lawrence, Nov. 19, 1869, to Joy.

[75] Geo. H. Vickery, Washington, D.C., Feb. 23, 1870, to Cherokee Delegates with memo by Cox, National Archives.

[76] Act of May 11, 1872, 17 *Stat.*, 98.

[77] 19 *Stat.*, 265, Act of Feb. 28, 1877.

FOR SALE!

308,000 ACRES

Valuable Lands
IN KANSAS.

By direction of the Honorable Secretary of the Interior, the undersigned will receive sealed bids for the purchase of any or all of the unsold lands west of the Neosho River, along the southern line of the State of Kansas embraced within what is generally known as the "CHEROKEE STRIP."

These lands are offered for sale in compliance with the provisions of an act of Congress approved May 11, 1872, [U. S. Statutes at Large, vol. xvii, pp. 98 and 99.]

They will be sold to the highest bidder for cash, in quantities not exceeding one hundred and sixty acres, at not less than two dollars per acre for all of said lands lying east of the Arkansas River, and one dollar and fifty cents per acre for such lands as lie west of said River.

Printed lists, describing the lands hereby offered for sale by their proper legal subdivisions and indicating the minimum price at which each tract is held, will be sent by mail to the address of any person making application therefor to the Commissioner of the General Land Office, or to the Register and Receiver of the local offices at Wichita and Independence, Kansas.

Persons offering to purchase may bid for as many tracts as they may desire, but each bid must be separately made and sealed, and must be for not more than one hundred and sixty acres, (and conform to the legal subdivisions embraced in the list.)

Bids must be accompanied by 10 per cent. of the amount bid as a guarantee of the good faith of the bidder, which sum, in case the land is awarded and the balance not paid, will be forfeited. Should any bid be rejected, the sum deposited will be returned to the proper party.

Parties whose bids are accepted will be notified of such acceptance as soon after the opening of the bids as practicable, and if within forty days after such notice has been duly mailed payment in full be not made to the Commissioner of the General Land Office of the amount bid, the land upon which such bid was made will be again subject to sale.

The ten per cent. deposit required to accompany bids may be remitted in Post Office orders, certificates of deposit, certified checks on some Government depository payable to the order of the Commissioner of the General Land Office, or in currency.

The right to reject any and all bids is expressly reserved.

All bids must be sealed and addressed to the "COMMISSIONER OF THE GENERAL LAND OFFICE, WASHINGTON, D. C.," and indorsed "BIDS FOR CHEROKEE STRIP LANDS."

Bids will be received as above invited until 12 o'clock noon of the thirtieth day of November, 1875, after which they will be duly opened and acted upon.

S. S. BURDETT,
Commissioner of the General Land Office.

WASHINGTON, D. C., *September 15, 1875.*

A government advertisement of the sale of Cherokee Strip lands, 1875. (Courtesy, Collection of Regional History, Cornell University)

Table 15. LAND SALES IN THE CHEROKEE STRIP [78]

Year (end June 30)	Eastern portion sold at Independence Office		Total sales
	Acres sold	Price per acre	Acres
1873	19,570	$2.00	83,732
1874	50,835	2.00	71,000(?)
1875	3,018	2.00	3,015
1876	1,919	2.00	1,919
1877	899	2.00	5,189
1878	329	1.25	30,400
1879	4,876	1.25	80,881
1880	9,851	1.00	
1881	5,111	1.00	20,086
1882	5,922	1.00	29,508
1883	12,225	1.00	59,800
1884		1.00	68,961
1885		1.00	267

after to reduce the price still further. The lower price brought out some increase in purchasing, but active buying had to wait on better times and the increasing pressure on the land supply which came in 1879 and later.

Treaties had been previously arranged with the Quapaws,

[78] Unlike public lands in unoffered areas which could be sold only as pre-emptions, there were no limits on the amount of land individuals could buy in the Cherokee Strip. Largest acquisition in the eastern part was made by George Storch who acquired 2,400 acres. Some of the larger acquisitions in Cowley and Sumner Counties were U. S. Mendenhall, 4,575 acres, Ira King, 3,388 acres, John A. Young, 3,164 acres, C. M. Scott, 2,400 acres and Isaac and Anne C. McDowell, 2,144 acres. Compiled from abstracts of land purchases in the Cherokee Strip at the Independence and Wichita offices, National Archives. C. W. McCampbell has described the extensive land and cattle business of "W. E. Campbell, Pioneer Kansas Livestockman" in *Kansas Historical Quarterly* (Aug., 1948), XVI, 245 ff. Campbell had a ranch of 14,000 acres which was part of the former Strip and Osage reserve. Commissioner of the General Land Office, *Annual Report*, 1878, *House Ex. Doc.*, 45 Cong., 3 Sess., IX, part 1, 53.

the Ottawas, the Peoria, the Sac and Fox of Missouri, the Sac and Fox of Mississippi, the Kansas, the Miami, and a number of other small groups for the disposal of those portions of their Kansas reserves that were not to be allotted. Generally, the lands were ceded in trust to the government or were sold to the government which in turn was to sell them for not less than $1.25 an acre plus the appraised value of any improvements. After 1875 a few Indian allotments, such as the tiny Black Bob reserve of the Shawnees and the claim of the New York Indians for compensation for their rights, continued to bedevil Kansas settlers, tax, probate, and other law officers, the Federal Congress, and the officers of the Indian Office. Not for many years were these issues to be entirely settled. Meantime lawyers had a Roman holiday with these disputes, as well as with most of the conflicts in Kansas involving Indian titles and the transfer of Indian ownership to whites; and settlers found the cost of buying their land and making their farms greatly increased.

CHAPTER VII

Ho for Kansas
and Free Land

LAND reformers looking at Kansas after 1862 could take little comfort from the progress which had been made in liberalizing the public land system; farm ownership had not been made notably easier for immigrants then pouring in from Europe and from eastern sections of America. The Homestead Act, which has been called one of the two "most important land acts in the history of the world. . . ." [1] was expected by its authors to halt the process of concentrating land-ownership in great estates, speculative groups, and individuals, a process that had been going on since the establishment of the Federal government. Free land was likewise expected to enable the poorer class to commence farming

[1] Addison E. Sheldon, *Land Systems and Land Policies in Nebraska* (Nebraska Historical Society, *Publications*, XXII; Lincoln, 1936), p. 75.

operations in the West without the great burden of debt which had earlier accompanied pioneering on the frontier. In Kansas, the expectations of the reformers were to be fulfilled only in part.

The area open to free homestead lay for the most part beyond the 97th meridian, far from markets, and much of it distant from railroads. Through the better part of this homestead region the Santa Fe and the Kansas Pacific Railroads owned alternate sections for a distance of twenty miles on either side of their lines; and these sections, of course, were not open to homesteading as free land. Within the primary area of railroad land-grants, homestead units were permitted on the reserved land but they could be only 80 acres in size. There were, then, two strips of territory, each twenty miles wide and stretching all the way across the state, in which each alternate section was held by the government (save sections 16 and 36 reserved for schools) and could be acquired by settlers only in 160-acre lots for $2.50 an acre or in eighty-acre lots as homesteads.[2] All of southern Kansas for a depth of 52½ miles and extending as far west as the 100th meridian, since it was Osage or Cherokee land, had to be sold under the treaty-making policy or special implementing acts.[3] Disposal of Indian lands by treaty had also assured that a considerable portion of eastern Kansas should not be thrown open to homestead entry. Altogether some 20,000,000 acres—more than a third of the State—were barred to homesteaders after the enactment of the Homestead Law. Stating the matter a little differently, 47 per cent of the area of Kansas was either sold as Indian reserves and

[2] By the Act of March 3, 1879 homestead units of 160 acres were permitted on reserved land within the primary grant area of railroads in Kansas and other public-domain states. 20 *U.S. Stat.*, 472.

[3] Maps showing the location of the primary-grant and lieu-land areas of the Kansas railroads are found in Thomas Donaldson, *The Public Domain*.

never became a part of the public domain or was granted to railroads or to the State for education.

The remaining 53 per cent of Kansas lands passed to private ownership under the general public-land laws that provided for sales to, or entries with scrip and warrants by, persons, partnerships, or companies; and for pre-emption, homestead, and timber-culture entries of 160 acres each by persons residing upon and improving their lands. A considerable portion of the cash sales and warrant and scrip entries, some of the pre-emptions, and even some of the homestead and timber-culture claims were acquired by speculators attempting to anticipate future immigrants' needs.

Vacant government lands were open to inspection, selection, and entry, but because of their scattered location immigrants usually had to secure the aid of professional land-lookers to direct them to desirable locations.[4] Few had time or inclination to devote to extensive search of the plat books, and to even more extensive examination of available tracts —tracts which, more often than not, were hard to find. While the official government policy was to permit selections on a completely *laissez-faire* basis of any unreserved land on which Indian title had been surrendered, the land companies, individual speculators, and land-grant railroads concentrated upon attracting settlers to their lands who would buy on credit and commence improvements.

[4] George L. Anderson has made good use of previously neglected records relating to efforts of settlers in western Kansas to acquire land in his "The Administration of Federal Land Laws in Western Kansas, 1880–1890: A Factor in Adjustment to a New Environment," *Kansas Historical Quarterly* (Nov., 1952), XX, 233 ff. Good as the article is, it is quite incomplete, for it leaves untouched farm making and land entries on the Osage Reserve and the Cherokee Strip, much of which lies west of the ninety-eighth meridian. The important story of pioneering on the grants of the Kansas Pacific and the Santa Fe also is not covered. The professional locators, in whom he is interested, were in keen competition with agents of the railroads who were equally anxious to make their fees from sales.

Office of EATON & OLNEY,

LINDSEY, KANSAS,

DEAR SIR: Having 100,000 acres of the best Homestead Land yet vacant in our County, we have prepared ourselves for locating SOLDIERS' HOMESTEADS thereon, under the Act of Congress of June 8, 1872.

These lands are located in the far-famed Solomon Valley and its tributaries, and within twenty miles of the Kansas Pacific Railway. There are now in the County, 2 Papers: 25 Stores: a dozen Post Offices, and dozens of School Houses, some costing from $3,000 to $5,000: $30,000 worth of Bridges, and 5,000 inhabitants.

Two other Railways through the County are almost certain to be built within two years. Over 15,000 acres of "School Land" that cannot be sold for less than $3 per acre will make a School Fund that, with the splendid State Fund, will provide a good education for every child in the County.

The recent law requires that the person taking a Homestead through an Agent, must settle upon it within six months thereafter, The Agent must produce a Power of Attorney from the Principal, authorizing him (or them) "to select a Homestead for him and in his stead."

Our fee for looking up the land, making papers, and paying fee at the Land Office, is only $10, for which the person gets choice of claims six months ahead (which is well worth $100), and when he is ready to come, has his claim ready for him and knows where to find it. We will, also, see to having houses erected on claims if wished.

We, also, have over 100,000 acres of Railway Land for sale, at about $3 per acre, one-fifth down: balance in 2, 3, 4 and 5 years, with interest at six per cent,

Also, a large number of Claims, the improvements on which are for sale at less than cost—after buying which the party may homestead the Claim.

A large list of Improved Farms, City Lots and Property upon our Books.

By permission we refer to

JOHN GEIS & Co., Bankers. - - - - - - - - - - - - - - Salina, Kansas.

FIRST NATIONAL BANK. - - - - - - - - - - - - - - - Topeka,   "

KANSAS INSURANCE COMPANY. - - - - - - - - - - - Leavenworth.   "

HARRIS, ABRAMS & Co., Gen'l Ag'ts K. P. R'y. - - - - - - Lawrence,   "

Respectfully Yours.

EATON & OLNEY.

DEAR SIR: Above we hand you a note respecting the location of Soldiers' Homesteads by us. If you will co-operate with us in soliciting this business we will allow you to retain one-fourth of our regular fee—$10. We have to pay about $2 at the Land Office: and, for the balance, must survey out the country to obtain good Claims, make papers, &c., &c. You will make the additional fee for making Powers of Attorney, which must be acknowledged and witnessed. If you wish, we will forward you the blanks.

Yours Respectfully,   EATON & OLNEY.

Eaton & Olney advertise 100,000 acres of homestead land. (Courtesy, Collection of Regional History, Cornell University)

Immigrants arriving during the sixties and seventies in Kansas where they hoped to find suitable land available free to them under the Homestead Act were met with posters, flyers, newspaper ads, and runners and agents for numerous land agencies and land-grant railroads, all calling attention to quantities of the "best" Kansas land for sale. Among the individual and partnership offerings that were thrust at the incoming land-seekers were: Robert S. Stevens, 60,000 acres; Thaddeus H. Walker, 100,000 acres; the Amos A. Lawrence estate, 45,640 acres at $1.80 to $3.00 per acre; Hendry & Noyes, 50,000 acres; Stebbins and Porter, 46,000 acres; and Van Doren & Havens, 200,000 acres at $3 to $10 an acre.[5] Gorrill, Dunbar & Stevens of the Kansas Land Company offered 211 parcels of land, most of which were improved farms and unimproved land outside towns, comprising 17,-475 acres at prices from a few dollars to as high as $70 an acre for choice improved land. For "cheap lands" they had "many thousand acres in Greenwood and Butler Counties which we can furnish certificate for patent at $1.50 per acre." [6]

A firm in Ottawa County, close to the 99th meridian, advertised that it had over 100,000 acres of railroad land

[5] *Emporia News,* April 10, Dec. 4, 1868; Feb. 10, 1869; Leavenworth *Conservative,* May 11, 1864; *Leavenworth Bulletin,* Feb. 7, 1871; *Marysville Enterprise,* May 2, 1868; *Kansas Farmer* (May, 1868, and Nov., 1869), V, 80 and VI, 192.

[6] Gorrill, Dunbar & Stevens, *Real Estate Register of the Kansas Land Company, Comprising Improved Farms, Raw Lands, and Town Property* (Lawrence, 1869), *passim.* The Capital Land Agency of Topeka, consisting of H. H. Wilcox, R. R. Adams, and W. C. Fitzsimmons, stated on its letter head (letter of July 15, 1871, to E. S. Parker, Commissioner of Indian Affairs, Bid File, Indian Office Archives, National Archives), "We have 1,000,000 acres of Kansas land for sale." The Lawrence lands were sold to the big Chicago land agency, W. J. Barney & Co., and were thereafter sold by it. See advertisement of Barney in the *Lincoln Herald* (Lincoln, Illinois), October 24, 1867.

and 15,000 acres of school land for sale at $3 an acre, and a large number of claims on which homesteaders had made improvements but without completing the residence requirements and which were now for sale. Buyers of these claims would have to conform to the provisions of the Homestead Law before they could get title. In addition, 100,000 acres of vacant homestead land were available in the county, on which the firm would select quarter-sections, file soldiers' additional homestead entries, and hold them for prospective customers for the price of $10.[7] The firm could hold the land under the entry for six months, and it did "look up" the land to the extent that it secured the information from the tract books in the neighboring land office, but otherwise its service was small. Nevertheless, many land-seekers found it desirable to employ the aid of such agents.

Most vigorous of the railroads in pursuing purchasers for their lands were the Union Pacific, Central Branch, which offered 1,280,000 acres including the "celebrated Kickapoo Indian Reservation" at $1 to $10 an acre; the Union Pacific, Southern Branch (Katy), which offered 1,300,000 acres at $2 to $8 an acre; the Santa Fe, which advertised 3,000,000 acres for sale; the LL&G which claimed to have 500,000 acres for sale; and the Kansas Pacific which announced 6,000,000 acres for sale. In addition, a number of railroads with smaller grants were vying for customers for their lands.[8]

---

[7] Undated circular of Eaton and Olney, Lindsey, Kansas, around 1873, Land Papers, Regional History, Cornell University. One suspects that these landlookers did little more for their patrons than to study the tract books at the local land office, determine quarters on which no filings had been made and then to file on them.

[8] Representative pamphlets advertising lands of the Kansas railroad are: *Lands of the Missouri, Kansas and Texas* (1877); *How and Where to Get a Living. A Sketch of the 'Garden of the West.' Presenting Facts Worth Knowing of the Atchison, Topeka and Santa Fe Railroad Co., In Southwestern Kansas* (Boston, 1876); *Homes for All, and How to Secure Them. A Guide to the Leavenworth, Law-*

To these selling agencies should be added the State of Kansas which was advertising for sale its 90,000 acres of "choicely selected" Agricultural-College lands and 38,400 acres of normal-school land.[9]

In Marion County, through which the 97th meridian runs, prominent speculators from Providence, Rhode Island; Boston, Massachusetts; and Bloomington, Illinois, had engrossed so many thousands of acres that agents were advertising in 1874 that immigrants henceforth would have to buy from the Santa Fe Railroad or from these absentee speculators, though the county still was but slightly developed.[10] One firm offered 31,000 acres of the best grain and stock land for rent in 1876. Numerous ranches were being developed that in later years were to be cut into small farms. In Butler County the Lawrence and Potwin lands, running to many thousands of acres and said in 1870 to comprise the pick of lands, were held for $3 to $10 per acre. They were sold on time with interest at 10 per cent. Homestead lands were about gone and the Osage lands were available only under the pre-emption principle.[11] Farms were being offered for rent in Butler as early as 1875.[12] North of Marion in Dickinson

---

rence and Galveston Railroad and Its Lands in Southern Kansas (Lawrence, 1872); *Emigrants' Guide to the Kansas Pacific Railway Lands. Best and Cheapest Farming and Grazing Lands in America, 6,000,000 Acres for Sale by the Kansas Pacific Railway Co.* (Lawrence, 1871). See also *The Homestead Guide. Describing the Great Homestead Region in Kansas and Nebraska and Containing the Homestead, Pre-emption and Timber Bounty Laws and a Map of the Country Described* (Waterville, Kansas, 1873), pp. 122–124 and elsewhere.

[9] *Emporia News,* April 10, 1868.

[10] Stephen C. Marcou, *Homes for the Homeless. A Description of Marion Co., Kansas, and the Cottonwood Valley: The Garden of the State* (Marion Centre, 1874), p. 2; advertisement of Case and Billings, *Marion Record,* Dec. 15, 1876.

[11] Eldorado *Walnut Valley Times,* Nov. 25, 1870.

[12] *Ibid.,* April 2, Sept. 3, 1875.

County farms were being advertised for rent in the later seventies.[13] Along the line of the Union Pacific, Central Branch, James MacDonald found in 1877 "the main portion of the land is held by the Railway Company and land speculators, and is for sale at from one to five dollars . . . per acre." [14] MacDonald also observed that good homestead land in central Kansas was "mostly all taken up" except at a great distance from railroads; and he stated that new settlers coming in would have to buy land.

Kansas railroads having land grants were anxious to have developed the government-held lands in their vicinity, and were not distressed that many settlers chose them instead of railroad land, realizing as they did that the homestead lands would soon disappear. As early as 1881 the Santa Fe announced in its advertising circular: [15]

All the Government land that can be cultivated, and far enough east to be adapted to general farming has long since been occupied. To find vacant homestead land the emigrant must go beyond the present frontier of settlement, and to utilize it he must have capital enough to stock it with sheep and cattle.

Two years later the State of Kansas published statistics in its immigrant promotion literature showing 19,495,807 acres of vacant lands held by the Federal and State governments and the railroads. Of this amount 9,238,247 acres were avail-

[13] Enterprise *Kansas Gazette,* July 14, 1876; *Abilene Gazette,* Aug. 24, 1878; and April 25, 1879. Wm. H. Steward advertised in the *Abilene Reflector,* Feb. 26, 1885, that he wanted to rent a good farm with buildings on it.

[14] James MacDonald, *Food from the Far West or American Agriculture with Special Reference to the Beef Production and Importation of Dead Meat from America to Great Britain* (London and Edinburgh, 1878), p. 74. MacDonald estimated that a minimum of £500 capital was necessary to buy and equip a farm in central Kansas, p. 87.

[15] *Description of the Atchison, Topeka & Santa Fe R.R. Cos. Lands in South Central & South West Kansas* (Topeka, 1881), unpaged.

able only on purchase, and 10,167,580 acres were open to homestead. More than nine-tenths of the homestead lands were beyond the 100th meridian in the far western counties of the state. Equally distressing to the land reformers who sought to make vacant land available cheaply to the immigrant was the listing of 13,833,842 acres of unoccupied "vacant private lands" priced at $1.25 to $20 and $30, much being held at $5 and $10 per acre.

Table 16. FEDERAL, STATE, AND RAILROAD LANDS IN KANSAS, 1882 [16]

Federal lands open to homesteading			10,167,560
Osage and Cherokee Strip lands available at $1 to $1.25 an acre	3,451,178		
State lands open to purchase	1,043,000		
Total Indian trust and state lands		4,494,178	
Railroad lands open to purchase			
Santa Fe (at $3.25 average)	1,850,365		
Kansas Pacific (at $3.50 average)	2,655,860		
Katy (at $2.75 average)	27,844		
Total railroad lands		4,534,069	
Aggregates: Indian trust, state, and railroad land open to purchase; Federal land open to homesteading		9,238,247	10,167,560

This is not to say that the Homestead Law and its later variation the Timber-Culture Act, were unimportant in Kansas.[17] Nothing, except possibly the lavish advertising campaigns of the land-grant railroads, so attracted people to the West as the offer of free land embodied in these two measures. Under the Homestead Law five years of residence and improvement won the farm maker the right to acquire title

[16] Compiled from *Kansas: Its Resources and Capabilities, Its Position, Dimensions and Topography* (Topeka, 1883), pp. 6–20.

[17] There is much of value concerning homesteading, settler purchases of the Santa Fe Railroad, and mortgage indebtedness in Allan G. Bogue, "Farmer Debtors in Pioneer Kinsley," *Kansas Historical Quarterly* (May, 1952), XX, 82 ff.

to a quarter-section. The Timber-Culture Act permitted settlers to gain title to an additional quarter-section free, provided they set out and maintained forty acres (later reduced to ten acres) in trees. Title could be gained at the end of ten, later eight years. Under both laws settlers could commute their entries to cash entries before the required period of improvement was up, and purchase the land for $1.25 an acre. The table of acreages entered, "proved up," commuted, and forfeited is adequate evidence of the wide use to which these laws were put.

Table 17. HOMESTEAD AND TIMBER CULTURE ENTRIES IN KANSAS, 1863–1934 [18]

	Original entries (Acres)	Final entries (Acres)	Commuted (Acres)	Forfeited (Acres)
Homestead Act	26,336,705	12,640,705	3,574,001	10,121,999
Timber-Culture Act	9,001,858	1,902,492	140,536	6,958,830
	35,337,563	14,543,197	3,714,537	17,080,829

Between 1863 and 1890 a total of 20,881,818 acres in Kansas were filed on by homesteaders, and 8,805,990 acres were entered under the Timber-Culture Act. Of the total acreage, approximately 12,000,000 acres were carried to patent as free grants, while 3,191,377 acres were commuted to cash entries and purchased at $1.25 an acre. If we assume that each homestead and timber-culture entry was 160 acres and that each became a going farm of that size, we arrive at a total of 94,488 farms that were acquired or were in process of being established either as free grants or at a cost of $1.25 an acre under the government's plan of land disposal. Since the Census Bureau listed only 166,617 farms in Kansas in 1890, it would appear that the free grants and delayed payments made under these two laws were responsible for more

[18] Compiled from Commissioner of the General Land Office, *Annual Reports*, 1863–1934.

than half of the farms in Kansas. Undoubtedly this was a great achievement, and full credit should be given the Homestead Law as a major factor in making possible this great development of new farms.[19]

Unfortunately, the ownership of the homesteads as thus established in Kansas was by no means stable. The number of tenant-operated farms more than doubled in the eighties, while the number of farms only increased by one-fifth. Fully 28 per cent of Kansas farms were tenant-operated in 1890. Also three-fifths of all taxed land in Kansas was mortgaged, a statistic which would probably mean that an equal proportion of farms was mortgaged. On the bulk of the mortgages the Census Bureau found that the interest ranged from 9 to 12 per cent.[20] Kansas land was mortgaged in 1890 to the amount of $174,160,000; and more than three-fourths of this debt was incurred either for the purchase of land or for improvements.[21] The great number of foreclosures that occurred after 1890 and the high percentage of failure among the principal lending agencies indicate how hazardous was this borrowing.

More striking than the increase in tenancy and the great

[19] This method of appraising the significance of the Homestead and Timber-Culture Acts is rough indeed and is subject to numerous reservations. Homestead and Timber-Culture claims were by no means always the maximum the law allowed. Many homesteaders established timber-culture claims, as the law authorized, thus acquiring 320 acres. Some of the claims under both laws were passed quickly into the hands of cattle barons and were not intended as farms. Doubtless some claims were divided. Statistics of acres entered under the two acts are compiled from the *Annual Reports* of the General Land Office.

[20] Statistics concerning the number of farms in Kansas, concerning tenancy, and concerning mortgages are from the *Eighteenth Census of the United States, Statistics on Agriculture* (Washington, 1895), pp. 116–117, and Report on *Real Estate Mortgages in the United States* (Washington, 1895), pp. 310 and elsewhere.

[21] *Ibid.*, pp. 95, 282.

extent of mortgaging by farm makers was the high rate of failure among those trying to take advantage of the free lands the government offered. Of those who sought free land in Kansas, 10 per cent found it advisable to commute their entries to cash purchases, perhaps to get title on which they could borrow; 41 per cent succeeded in "proving up" on their claims and getting title; and 49 per cent failed and relinquished their rights.

In neighboring Nebraska, where settlement was permitted at the same time that Kansas was opened, a much larger acreage went into private ownership through the free-grant route.

Table 18. COMPARISON OF HOMESTEAD AND TIMBER-CULTURE ENTRIES IN KANSAS AND NEBRASKA

	Total Acreage	Original Entries	Final Entries	Com- muted	Forfeited
Kansas	52,335,360	35,337,563	14,543,197	3,714;537	17,080,829
Nebraska	49,157,120	50,905,255 *	24,670,847	2,838,318	23,396,090

* Because of forfeitures many tracts were entered more than once.

Comparing the statistics of Kansas land sales by the Federal government, the State of Kansas, and the Railroads against the original homestead entries from the adoption of the Homestead Act (1862) to 1873 shows that in every year except 1863, 1864, and 1872 more land, and in some years much more, was being acquired for settlement or speculation through purchase or its equivalent than was being homesteaded. Although the statistics of sales for the years after 1873 are by no means complete (as they are not for sale in the table), they show that for most of the seventies and eighties the cash purchases continued to be in much greater volume than was the acreage being homesteaded. Clearly, the Homestead Act had not displaced other routes to ownership in Kansas.

Table 19. COMPARISON OF LAND SALES, INCLUDING WARRANT AND SCRIP ENTRIES BY UNITED STATES, STATE OF KANSAS, AND KANSAS RAILROADS WITH NUMBER OF ORIGINAL HOMESTEADS (IN ACRES) [22]

	United States Cash, Warrant & Scrip	Indian Lands	State of Kansas	Railroads	All Sales	Original Homesteads
1863	1,367				1,367	169,221
1864	2,670	18,468			21,138	98,619
1865	69,535	296,836			366,371	52,972
1866	146,208	12,503			158,711	146,989
1867	281,590		1,920		283,510	154,675
1868	187,151	50,788	5,279	111,271	354,489	165,976
1869	85,180	26,044	76,187	473,262	660,673	228,137
1870	336,005	93,625	62,372	318,193	810,195	647,186
1871	265,232	744,735	74,086	265,642	1,349,695	1,191,622
1872	133,113	768,870	50,663	195,861	1,148,507	1,227,376
1873	123,146	563,911	34,300	245,995	967,352	817,124
	1,631,197	2,575,780	304,807	1,610,224	6,122,088	4,899,897

As most of the homestead lands were distant from railroads and in the more western part of Kansas, farm making on them was hazardous, being accompanied by a relatively high rate of failure. From a comparison between the original homestead entries and the final entries of five years later it appears that the figures of original entries are not accurately indicative of the amount of land going into private ownership. The figures of original entries are an indication of settlement activity by people attempting to take advantage of the government's bounty, but the final entries are the real test of the significance of the Homestead Act. Settlers who failed

[22] Statistics of warrant entries and of sales by the State of Kansas for certain years are unavailable. 27,741 acres of Neutral-Tract lands and 89,690 acres of "free" or State lands given to the Missouri River, Fort Scott, and Gulf Railroad and sold in 1871, 1872 and 1873 have been equally divided between the three years because the annual sales were not available. The table does not include all the State sales, nor the land sales of a number of the railroads holding smaller grants and Indian reserves. The sales of Indian land to railroads have not been included.

in gaining ownership or who felt compelled to buy their claims in order to acquire an equity on which to borrow capital for improvements had only enjoyed the right of occupancy or essentially the right of pre-emption. True, some purchasers of state and railroad lands had their contracts forfeited for failure to meet their payments, but the proportion of failure was less than among homesteaders.

Table 20. ORIGINAL AND FINAL HOMESTEAD ENTRIES IN KANSAS, 1863–1873

Year	Original Entries	Final Entries of Five Years Later
1863	169,221	68,603
1864	98,619	48,571
1865	52,972	37,144
1866	146,989	39,347
1867	154,675	65,086
1868	165,976	156,270
1869	228,137	216,674
1870	647,186	344,880
1871	1,191,622	457,593
1872	1,227,376	568,153
1873	817,124	670,337
Totals	6,024,109	2,604,658

Notwithstanding the factors that made Kansas something other than an ideal community in which to begin farm making on unimproved land of the public domain (among these factors were the railroad grants and the high prices they brought about, speculator acquisitions which diffused population widely, Indian reserves that were not subject to public-land policies, and the remoteness of public land open to homesteading), no other part of the new West drew immigration in the volume that was attracted to Kansas between 1865 and 1880. Even during the territorial period Kansas had been the focus of attention for its brawling over slavery, land claims, railroad charters, and rights of way. Now, because railroads were being rapidly built, because they conducted extensive advertising campaigns to draw immigration, because stories were being widely repeated of appreciation in land values that was bringing wealth to extensive holders, and because Kansans were writing optimistic letters to eastern friends and to the press, the state continued to be the center of attraction for immigrants.[23] The growth of Kansas population was astonishing; the number of Kansans rose from 107,206 in 1860 to 996,096 in 1880.

In this great movement of people to Kansas, the older Middle West was being drained of its unsuccessful farmers who were debt-ridden, tenants, or agricultural laborers. The Census of 1880, for example, showed that more than 215,000 people born in the corn-belt states of Ohio, Indiana, Illinois, and Iowa had emigrated to Kansas in the previous decade. These emigrants, in turn, were replaced by recent arrivals from central Europe who were willing to accept tenant and farm-labor positions that older Americans rejected. In this migration of the defeated, the failures, and the unsuccessful lies an explanation of why Populism won so few converts in the corn belt.[24] It also aids in explaining the intensity of

[23] A letter from the Osage lands in Sumner County published in the *Bloomington* (Ill.) *Leader,* May 22, 1872, is worthy of quotation: "It is a mystery to me why so many men with limited means will stay East, eke out a miserable existence, and pay a rich, miserly, contemptible flint-hearted, cunning landlord more in a year than it would take to get one hundred and sixty acres of rich land here.

"My advice is to quit paying high rents, come to Sumner County, preempt a quarter section of land, improve and enter it, and make a home where you can enjoy all the comforts of life; where you will feel independent, and by energy will soon gain a fortune."

[24] Chester McA. Destler mentions this same movement of tenants from the corn-belt counties of Illinois in the late eighties and nineties, the result of increasing rents and the high price of land, and maintains that this emigration "served to a limited extent as a safety valve

the Populist fervor in Kansas, for the people who there took part in it were those who had failed twice on successive frontiers.

Having failed to move up the agricultural ladder in communities where rapidly rising land values made the attainment of ownership increasingly difficult if not impossible, tenants and agricultural laborers migrated by the tens of thousands to areas that seemed more promising, where cheap or free land might still be found. It was to Kansas that they turned more than any other state. Rural papers of corn-belt counties in Illinois and Iowa for the seventies frequently mention tenant unrest as a cause of emigration to the Sunflower State.[25]

"High rents are leaving renters with nothing but a chance to make a bare living, and it is not likely to ever get better," wrote a former resident of "Scullyland," Logan County, Illinois.[26] A settler in Mitchell County, Kansas, commented on the immigration which was pouring into the area from Mills County, Iowa, where the Burlington Railroad was having trouble over titles with local people, who claimed they had settled on county-owned swamp land.[27] Illinois tenants complained bitterly of low grain prices, of the heavy debts

---

for much of the rural discontent that otherwise would have found expression within Illinois." "Agricultural Readjustment and Agrarian Unrest in Illinois, 1880–1896," *Agricultural History* (April, 1947), XXI, 111–112.

[25] *Glenwood* (Iowa) *Opinion,* May 25, 1872; *Lincoln* (Ill.) *Herald,* May 1, 1873; Feb. 17, 1876; Feb. 22, March 8, 1877; *Watseka* (Ill.) *Republican,* Dec. 13, 1877; Feb. 14, 1878; March 20, 1879. See also *Lincoln Times,* Jan. 13, 1881; *Lincoln Herald,* Dec. 6, 20, 1883; and *Bloomington Pantagraph,* Feb. 26, 1887.

[26] *Lincoln Herald,* May 1, 1873. A land advertisement of the Chicago, Burlington, and Quincy Railroad in the *Pontiac* (Ill.) *Sentinel,* May 21, 1879, advising people not to rent in Illinois but to own in Nebraska said: "Life is too short to be wasted on a rented farm."

[27] *Glenwood Opinion,* May 25, 1872.

they owed farm-implement dealers, of chattel mortgages, the heavy capital needs for improvements, and the high cash rents. A significant cause of their distress was the fact that immigrants coming in from Europe were willing and anxious to take over their rents and were actually bidding for them.[28]

"The moving fever has seized the renters," said the Aetna correspondent of the *Lincoln Herald*. As they set out for Kansas he noted that their "worldly possessions consist of a pair of wretched horses and a shabby covered wagon, and children enough to fill one end of it and household goods the other end. . . ." [29] The *Ottawa Free Trader* of August 10, 1878, commented on the "innumerable caravan" of Illinoisians who were moving to Kansas. A year later the *Bloomington Pantagraph* expressed regret at the two or three thousand people who had journeyed through its city on their way to Kansas, the result of mortgage foreclosures.[30] From Ford County, Illinois, it was reported in 1878 that seventeen car loads of freight and 121 people were leaving the area for Kansas. A few were land owners, but most of the migrants were renters.[31] In Glenwood, Iowa "the Kansas fever continues to rage" in 1879. "There seems to be no preventative," lugubriously commented a local reporter.[32]

In attempting to account for the great "hejira from Illinois and Indiana," one observer added to the usual story of crop failures, crushing debts, and depressed prices the "flaming hand-bills" that had been "posted in every railroad station, post office, and cross road from Maine to Mexico, headed 'Ho! for Kansas,' and setting forth in glowing colors the

[28] *Hoopeston* (Ill.) *Chronicle*, Aug. 26, 1875; *Lincoln Herald*, Jan. 17, 1876; *Bloomington Pantagraph*, Jan. 27, Feb. 7, 1879; *Champaign Gazette* in *Bloomington Pantagraph*, Jan. 23, 1879.

[29] *Lincoln Herald*, May 8, 1877.

[30] *Bloomington Pantagraph*, Feb. 18, 1879; and Jan. 23, 1878.

[31] *Paxton Weekly Standard*, Feb. 9, 1878; *Atlanta* (Ill.) *Argus*, Aug. 2, 23, 1878; Feb. 7, 1879.

[32] *Glenwood Opinion*, Aug. 16, 1879.

'wonderful fertility of its plains,' 'its salubrious climate,' and 'the cheapness of its lands.' " [33] To counteract this type of advertising the same paper earlier warned that "cheap lands means cheap crops and hard times. It looks inviting at the start, but we have been there ourselves and know that cheap lands and a good soil do not necessarily make a man prosperous, nor even contented." [34]

Unceasingly this flow of immigration swept westward in the seventies over the central portion of Kansas and penetrated beyond the 99th and the 100th meridian into the dryer plains. Free or cheap land, always its goal, was becoming more remote and less attractive. The building of the railroads, combined with this great immigration and the pressure on the land supply, placed railroad- and speculator-owned land beyond the reach of many who were driven to even more inaccessible areas in their search for the elusive cheap land.[35] At the same time, disillusionment was being expressed by some who had ventured into the Osage reserve where they had to buy the land. One distressed settler wrote in 1871 that southern Kansas was not suitable for corn, was not even first-rate wheat country. He held that a renter in Iowa was better off than a land-owner in Kansas.[36] Allusion has already been made to Walter Denning's discouraging report of the large number of mortgaged farmers in southern Kansas who in 1877 were without hope of meeting their obligations.[37] At this juncture railroads having land grants

[33] E. Sanford in *Watseka* (Ill.) *Republican,* April 24, 1879; *New York Tribune,* Dec. 27, 1880.

[34] *Watseka Republican,* Feb. 14, 1878.

[35] S. E. Pendleton, writing from Cottonwood Falls, in Chase County, on Feb. 2, 1872, (*Atlanta Argus,* Feb. 17, 1872), deplored the high price of land which drove people farther west. He attributed it in part to railroads and speculators who had bought up much land that they held vacant for years and on which few taxes were paid.

[36] *Glenwood Opinion* (Glenwood, Iowa), Feb. 11, 1871.

[37] *Iroquois County Times,* Nov. 24, 1877.

in those neighboring states which had earlier been somewhat neglected by immigrants began to look upon Kansas as fertile ground in which to advertise their lands. The *Manhattan Beacon* in 1873 carried advertisements of 3,000,000 acres for sale in Nebraska by the Union Pacific Railroad, 10,000 prairie farms or 1,700,000 acres for sale in Iowa by four railroads, "cheap farms" for sale among the 1,200,000 acres of the Atlantic and Pacific Railroad in Missouri, and 1,000,-000 acres for sale in Arkansas by the Little Rock and Fort Smith Railroad.[38]

Kansas, like Illinois, Indiana, and Ohio, had thus become a state in which migrants might be recruited for other regions; though, unlike them, it still retained in its western portion large areas untouched by the plow. To counteract any losses sustained through the advertising of land-grant railroads and settlement agencies working for other states and territories, the Kansas Pacific, the Santa Fe, and other land agencies in Kansas had to increase the tempo of their advertising and land-settlement work.

[38] *Manhattan Beacon,* March 22, April 19, 1873.

CHAPTER VIII

Railroad Land Policies
in the Agrarian Crusade

WESTERNERS early adopted the notion that all land of value for agriculture should, as soon as there was any white pressure for it, be divested of its aboriginal title and made a part of the public domain. As such, it should be subject to settlement with a pre-emption right to all comers. After 1862 the right to acquire a free homestead anywhere on the public lands was added to the previous pre-emption right. The fulfillment of these deeply ingrained notions was jeopardized particularly in Kansas by the treaty-making policy of disposing of Indian land and the action of the Kansas railroads in grabbing the Indian reserves over which hordes of incoming settlers had swept.

The railroad land-grab, including the much greater scramble for grants, and the greedy land policies of the railroads produced a swift and violent reversal of the previously favorable attitude toward the developing transportation companies. Whereas earlier Kansans had willingly, even anxiously, given liberal charters and rights-of-way, whereas the counties and municipalities had voted lavish bond subsidies to bring railroads to their communities, and the state had bestowed nearly half a million acres on four railroads under construction, now the railroads became subject to sharp attack; they were threatened with heavy taxation and even forfeiture of their lands, with loss of further subventions, and with restrictive legislation. Contributing to the reversal of public opinion were the financial malpractices of the railroads, their high freight rates, and their increasingly menacing political power. The latter issues have received adequate attention at the hands of historians and economists, but the land-policies which produced settler-railroad warfare, as bitter in feeling and as violent in action as almost any other American social conflicts, have for one reason or another been neglected. One can search the histories of late-Nineteenth-Century agrarianism and find few allusions to the subject that most absorbed settlers on the frontier.

No aspect of Federal land-policy created so many great issues or such complex legal and political controversies for the West, for the courts, for Congress, and for public opinion as did the railroad land-grants. In initiating the land-grant policy, Congress had defined no precise procedures to provide for selecting the lands, for determining the time when they should be patented after being earned, for forfeiting them if they were not earned, and for deciding when lands withdrawn temporarily from entry to enable the railroads to make their selections might or must be returned to the public domain.

Congress had been doubly generous in giving Kansas land and loans to aid in building its railroad network. The largest aid was given the LP&W, later the UP, Eastern and still later the KP, for the construction of a line from the Missouri

River through the state to Denver. Kansas' most important railroad, the Santa Fe, had a somewhat smaller grant for its line from the Missouri River in a southwestern direction all the way across the state. Two other railroads projected westward from the Missouri River (the Union Pacific, Central Branch, and the St. Joseph and Denver) had small grants. Three north-south lines running from the Kansas River to the southern border, namely the LL&G, the Fort Scott Line, and the Katy, completed the list of Federally-aided railroads.

Table 21. FEDERAL LAND GRANTS TO RAILROADS IN KANSAS [1]

	Primary and lieu grants limits	Acres received
Atchison, Topeka and Santa Fe	10 and 20	2,944,788
Kansas Pacific	20	3,925,791
Missouri River, Fort Scott and Gulf	10 and 20	21,341
Missouri, Kansas and Texas	10 and 20	705,623
Leavenworth, Lawrence and Galveston	10 and 20	62,510
St. Joseph and Denver City	10 and 20	463,409
Union Pacific, Central Branch	20	223,141
		8,346,603

Also the State of Kansas gave to four railroads included in this table the proceeds from the sale of 500,000 acres of land which the state received for internal improvements from the Federal government.[2] The four railroads were permitted to buy the lands if they desired, though in effect the land was donated to them. If we add to the Federal land-grants 1,953,909 acres representing land bought at moderately low prices from Indians and from the United States plus acreage given by the State of Kansas, and then add to the total the

[1] Compiled from Donaldson, *The Public Domain,* pp. 269–279; and Commissioner of the General Land Office, *Annual Report,* 1932, pp. 44–45.

[2] Act of Feb. 23, 1866, *Laws of Kansas,* 1866, pp. 142–145.

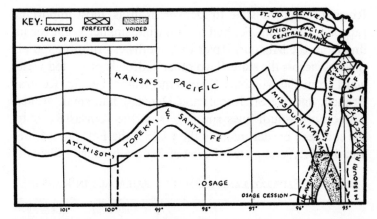

KEY: GRANTED · FORFEITED · VOIDED
SCALE OF MILES ■■■■■ 50

Railroad land grants in Kansas: Primary grant area. Alternate sections were reserved by the government. (Drawn by Mary Young)

40,000 acres given for right-of-way through the public lands, we have a grand aggregate of 10,340,512 acres controlled by railroads in Kansas, or about one-fifth of the state.

Table 22. RAILROAD PURCHASES (GIFTS) FROM KANSAS OF
INTERNAL-IMPROVEMENT LANDS [3]

Railroad	Acres Acquired
Missouri River, Fort Scott, and Gulf	89,691
Missouri, Kansas, and Texas	89,905
Leavenworth, Lawrence, and Galveston	123,543
St. Joseph and Denver City	104,632

[3] The Land-Grant Railway and Trust Company of New York, a subsidiary or affiliate of the Katy, bought 89,095 acres for $396,252, according to an instrument in Cloud County Deed Records, A:537, and conveyed 80,416 to the Katy. P. F. W. Peck and James F. Joy bought the land for the Fort Scott and LL&G Railroads. Butler County Deed Records, B:487–500.

Dudley M. Steele, president, and Milton Tootle, vice-president, of the St. Joseph and Denver City Railroad bought 104,632 acres, mostly in Cloud and Republic Counties. Whether this acreage was

Most early Kansas railroads were then land as well as transportation companies. As land companies they were concerned to sell their lands at the highest possible price and with the least possible expense. But as transportation companies they sought to have their areas developed as speedily as possible by settlers who would provide traffic. The resulting teetering between the two positions is reflected in the advertising literature of the railroads. Fairly typical is the statement of the LL&G: [4]

We are not real estate agents or land speculators, whose only interest is to obtain purchasers for the land we have to sell, and obtain the highest possible price for it—careless of whether you prosper or suffer after the sale has been made to you. On the contrary, we have the largest and keenest interest in your welfare and

------

retained by them as part of their compensation for construction work and financial aid to the railroad of which they were officers is not clear, but keep it they did. Steele and Tootle each had 9/40 of the total, Thomas E. Tootle received 6/40 and the remainder was scattered among a number of associates. Both Steele and Milton Tootle retailed much of their land to settlers, but Tootle retained a substantial acreage which was developed into a large farming operation. In 1940 the Tootle family holdings in Cloud County were 4,260 acres, constituting the largest farm holding in the county. Information concerning the Steele and Tootle land business was gathered from numerous deeds and assessors' records in Cloud County courthouse, Concordia.

It should be remembered that the Santa Fe had lands granted it in Arizona and New Mexico, the Kansas Pacific grants in Colorado were larger than those in Kansas, the Katy had extensive grants in Texas, and the St. Joseph and Denver City was given lands by the State of Nebraska.

In addition to the large grants of land generous Federal loans were made to the Kansas Pacific and the Union Pacific, Central Branch, and loans were made by many counties and cities to all the lines included in the table.

[4] *Homes for All, and How to Secure Them. A Guide to the Leavenworth, Lawrence & Galveston Railroad and Its Lands in Southern Kansas,* prepared by John W. Scott, Land Commissioner, pp. 1–2.

prosperity, both present and future, for upon your welfare and success, year by year, depends our own success and prosperity.

As railroad policy vacillated between the two extremes, the homestead element now approved, now disapproved of land grants as a means of reaching the goal of cheap land. Land grants could be justified in the pioneer period because they were considered necessary to build railroads. Some people even justified the purchase of Indian reserves on the ground that it made possible railroads in regions where the lack of public lands available for grants would otherwise have barred them for some time. Once the railroads had their lands, they had to conform to an acceptable pattern of managing them or run the risk of antagonizing the homestead and land-reform elements; and these elements, like the railroads themselves, were to prove tough customers. Arrogant and self-assured railroad managers, accustomed to operate in the tradition of the Gilded Age, felt it unnecessary to bow to public opinion. Their actions created increasingly hostile feelings among many, and eventually arrayed against them powerful groups that could not be easily defeated, bought off, or destroyed.

In the resulting conflicts the railroads had major weapons in their arsenal. The advertising patronage which they dispensed among newspapers assured generally favorable support; the liberal suspense accounts and fees which they distributed among politicians, state, and Federal judges assured that, with some exceptions, they would stand firmly for the rights of private property, especially railroad property, against encroachments by "wild eyed radicals"; the conservative and "railroad-minded" United States Senate resisted agrarian demands until the pressure of public opinion burst through its dikes; and, finally, the railroads made liberal use of their best weapon, the pass. On the other side the homestead element also had good cards to play. The rugged pioneer was a sentimental stereotype in the mind of the average American, and the frontier tradition could easily be invoked to encourage further land-reform; many people outside agriculture were coming to dislike railroads because of rate discrimination; the arrogance of railroad magnates had provoked widespread hostility; and the age-old cry of monopoly would always gain a hearing.

The settlers' protective associations became the first organized groups in Kansas to place themselves squarely in opposition to the growing political and economic power of the railroads. They early concerned themselves with opposition to the sales of the Neutral Tract and of the Osage trust and diminished reserve, as well as to the extension of railroad land-grants into the Osage-ceded tract. Then came the squabbles between the Katy and the KP Railroads that threatened settler interests, and the conflict between the LL&G and homesteaders over ownership of tracts which the settlers claimed as lieu lands. At the same time settlers on the Black Bob, Miami, New York, Kansas, Quapaw, and Cherokee Strip tracts were attempting to wrest from the Federal government the right to pre-empt at a fair appraisal the lands on which they had been squatting for years. Railroad efforts to acquire these reserves were unsuccessful, but the squatters feared and hated the railroads for trying to purchase them.

The strangling power that the railroads were exercising in Kansas affairs, in the operation of the Indian Office, and to some degree in the General Land Office led to increasingly sharp attacks upon them. To unite the movement for land-reform, the scattered land leagues came together to organize the Liberal Land League of Kansas. With its 2,000 members, mostly in southern Kansas where the power of the railroads was most acutely felt, it carried on the fight to have the remaining Indian reserves and public lands withheld from the railroads' grasp for the benefit of homesteaders. The *Workingman's Journal* of Columbus and the *Fort Scott Monitor*, the latter under the editorship of Eugene Ware after 1872,

were flaming organs of land-reform and anti-railroad sentiment.[5] Delegations and representatives were sent to Washington to lobby for the homestead element. When these
official delegations were frustrated by the coolness of the
Kansas legislators and their cohorts in the "Indian Ring,"
the "Land Ring," and the "Railroad Ring," the land-reformers
entered politics to achieve their aims. Local officers, members of the legislature, Governors, Representatives, and Senators who did not accept settler views were attacked and often
unseated, numerous instructions were forwarded to Kansas
representatives in Washington, and the issues were carried
into the halls of Congress.

Kansans had so effectively dramatized their Neutral-Tract
and Osage-Reserve conflicts with James F. Joy, the Fort
Scott, and the LL&G that Kansas matters received wide and
sympathetic attention in the press of the country. All well-
known land reformers, such as Julian and Holman of Indiana, Payson of Illinois, Butler of Massachusetts, Lawrence
of Ohio, and of course Greeley of New York had seized upon
the conflict to further their reform plans. These plans included halting further land grants to railroads and sales of
public lands to speculators. The reformers gave much publicity to the "prodigious," "enormous," "gigantic" grants
given the railroads, they showed how the grants made homesteading impossible in great areas, and they argued that the
grants were productive of tenancy, heavy mortgage-indebted-
ness, and, indeed, retarded development. By 1870 they had
amassed sufficient strength in the House of Representatives
to adopt a resolution declaring that "subsidies in public
lands to railroad and other corporations ought to be dis-

[5] Ware's attack upon Pomeroy, Clarke, and other Republicans for
their relations with the railroads and willingness to serve their interests is very bitter. See especially the *Fort Scott Monitor*, July 11,
20, Sept. 15, 1872. See also Lula L. Brown, *The Cherokee Neutral
Lands Controversy*, p. 25 ff.

continued. . . ." [6] In view of this resolution it is somewhat disillusioning to find Congress, the following year, giving a lavish and largely unjustified grant to the Texas and Pacific Railroad. A number of other land grants were renewed in the period from 1869 to 1871, but with the limitation that the lands were to be sold to actual settlers in quarter-section tracts at no more than $2.50 an acre.[7]

By 1871 opposition to further land grants had reached such a height that members of Congress, no matter how strongly inclined they were toward the railroads, dared not vote them additional lands. The land-reformers had won, but their victory came late. Complete disillusionment with land grants was effectively expressed by Eugene Ware in the *Fort Scott Monitor* in 1872. In an examination of the land-grant policy, he estimated the acreage given in Kansas and the price at which the railroads were selling these acres, and concluded that "land for the landless" was a false cry since all the good land had been given to the railroads. The "real cause of our financial blight" was the land grants and their management by the railroads.[8]

Railroad influence in the senatorial elections of 1871 and 1873, elections in which bribery played a well-established part, contributed to the growing disillusionment of Kansans and to the demand for greater integrity in public life. Following reports of outright bribery involving the expenditure of some $60,000 to $75,000 in the successful senatorial campaign of Alexander Caldwell, wealthy railroad magnate associated with the Missouri River Railroad which had bought the second Delaware Reserve (see above pp. 140–142), the State of Kansas and the United States Senate conducted extensive and revealing investigations. Carl Schurtz, Senator from neighboring Missouri, summarized the findings

[6] *Cong. Globe,* 41 Cong., 2 Sess., p. 2095.
[7] 16 *Stat.,* 47, 576, 580.
[8] *Fort Scott Monitor,* Aug. 10, 1872.

of the Senate Committee on Privileges and Elections in regard to the Caldwell election: "I find here bribery systematically organized; I find here a bacchanalian feast and riot of corruption. And when you read the testimony your imagination will fairly recoil from the spectacle of baseness and depravity that presents itself." [9] Not only were the Missouri River and the Katy Railroads implicated through their officers, but the Kansas Pacific was shown to have been ready to spend a large sum for the election of Caldwell. The Joy interests, acting through Peter Abell, were working in behalf of Sidney Clarke; but when offered a generous bribe by Caldwell, Clarke withdrew and supported his former opponent. Only by resigning could Caldwell avoid the greater scandal of expulsion.[10]

A greater bombshell in Kansas politics and a heavier blow at railroad influence was the disclosure that Samuel Pomeroy had offered a bribe to influence voting on the Senatorial election in 1873. Pomeroy from his first appearance in Kansas had a somewhat unsavory reputation. Time after time he was accused of demanding a consideration in return for the many railroad, land, and Indian measures he had aided in putting through Congress. We have seen how he profited from land grants, financial subsidies, and Indian reserves which he secured for favored railroads. Pomeroy's re-election in 1867 was commonly attributed to the lavish use of funds by him and his associates. Known colloquially as "Old Beans," "Old Pom the Pious," "Old Subsidy," "the Christian Gentleman," and by other sobriquets, Pomeroy had by 1873 so posed as a friend of the pioneers, a defender of the Neutral Land

[9] *Cong. Record,* 43 Cong., Special Session of the Senate, p. 87. Much of the volume is taken up with discussion of the Caldwell case, with Morton of Indiana and Alcorn of Mississippi leading the fight for expulsion, and Carpenter of Wisconsin and Logan of Illinois leading the opposition.

[10] For the report of the Senate Committee see *Senate Reports,* 42 Cong., 3 Sess., no. 451.

League, and a supporter of the homestead policy, while at the same time appearing so regularly as the champion of special interests, that few had any illusions about him. It was not the news that he had resorted to bribery that shocked the Kansas legislature and produced his complete defeat. What surprised members of the state legislature, of the National Congress, and the people generally was that the tide of opinion against the railroads' misuse of corrupt wealth had so turned as to make possible Pomeroy's destruction and his replacement by a better man.[11]

Most of the federally-aided railroads in Kansas were slow to determine their routes and hence to make possible the restoration of withdrawn lands to homesteading; they were also unconscionably slow, most Kansans thought, in having their lands patented, placed on the tax roll, and sold. Rising indignation against the railroads, stimulated by their grab of the Indian reserves, was enormously increased by the management of their land grants.

Delay in laying out their routes and having the public lands in their vicinity withdrawn produced sharp clashes between settlers and the Union Pacific, Central Branch, (Senator Pomeroy's road) and the St. Joseph and Denver City Railroad. Some fifty settlers had selected lands along the Central Branch, filed their original entries, lived upon and improved the land for the required five years; then, when

---

[11] For Ex-Senator Ross's attack upon Pomeroy because of the boodle he had taken from railroads and Indians see Martha Caldwell, "Pomeroy's 'Ross Letter': Genuine or Forgery?" *Kansas Historical Quarterly* (Aug., 1945), XIII, 463. See also *Report of the Joint Committee of Investigation Appointed by the Kansas Legislature of 1872, To Investigate all Charges of Bribery and Corruption Connected with the Senatorial Elections of 1867 and 1871* (Topeka, 1872), p. 4 and *passim; Senate Reports,* 42 Cong., 3 Sess., no. 523. For a well-written and able account of the Pomeroy affair see Albert R. Kitzhaber, "Götterdämmerung in Topeka: The Downfall of Senator Pomeroy," *Kansas Historical Quarterly* (Aug., 1950), XVIII, 243 ff.

they went "to prove up," file their final entries, and get title to the land on which they had spent so much of their lives, they were informed that their entries had been cancelled; the land had been selected by the railroad. Efforts to reverse the ruling of the General Land Office and to have the homesteaders confirmed in their claims were fruitless.[12]

On the St. Joseph and Denver City route, several hundred homesteaders found themselves in similar difficulties with the railroad. Officials of the company had made a claim to their land fairly early but seemingly abandoned their rights when shown that prior settlement had been made. Lieu lands were selected instead. Years later a third party, claiming the right to the land under purchase from the railroad brought suit to recover from the homesteaders, who by now had patents for their land. The Federal courts, leaning over backward in their effort to protect property rights, delivered a decision upholding the plaintiff and requiring that all the contested land be confirmed to him. After fifteen years of residence on the land, which had been made valuable by their improvements and on which they had paid taxes for that time, the settlers were stripped of their rights by the Supreme Court. Whatever the legal rights, few could agree there was justice in the decision, which disregarded the positive instruction of Congress as expressed in the original act granting the land in 1866. Railroad responsibility for opening up the question at so late a date combined with the decision of the Court to add much to the ill will in Kansas against the railroads. Congress was urged to intervene, and proceeded to give partial redress by allowing settlers who had gained title and then had been required to purchase again many years later from an assignee of the railroad to recover up to $3.50 an acre for their improvements.[13]

[12] *Marshall County News* (Marysville, Kansas), Feb. 14, 1874.

[13] *Gage County Democrat,* (Beatrice, Nebraska), March 10, April 6, 1882. For the report of the Senate Committee on Public Lands on

A similar controversy with a wider basis of ill feeling arose over homesteaders in Allen, Woodson, Anderson, and Neosho Counties who had settled on lands that were later selected by the LL&G and the Katy Railroads as lieu lands or as part of the 500,000-acre grant given to the state for internal improvements. Among the issues were questions of priority of claim, a question whether either of the railroads had earned their grants because of failure to build all the mileage within the time prescribed by Congress and the State of Kansas, and a question whether the state could grant the internal-improvement lands to railroads in the face of a positive federal prohibition of such action.[14] As early as 1870, immigrants were grumbling against the high prices being charged for the railroad lands, and their journalistic spokesmen demanded that the lands be sold at the government price.[15] A local newspaper complained that the railroad charges for the lands were so high that no one could afford to buy them, and that as a result immigrants were going farther west in their search for reasonably priced land, leaving behind them retarded areas.[16] This was all bad enough, but then came a greater blow to the community. The railroads succeeded in upsetting homestead rights and having patents cancelled for lands to which settlers had already earned the full title. The railroads now sold to persons newly arriving in the community who were unaware of the dispute over titles. There were, then, two groups of settlers claiming title, with one supported by the railroads. The original homesteaders organized the usual land league for mutual protec-

the controversy over the lands see *Senate Reports,* 49 Cong., 1 Sess., IV, no. 96. The act providing relief to the settlers was adopted on March 3, 1887, 24 *Stat.,* 550.

[14] *The Settlers' Side of the Land Question,* a 19-page brochure apparently prepared by J. W. Pine, is useful.

[15] *Neosho Valley Register* (Iola), Oct. 1, 1870.

[16] *Ibid.,* April 23, May 3, 31, July 5, 1873.

tion against eviction by railroad agents or law officers and to protect themselves against new buyers.

There followed intermittent war between the two groups, accompanied by the destruction of fences, the burning of houses, mob scenes, and outright murder. Continued bickering and turmoil over some 64,000 acres in dispute between the two railroads and their customers on the one hand and the homesteaders on the other led the Kansas legislature to take up the issue. In 1881 and 1883 the legislature asked Congress to authorize litigation in the Federal Courts to test the validity of the railroad claim. Feeling against the LL&G reached such a height in 1883 that the legislature urged that steps be taken to forfeit its charter.[17]

By 1886 there were sufficient purchasers of railroad land in Allen County to make possible the organization of the Bona Fide Purchasers Association, which was planned to fight the League. At a meeting in September of that year "nearly 100" Allen County citizens came together to make plans for the defence of their claims against the squatters.[18] The immediate occasion for the meeting was news that the Secretary of the Interior seemed to have discovered grounds for bringing suit to cancel all patents to the two railroads for land in the county. Thus the railroad buyers were now faced not only with the opposition of the League but also with that of the government.[19] After the railroad title was upheld, the buyers pressed suits to evict the squatters.[20] It was reported in 1887 that fifty eviction cases were on the docket of the court. When the judge ordered the squatters removed and the buyers confirmed in their rights, the League violently dispossessed the buyers in turn, while committing other "out-

[17] References in previous note and *Iola Register*, April 6, 1878; *Kansas Laws*, 1881, p. 329 and 1883, pp. 246, 248; Andreas, *History of Kansas*, p. 671.

[18] *Iola Register*, Sept. 10, 1886.

[19] *Ibid.*, July 9, 1886.

[20] *Ibid.*, Jan. 28, 1887.

rages." [21] Continued litigation kept the county in turmoil for years and fattened the purses of the lawyers, one of whom said he could keep the Leaguers on the land for two more years but that eventually they must lose.[22] A recent writer in describing the land leagues that fought the Katy Railroad over the management of its lands reflects the company point of view: [23]

Hordes of immigrants, many of them honest settlers but a goodly proportion of them tough, land-speculating squatters who hoped to make fortunes by pre-empting railroad lands, were organized into "leagues" to fight for their "rights" throughout this period. Some of these organizations grew powerful; all were a thorn in the side of the Katy; most were a real deterrent to honest settlement and development, for the "hardest characters" usually obtained control of the leagues and were responsible for many outrages perpetrated during this period.

This generation-long dispute between the Katy and squatters on lands claimed by it did little to improve relations between the people of Kansas and the railroads.

The Kansas Pacific (KP) Railroad, with its great holding of 3,925,791 acres of donated lands, 223,960 acres of Delaware lands and 27,728 acres of Sac and Fox lands in Kansas,

[21] *Ibid.,* March 18, 25, April 8, 1887. *Atchison Champion,* Sept. 1, 1887.

[22] *Iola Register,* March 12, Sept. 10, Nov. 12, 1886, Jan. 21, April 29, and July 1, 1887. For another instance of a long feud between a settler on a tract he began improving in 1866 but which was later selected by the Katy as indemnity land see the *Atchison Champion,* June 25, 1887. Title passed improperly to the Katy in 1873; the settler continued on the land and in 1887 succeeded in getting the General Land Office to review his claim and to begin action to void the railroad patent.

[23] Masterson, *The Katy Railroad and the Last Frontier,* pp. 55, 82 and note. Masterson also says that "Immigrants, honest settlers, squatters, promoters, adventurers, all accompanied by the lowest riffraff of the frontier, were flooding into southern Kansas in the wake of the railroad."

was hated as much as the LL&G and the Katy Railroads because of its conflicts with settlers and its delay in taking title to the donated lands and in pushing them into market.

The Katy Railroad, whose land grant overlapped that of the KP, had secured its lands early and sold the bulk of them to settlers on long credit. The KP then brought suit, claiming 92,000 acres had been wrongly awarded the Katy.[24] Victory in the courts was followed by the ejection of numerous settlers in Morris, Dickinson, and Davis Counties who had made some payments on their land and erected considerable improvements. Much indignation was expressed at the action of the KP in demanding its "pound of flesh" from the innocent victims of a land-office blunder.[25] Ultimately, though only after many complaints had been aired and strong anti-railroad prejudices engendered, a compromise was worked out whereby the Katy agreed to transfer to the KP the contracts, receipts, and other assets relating to the disputed lands, while the Kansas Pacific was to deed to settlers on the completion of their payments.[26]

For years after the line of the KP across the state was surveyed, close to 10,000,000 acres in a fifty-mile-wide swath of territory through the heart of Kansas were closed to settlement by homesteaders, in order to permit the railroad to earn its grant and make its selections. The railroad was not at all anxious to take title to the western portion of its lands, even though they were earned, since to do so would assure their assessment and taxation before they were in demand by settlers. An amendment to the original Pacific Railroad Act of 1862, adopted in 1864, permitted the KP to delay the patenting of its earned grant by providing that titles should pass only when the railroad took the initiative in pay-

[24] *Council Grove Republican,* March 31, 1877.
[25] *Ibid.,* Dec. 28, 1878.
[26] *Ibid.,* Oct. 4, 1879.

ing the cost of surveying, selecting, and conveying the lands.[27]
Construction was completed in 1870, and surveying of adjacent lands was finished by 1875. All that was necessary to
have the patents issued and the lands placed on the county
tax-rolls was for the KP to pay the small cost of preparing the
lands for transfer of title. Since the initiative was left in the
hands of the officials of the railroad, they elected to tender
the necessary payment only on those lands which they had
sold and on which they would soon have to give title.

From the beginning, the KP and its predecessor, the Union
Pacific, Eastern Division, fought every effort to tax railroad
property. In 1867 the attorney for the railroad took the
astonishing position that the property of the railroad could
not be taxed since it was in effect created and its construction made possible by the land grant and financial loan which
Congress gave it. Because of the obligation thus assumed,
the railroad was in the same tax-exempt position as the
branch of the Bank of the United States had occupied when
the State of Maryland attempted to tax it. Said John P. Usher,
attorney, "no tax can be levied upon the road which shall in
the least, effect or impair the property of the United States,
and that it will be effected by any tax laid specifically on
the property." [28] This distortion of the Marshall doctrine
laid down in the McCulloch case was not to stand, but it
shows how far railroads had come to regard themselves above
the law.

Failing in their efforts to avoid taxation because they were
quasi-governmental enterprises, the land-grant railroads
sought other means of relieving themselves of taxes. The
exemption of their lands from taxation was a great boon,
but assessments on their right-of-way, rolling stock, and other

[27] Act of July 2, 1864, 13 *Stat.*, 365.
[28] Printed document signed by J. P. Usher, Attorney for the Union
Pacific, Eastern Division, Topeka, Feb. 4, 1867, and addressed to
the Governor of Kansas, College of Emporia Library.

improvements bore heavily upon railroads built through sparsely developed communities and would make it difficult for them to raise funds for the completion of their lines. Representatives of the KP came up with the bright idea of substituting an income tax on profits in place of the property tax. The substitution was urged upon the governor of Kansas and brought to the attention of the public in the hope that favorable action might be secured.[29] Readers may wonder whether the present-day officers of the Union Pacific are aware of the early attitude on taxation of their predecessors.

That the KP should not wish to subject its lands to taxation before they came into demand was natural; for this taxation would constitute a heavy liability. It was common knowledge that residents in thinly-developed frontier communities sought to place the burden of supporting local governments as largely as possible on railroads on the grounds that they were absentee and alien institutions. If the land grants as well as the right-of-way were taxable, the companies might not survive. In western-Kansas counties before settlers began to take title under pre-emption and homestead laws, there was actually little to tax except the right-of-way and lands (if title had passed) of the railroads.[30]

Most aggravating to the settlers in the western counties of Kansas was the practice of the railroads, notably of the

[29] Usher document cited in previous note and Edgar W. Dennis, Assistant General Solicitor for the Kansas Pacific, *Tabulated Statements Relating to Taxation of Railroads, 1873* (Topeka, 1873), copy in Kansas State Historical Society.

[30] James C. Malin in "J. A. Walker's Early History of Edwards County," *Kansas Historical Quarterly* (Aug., 1940), IX, 268–269, cites the experience of Edwards County, where a large proportion of the tax burden was born by the Santa Fe Railroad. Minnie D. Millbrook has an instructive article on the way county government was manipulated in frontier Kansas for the financial benefit of the few who organized it. "Dr. Samuel Grant Rodgers, Gentleman From Ness," *Kansas Historical Quarterly* (Feb., 1953), XX, 305–349.

KP, in delaying the request for patent until the buyer had completed payments upon his land. Thereafter any tax assessments were his responsibility.[31] For example, the KP began sales of its land in 1868, but no lands were patented and placed on the tax roll before 1873. By the end of 1879 it had sold 1,515,059 acres in Kansas and 199,202 acres in Colorado but had patents on less than half of these acres.[32] Furthermore, all the lands, though not patented, had been mortgaged to provide funds for building the road.

Table 23. KANSAS PACIFIC SALES AND ACREAGE PATENTED TO IT

Year	Sold in Kansas	Patented in Kansas	Sold in Colorado	Patented in Colorado
1868	111,271	0	——	——
1869	382,885	0	——	——
1870	124,168	0	32,613	0
1871	123,935	0	41,543	0
1872	62,851	0	19,959	0
1873	25,423	52,914	17,951	0
1874	35,395	378,989	10,918	0
1875	61,366	63,666	3,676	10,943
1876	74,554	36,506	4,364	0
1877	135,944	225,467	26,101	0
1878	207,938	15,491	34,523	0
1879	169,328	43,760	7,554	12,950
	1,515,059	816,793	199,202	23,893

Homesteaders watched with concern this delay of the railroad in taking title and in assuming a part of the cost of local government. Their own lands, the *Abilene Chronicle* pointed out, were entered on the tax roll on March 1, after final proof had been offered but before the patent was issued.[33] Settlers

[31] *Junction City Union,* Jan. 21, 1882.

[32] Statistics on sale and amount patented are from the Report of the United States Pacific Railway Commission, *Sen. Ex. Doc.,* 50 Cong., 1 Sess., no. 51, part 7, p. 4253 and part 9, p. 5244; Thomas Donaldson, *The Public Domain,* pp. 776–777.

[33] *Abilene Chronicle* quoted in *Junction City Union,* Feb. 11, 1882. In his valuable account of pioneering in Osborne County in the sev-

who were buying the Osage lands on time after 1880 had their lands placed on the tax roll after the first payment was made, though the final installment was not due for three years.[34] Not only was the railroad largely exempt from taxes on its lands, but its purchasers had the same privilege until they had made their final payment at the end of their ten-

---

READ AND CIRCULATE!
——ALL ABOUT——
The Great Arkansas Valley in Kansas.
RENO COUNTY STILL AHEAD!

150,000 Acres first-class **HOMESTEAD LAND,** and How to Get it.

The Place to locate under the Timber Tree Law, and How to do it.

300,000 ACRES ATCHISON, TOPEKA & SANTA FE RAILROAD LANDS at **$3 to $7 per Acre,** on 11 years time, at 7 per cent interest. No charge made for showing these Lands to purchasers by C. C. HUTCHINSON, at Hutchinson, County Seat of Reno County, exclusive agent for the *Choicest Lands in the Valley.*

HUTCHINSON has grown in 18 months to contain 1000 people, and is a city of the third class. Not a saloon or gambling house in City or County. C. C. Hutchinson offers for sale 500 beautiful residence lots (one-eighth acre) at *$15 to $30 each,* all within fifteen minutes walk of the Court-House. Will sell on time to suit purchasers. I am selling my own lots, and will do better by you than any other person can do. Also 5 and 10 acre out-lots at prices to suit.

☞ The Best opening for a Home in the West.☜ ☞ The place to invest your money and double it in one year.☜

DO YOUR NEIGHBOR GOOD BY SHOWING THIS CIRCULAR.

Circular advertising homestead land in the Arkansas Valley. (Courtesy, Collection of Regional History, Cornell University)

year contract; hence they were not inclined to push their payments as they might have if some incentives had been offered. As late as 1882, twelve years after construction was completed and twenty years after the lands were granted, the Kansas Pacific had taken title to little more than one-sixth of its lands.[35]

---

enties and eighties, John Ise relates how his parents delayed proving up on their homestead claim for two or three years beyond the five-year period in order to avoid earlier tax assessments. *Sod and Stubble* (N.Y., 1936), p. 81.

[34] 21 *Stat.*, 144, Act of May 28, 1880.

[35] *Junction City Union*, July 1, Aug. 12, 1882.

It is instructive to compare the land policies of the Kansas Pacific and the Santa Fe Railroads, for they differed sharply in some respects and in that difference lies the reason for the attacks upon the former and the more friendly attitude toward the latter.

The purchase of the Pottawatomie reserve by the Santa Fe aroused hostility in a settler-minded national House of Representatives and certainly in the squatters who had hoped to get homestead or pre-emption rights.[36] But the squatters on the Delaware reserve somewhat earlier had not liked any better the action of the predecessor of the KP in buying the tract and requiring those dwelling on it to come to terms with the railroad. In taking title to its lands and having them placed on the tax roll, however, the Santa Fe was far in advance of the KP. For example, in 1880 the KP had but 13 per cent of its lands on the tax rolls in contrast to 84 per cent of the Santa Fe lands. The Santa Fe also had an additional 6 per cent only waiting on the action of the government to have the patents issued and the lands taxed. Through 1886 the Santa Fe had paid $482,127 in taxes on its lands while the KP had paid only $160,927 on a grant that was one-third larger.[37]

The Santa Fe was much more vigorous in pushing its lands into market and getting them into private ownership. True, the KP commenced sales in 1868, and in 1871 published a 33-page pamphlet calling attention to the admirable features of the area through which it was built, especially the deep, rich prairie soil that brought forth high yields of grain and produced fruit in abundance, the short winters, the absence of swamp lands and of accompanying ague "that

[36] *Cong. Globe,* 40 Cong., 2 Sess., part 4, July 7, 1868, p. 3786.

[37] Compiled from *Annual Reports* of the Santa Fe and from the *United States Pacific Railway Commission, Sen. Ex. Doc.,* 50 Cong., 1 Sess., IV, no. 51, part 7, p. 4283.

great plague of almost all new countries," the moderate sum-
mers and abundant rain that came fortuitously in the early
part of the growing season. The lands were offered at prices
ranging from $2 to $6 on five years' credit.[38] After this initial
and promising start, which produced large sales for four
years, the KP showed less zeal to sell its lands, and increased
their price. The Santa Fe, on the other hand, started more
slowly, first opening its Pottawatomie lands to sale and then
its odd sections in 1871. From then on, in proportion to the
total acreage it held, the Santa Fe sales greatly exceeded
those of its rival. The lack of vigor shown by the KP in advertising its lands troubled Kansans, who complained about
it, as did the *Atchison Champion,* in 1887: [39]

The Kansas Pacific, now the Union Pacific, never did very much
to advertise our state or even its own lands. At first, almost, it was
managed by St. Louis men, and Missouri has never done any advertising. . . . The Union Pacific is now in the hands of eastern
men and is progressively managed, but it was passive while
Kansas was building.

In contrast the Santa Fe, the Fort Scott Line, the Katy, the
St. Joseph and Denver, and the UP, Central Branch, were
commended for their extensive advertising efforts to bring
their lands to the attention of immigrants and for the resulting beneficial effect upon Kansas. It should be said that a
larger proportion of the Santa Fe lands than of the KP lands
were in the humid section of central Kansas. This fact made
it possible for the Santa Fe to charge a higher price for lands
being sold in the seventies; but by 1882, when its better tracts
were taken up, its average price was substantially lower.
In fact the table of sales of the two railroads shows the Santa
Fe prices declining while those of the KP were rising. Be-

[38] *Emigrants' Guide to the Kansas Pacific Railway Lands. Best and
Cheapest Farming and Grazing Lands in America. 6,000,000 Acres
for Sale By the Kansas Pacific Railway Co.* (Lawrence, 1871), *passim.*
[39] *Atchison Champion,* May 8, 1887.

cause it maintained a high price-level in the eighties the KP attracted few buyers.

Table 24. COMPARISON OF LAND SALES BY SANTA FE (2,944,788 ACRES IN KANSAS) AND KP (8,997,713 ACRES IN KANSAS AND COLORADO) [40]

Year	Santa Fe (in Kansas)		Kansas Pacific (Kansas only)	
	Acres	Average price	Acres	Average price
1868			111,271	$2.96
1869			382,885	2.91
1870			124,168	3.19
1871	71,801	$5.91	123,935	3.50
1872	45,328	5.90	62,851	2.92
1873	133,507	5.61	25,423	3.67
1874	200,459	4.54	35,393	3.29
1875	75,415	5.59	61,366	3.57
1876	122,201	5.44	74,554	4.23
1877	85,047	4.98	135,944	3.31
1878	267,122	4.52	207,938	3.38
1879	104,744	4.72	169,328	4.09
			(Kansas and Colorado)	
1880	78,241	4.98	100,383	4.03
1881	50,033	5.22	99,369	4.28
1882	189,830	4.71	105,915	4.93
1883	431,755	3.56	298,478	4.41
1884	353,090	3.36	475,007	4.21
1885	770,494	2.66	711,960	4.08
1886	347,321	2.44	230,387	4.68

The Santa Fe cancelled a slightly smaller proportion of the acreage in its sales contracts in the period through 1886 for which comparable statistics are available, but the difference would not materially affect the figures in the table. At the end of 1886 the Santa Fe had only a scattered 33,390 acres unsold while the KP had 1,174,700 acres unsold in Kansas and 2,200,000 acres unsold in Colorado. In addition to its more popular tax and sales policies, the Santa Fe managed

[40] Compiled from *Annual Reports* of the KP and Santa Fe Railroads. For 1880 to 1886 the KP sales include also the sales of the Denver Pacific. Before that period the sales of the Denver Pacific were kept separate and are not included in the table. The KP grant in Kansas included 3,925,000 acres.

to avoid more successfully than did the KP clashes over lieu lands on which settler rights might have been established before the lands were officially withdrawn from entry. Finally, the Santa Fe never found itself in as awkward a situation as was the KP when it won its land case against the Katy Railroad and proceeded to evict settlers who had bought their land from that railroad.

Table 25. LAND SALES AND CANCELLATIONS OF KANSAS PACIFIC AND SANTA FE RAILROADS THROUGH 1886 [41]

	Sales		*Cancellations*		*Percentage of Cancellations*
	Acres	*Purchase Money*	*Acres*	*Purchase Money*	
Kansas Pacific	3,741,927	$14,798,360	487,255	$2,064,233	12.7
Santa Fe	3,326,397	12,717,831	396,621	1,851,394	11.9

Readers should not be unmindful of the pressures the railroads were under in handling their land grants, and of the fact that historians attribute to the advertising and colonization activities of these companies responsibility for the plight of the Kansas wheat-farmer in the period of the Populist revolt. Westerners wanted the lands sold, their titles passed, the tracts assessed, and the land developed as rapidly as possible. The railroads felt the constant pressure of tax assessments and other influences, and for this reason they did not wish to retain ownership of land for any very long period of time. They certainly preferred to sell at their price and get the land into cultivation. The railroads spent great sums of money in advertising their lands and attracting settlers to them. A writer in the *New York Tribune* in 1880, commenting upon the condition of many farmers in western Kansas following two drought years, alluded to this advertising of the railroads: [42]

[41] Computed from *Sen. Ex. Doc.,* 50 Cong., 1 Sess., no. 51, part 9, p. 5244 and *Annual Reports,* Santa Fe Railroad.

[42] Correspondent writing from Wa-Keeney, Kansas, *New York Tribune,* Feb. 27, 1880.

Attracted by glaring railroad advertisements and glowing descriptions of the country, thousands upon thousands of immigrants came into the State; crossing the Missouri River, they rushed for the Western frontier line, which during 1877 and 1878 moved fully 100 miles each year nearer the Rocky Mountains. Many came who had no business here; who after paying their land-entry fees—the first settlers being always those upon the public lands—had little and in many instances no money left.

This great flow of population into Kansas and other plains states vastly increased the area under cultivation to wheat, and created during the eighties and nineties marketing difficulties and low prices that had a bearing on the recrudescence of agrarian radicalism.[43]

It should be remembered that the advantage of tax exemption was passed on to the purchasers of railroad lands who for the five or ten years in which they were attempting to meet their payments to the railroads had no taxes to pay if the patent had not been issued. This exemption from taxes, combined with the low interest rate the railroads charged for the credit they granted their purchasers—6 per cent compared with the 9–12 per cent charged by local lenders—placed the purchasers in a preferred position and weighed considerably in their favor. Also, the railroads did not press their debtors so sharply for collections as did the loan and trust companies; for railroad officers could not forget that they were primarily operating a transportation business and that leniency toward farmers developing their lands was desirable. The Kansas correspondent of the *New York Tribune* found in 1881 that the loan agents and representatives of

[43] Hallie Farmer describes the railroad's part in the settlement of the plains states and its relation to the Populist movement in "The Economic Background of Frontier Populism," in *Mississippi Valley Historical Review* (March, 1924), X, 406 ff. See also an illuminating article by Raymond C. Miller, "The Background of Populism in Kansas," *Mississippi Valley Historical Review* (March, 1925), XI, 469 ff.

the trust companies were so disturbed at the greater leniency of the railroads toward their purchasers that they urged the agents of the railroads to be more stringent in requiring payments.[43a] Since the purchasers of railroad lands were in a minority in almost every community, the more favorable attitude they may have felt toward the railroads because of the lower rate of interest, consideration in extending time payments, and the tax exemption did not offset the ill-feeling engendered among those not benefiting from these policies.

Nearly half the land in KP counties was tax-exempt; and even though a part of these lands might be sold on credit and in process of development, this condition placed heavy burdens on homesteaders and doubtless contributed to the high rate of failure among them. It was natural, therefore, that they should attempt to make railroad lands subject to taxation. In the seventies numerous efforts were made to bring the matter to the fore.

In 1872 and 1873 meetings of county commissioners and farmers' clubs adopted resolutions urging that all railroad property be taxed as was other property and urging Kansas representatives in Congress to introduce legislation that would compel forfeiture of lands withdrawn for railroads and not earned.[44] At the same time Sidney Clarke, who despite his efforts to play both sides of the railroad question, had been defeated for re-election to Congress, joined the anti-monopoly forces in a campaign to shift a larger part of state and local taxes to the railroads on the ground that they were evading their fair share of the burden. In a speech at Lawrence, Clarke provided "A Startling Array of Facts and Figures," to prove his indictment. He described the railroad scheme of tax-evasion and the railroad influence in politics as follows: [45]

[43a] *New York Tribune*, Jan. 22, 1881.
[44] *Manhattan Beacon*, May 10, 1873.
[45] *The Taxation of Railroads in Kansas. Speech of Hon. Sidney Clarke Delivered Before the Anti-Monopoly Clubs of Lawrence*

Our politial parties, our influential politicians, our political conventions and legislatures, and many of our courts, have been the willing tools of the Railroad corporations ever since Railroad property has had an existence in Kansas, and in open defiance of the constitution, and of every principle of equity and justice, they have deliberately secured, enacted and interpreted a system of special laws by which the masses of the people are cheated and swindled, and through which the great body of the railroad property of this State is entirely exempted from the little inconvenience of paying its just proportion of taxes. This result has been accomplished by the monopolists step by step. The monopoly shackles have been placed upon us one by one, till we are pinioned and bound by a half-dozen Legislative enactments and court decisions, more offensive to sound public policy and common sense, than many of the enactments and decisions of the Slave Oligarchy when that monstruous [*sic*] power reigned supreme.

The first definite move to compel taxation of the unpatented lands held for the railroads was made in 1874 when the House of Representatives adopted a measure to strip from the railroads the tax-exemption they enjoyed because of failure to take title to earned lands. When action by the Senate appeared unlikely, the Kansas legislature forwarded a memorial urging adoption of the bill, but the Senate remained unmoved.[46] In 1876, 1881, 1883, and 1887 similar memorials were forwarded to Congress by the Kansas legislature urging that the lands of the KP be made taxable.[47]

(Lawrence, 1873), p. 31. In reply to the attacks upon it for the light taxes it paid, the Kansas Pacific published *Tabulated Statements Related to Taxation of Railroads, 1873,* by Edgar W. Dennis (Topeka, 1873), p. 2, wherein it compared the percentage of gross and net receipts it paid in state and local taxes with that of eastern railroads enjoying much greater density of traffic; and amazingly, it may be said, the view is expressed in a treatise on railroads that "the only just basis" for taxation of railroads "is that it be imposed upon profits."

[46] *Cong. Record*, 43 Cong., 1 Sess., II, part 4, 3773, May 11, 1874; *Laws of Kansas,* 1875, pp. 240–241, Feb. 2, 1875.

[47] *Laws of Kansas,* 1876, p. 322; 1881, p. 331; 1883, p. 251; and 1887, p. 347.

Failing to secure legislation in Washington, Kansas turned to direct action. Some counties placed the earned but un-patented lands of the KP on the tax rolls even though the title remained technically in the United States. As early as 1872 Ellsworth County advertised its KP lands for sale for tax delinquency. Attorneys for the KP had no difficulty in persuading the courts to declare all such efforts illegal. That railroad ownership of its lands was sufficient to permit mort-gaging and yet not sufficient to permit taxing was too subtle a legal distinction to the people but not to the judges.[48]

By keeping the issue of tax-exemption before the people, western Kansas won increasing support for its demands. A meeting of a congressional convention of the Greenback Party in Beloit on August 4, 1880 expressed opposition to the local congressman—John A. Anderson—for his hard-money votes, and urged him to favor taxation of railroad lands and legislation to prevent the railroads from passing taxes on to the people.[49] Two years later at Clay Center the Greenback Labor Party demanded that railroads forfeit earned lands on which the survey fees were not paid and the taxes assessed, as well as the opening of the lands to pre-emption. Great mass meetings of settlers were held at which petitions were circulated calling upon Congress either to forfeit the earned but untaxed lands or to compel the patent-ing of all earned lands. Petitions from Lincoln, Ellis, and Osborne Counties where the KP held much land—one peti-tion being signed by 769 citizens—condemned "this con-tinuous and perpetual non-taxable condition of the Kansas Pacific lands" which "is an outrage not to be tolerated" by governments anywhere. The petitioners declared that some counties were forced to levy taxes as high as 5 per cent be-cause of the exemption on railroad land which constituted

[48] *Ellsworth Reporter*, Mar. 28, 1872; *Junction City Union*, Jan. 21, 1882.

[49] *Ibid.*, July 6, 1882.

a large part of the privately owned property.[50] At the same time the State of Kansas appointed an agent to seek forfeiture in Washington of unpatented lands which the railroads claimed but were not willing to have taxed.[51]

Henry M. Teller, Secretary of the Interior and prominent Colorado figure, who in his own state had felt the tax burden caused by the exemption of the KP lands, threw his influence behind the move. In his *Annual Report* for 1882, he said of the earned but unpatented lands: [52]

The companies permit these large bodies of land to rest in this situation, and grow valuable by the lapse of time and the settlement of the country, thus obtaining all the advantages of public protection and enhancement of values, without contributing to the maintenance of the public authority or of the common institutions of municipal organization by the aid of which such enhanced values may be secured.

A year later Teller returned to the question, charging that continued tax-exemption of railroad lands retarded the development of neighboring government lands and imposed "the full burden of taxation upon purchasers of railroad lands and other settlers who homesteaded lands in the same neighborhood. . . ." He "urgently recommended" that Congress take prompt action to make the lands taxable.[53] At this late date few expected relief from the provision in the original Pacific Railroad Act which stated that all lands not sold within three years after completion of construction should be subject to sale at a maximum price of $1.25 an acre; previous hostile decisions of the Supreme Court had discouraged men from looking for help in that quarter.

John A. Anderson, who was campaigning for re-election

[50] *Cong. Record,* 47 Cong., 1 Sess., II, 1696, 1928, and III, 2095.

[51] *Clay City Times* in *Junction City Tribune,* Nov. 22, 1883. See also the *Junction City Tribune,* Dec. 27, 1883.

[52] *House Ex. Doc.,* 47 Cong., 2 Sess., I, no. 1, part 5, xxxi.

[53] Donaldson, *The Public Domain,* p. 1265.

to the national House of Representatives in 1882, was now under the pressure of agrarian politics taking a more favorable attitude than earlier to the movement for inflation, for railroad regulation, and for the taxation of railroads.[54] On the tax question he became the leading advocate in the House of a bill to make all railroad lands taxable. With the aid of Senator Preston B. Plumb, who likewise was induced by public opinion in Kansas to change his attitude, at least in the open,[55] four bills were introduced into Congress to compel the transfer of title to all donated lands of the KP and to require sales by the railroad at $1.25 an acre.[56] Anderson's efforts to make taxable the Kansas Pacific lands brought him great popularity so that despite the opposition of conservative Republicans he continued to run far ahead of his ticket in the western-Kansas district.[57] Though the effort to compel the patenting of the KP lands and their sale at $1.25 an acre was easily defeated in 1882, it did produce some action. Not wanting to incur too much ill will, officials of the KP in the midst of the fight made the necessary payments for survey and had the patents issued for part of the earned lands, making certain at the same time that their action received proper attention in the press. In 1884 219,747 acres were added to the tax rolls in twelve Kansas counties, thus providing considerable new taxes for schools.[58]

[54] A friendly and uncritical sketch of Anderson by George W. Martin in the Kansas State Historical Society, *Collections,* VIII, 315–323, summarizes his achievements as representative.

[55] The *New York Herald* called Plumb "an active and very shrewd friend of land-grant corporations." Quoted in the *Junction City Tribune,* April 14, 1887.

[56] *Cong. Record,* 47 Cong., 1 Sess., I, 660–665; VI, 5905–5910; and Appendix, p. 3.

[57] *Junction City Tribune,* Nov. 6, 1884; Andreas, *History of the State of Kansas,* pp. 230, 1308.

[58] *Junction City Tribune* (Sept. 30, 1886), gave Anderson credit for this improvement.

During the eighties the cry "Tax the Railroad Land Grants" went up all over the West, being taken up by the Grangers, the Farmers' Alliance, and the Democrats.[59] Defeat of the move to make taxable the earned but unpatented lands of the KP only increased the pressure for a general measure that would apply to all earned but unpatented lands. Supporters of the move pointed out that on the three main branches of the original Pacific Railroad, the Union, Kansas and Central Pacific, 19,039,490 acres remained to be selected and patented before they could be taxed, and the unselected land on the Northern Pacific and the Atlantic and Pacific Railroads would greatly augment that figure.

Table 26. RAILROAD LAND GRANTS [60]

	Completed Grant	Patented in 1886	Selections Pending	Unselected
Central Pacific	7,449,725	1,040,210	546,076	5,863,439
Kansas Pacific	6,176,383	963,714	824,538	4,388,131
Union Pacific	11,935,603	2,616,178	531,504	8,787,921
				19,039,491

Kansas was in the forefront of the movement, with Representative Anderson and Senators Plumb and Ingalls joining actively with Holman of Indiana, Payson of Illinois and Van Wyck of Nebraska in the fight. They exploited the inconsistency of the courts in refusing to allow the taxation of earned lands which had not been patented but permitting the railroads to mortgage them.[61] Railroad lands were being

[59] *Gage County Democrat,* July 25, 1884.

[60] Report of the United States Pacific Railway Commission, *Sen. Ex. Doc.,* 50 Cong., 1 Sess., no. 51, part 7, pp. 4250–4257.

[61] Similar confusion was shown in the matter of taxing the Agricultural-College lands of Kansas. These lands were sold on the usual seven years' credit and with the assurance that they would not be taxable until the final payment was made. Some 16,000 acres, located in a few townships in Marshall County where the Central Branch, Union Pacific held many thousand acres of tax-exempt lands,

sold on a ten-year contract, and during that entire period the purchaser was under no tax-obligation, while his neighbor on a homestead was taxed after making his original entry and for five years before he got title. Only by congressional action could the railroads be compelled to pay taxes on lands which were rising in value as a result of improvements being put upon neighboring tracts.[62]

Representatives of the railroads fought to defend their tax-exemption and prevent the forfeiture of unearned grants. In 1882 it was estimated that exemption was worth $250,-000 a year to the Kansas Pacific.[63] Advertising patronage was denied newspapers which urged hostile legislation, and favorable publicity was liberally supplied friendly papers. The railroads tried to cast blame for the delay in taking title and having lands placed on the tax rolls on the General Land Office and its officials who pushed surveys slowly.[64] In 1886 Congressman Anderson was refused renomination by regular Republicans who found unbearable his criticism of railroad sales, tax exemption, and unearned land grants and other instances of his financial heterodoxy. But the tide was now running so strongly against the railroads that Anderson won "an unexampled victory . . . over machine politics. . . ."[65]

---

were sold in 1869. At the earliest they would not be taxable until 1876. With so much of the area not contributing to the support of local government, schools, and roads, the owners of taxable land felt their burdens keenly and attempted to overthrow the exemption agreement for the Agricultural-College lands. An unfavorable opinion by the state attorney general was followed by a favorable court opinion which in turn was qualified by subsequent law and a later attorney general. See broadside: *Taxation of College Lands. Attorney General Randolph's Opinion*, 1876, Kansas State Historical Society.

[62] *Cong. Record*, 49 Cong., 1 Sess., III, 2201 *et seq.;* VII, 6165, 6266.

[63] *Junction City Union*, Aug. 12, 1882.

[64] *Junction City Union*, Jan. 21, 1882.

[65] *Junction City Tribune*, Sept. 30, Nov. 11, 1886.

Tax reformers secured their objective in the same year, not only for Kansas but for all the public-land states in which railroad land grants lay, when Congress provided that all lands granted to railroads that had been surveyed should be subject to local taxes.[66] Perhaps no measure other than forfeiture and re-opening of the railroad lands to homesteading could have done so much for the states of Kansas, Nebraska, North Dakota, and Montana as well as other states in the Interior Basin and on the Pacific Coast.[67]

Meantime, Kansas had come to dispute the amount of land claimed by the Santa Fe and the Kansas Pacific and sought to have that amount pared substantially. Former Governor Samuel J. Crawford, who had earlier taken an active part in the fight against James F. Joy's purchase of the Neutral Tract, was employed by the State to prosecute its case before the Department of the Interior and was successful in gaining some benefits.[68]

The slowness with which many land-grant railroads established their lines, built them, took title to donated lands, and pushed them into market led critics to hold that the policy of giving land bounties to railroads tended to lock up resources in new regions as much as to promote development. As late as 1885 it was estimated that close to 100,-000,000 acres of land were waiting on construction before

[66] 24 *Stat.*, 143.

[67] Addison E. Sheldon has a useful section on "Exemption of Railroad Lands from Taxes" in *Land Systems and Land Policies in Nebraska* (Nebraska State Historical Society, *Publications*. XXII; Lincoln, 1936), 98–103.

[68] See Crawford's *In The Matter of the Kansas Pacific Railroad Grant and Withdrawal of Lands* (Topeka, 1883), *Argument Before the Commissioner of the General Land Office in the Matter of the Atchison, Topeka and Santa Fe Land Grant* (Washington, 1883), and *Adjustment of Railroad Grants Within the State of Kansas* (no place, no date), and *Kansas in the Sixties* (Chicago, 1911), pp. 354 ff. Crawford's arguments are given in summary form in *Junction City Tribune*, Jan. 20, 27, Feb. 3, 1887.

they could be acquired either as free homesteads from the government or by purchase from the railroads. Lax administration and perhaps a predilection of the General Land Office in favor of the railroads permitted these withdrawn lands to remain dormant for a long time.

The Kansas legislature in 1887 summarized the major grievances of the State concerning the administration of the railroad land grants: [69]

1. Lands had been patented to railroads though the land rightfully belonged to settlers.

2. Lands had been patented to railroads in excess of the amount to which they were entitled.

3. Lands were withdrawn and withheld from market for the benefit of railroads without authority.

4. Parts of subsidized lines had been abandoned and the grants applied to others in violation of the law.

5. Railroads had sold land to citizens who were entitled to them as homesteads.

6. After the indemnity lands had been patented to the railroads they had selected others on which settlers' rights had been established and unseated the settlers.

In addition to the large acreage of withdrawn lands that remained unutilized a sizable amount of earned land was still held by railroads at prices that delayed sales and development. In some of the later land grants, provisions had been included that required the lands to be sold to actual settlers only in tracts of 160 acres; but the Kansas railroads were immune from this condition. The railroads undoubtedly wished to get their lands into the hands of people with capital who would develop them and thereby provide traffic, but

[69] *Laws of Kansas,* 1887, p. 347. There is much information bearing on these questions raised by the Kansas legislature in a reply to a request for data on railroad land-grants in Kansas that was submitted to the Secretary of the Interior by the United States Senate, *Sen. Ex. Doc.,* 50 Cong., 1 Sess., no. 194, *passim.*

their officials, anxious to make as good showing as possible in land sales, sold on occasion to people interested only in speculation or, in one notable instance, to a much-hated person who was involved in creating America's greatest individually-owned landed estate—William A. Scully.

In the homestead area west of the 97th meridian it was legally possible for a man to secure from the Federal government only one pre-emption claim, one homestead claim, and one timber-culture claim, altogether 480 acres. He could also purchase from the State of Kansas part of the school sections, 16 and 36. These restrictions on land entries were in sharp contrast to the situation farther east in Kansas where unlimited quantities of land could be bought by anyone with the means. Land reformers had to this degree succeeded in revising Federal policy in the direction of reserving the public lands for actual settlers and preventing the accumulation of those large speculative holdings and great estates that had been created in other prairie areas, notably in Iowa and Illinois. They did not succeed, however, in preventing men of capital from buying the small tracts of homesteaders and the large acreages of railroads.

Two of the largest sales to individuals in central Kansas were made in 1869 when the Fort Scott Line sold to a Mr. Balis, not otherwise identified, 40,000 acres; and when the KP sold to Alexander McDonald of Scotland 46,823 acres. The latter sale presumably was for the development of the cattle industry and the former for speculation and resale.[70] In 1870 Charles Potwin, a land dealer, bought 34,683 acres in Butler and Marion Counties from the LL&G. In 1872 the KP sold 13,160 acres in McPherson County to the First Swedish Agricultural Company. This sale was doubtless made primarily for settlement, but as with most such colonies there may have been a speculative element in it. The Santa

[70] Kersey Coates, Kansas City, July 25, 1869, to Joy, Joy MSS.; Dickinson County Deed Records, L:48.

Fe made sales of 10,000 to 20,000 acres to at least four people. Similarly, the Katy Railroad sold 11,500 acres to Robert Chapin of Ontario County, New York, with whom T. C. Henry was associated.

Biggest of the sales of railroads to individuals may have been that of the KP to James Grant. In 1873 between 100,-000 and 150,000 acres in Ellis County were sold to Grant, on which he established the Victoria colony of Englishmen. The spectacular size of the operation and its early success in attracting immigrants brought much attention to the colony; its ambitious promoter pushed large-scale farming operations energetically, rented to tenants, and sold in 640-acre lots.[71]

Many of the large farms in central Kansas were built up through purchases made from railroads. John Marsh, Marcus Field, and George Brooks, all of Cooperstown, New York, bought from the KP 8,000 acres which were being fenced in 1883.[72] The Christie Ranch in Marion County and the wheat farm of T. C. Henry, perhaps the most widely advertised wheat ranch in America at the time, were acquired from the Katy Railroad.[73] Aside from his extensive farming operations, which have been described by James C. Malin, Henry was the great booster for the wheat belt of Kansas, as part of his activities as a real-estate agent. In fact, one is led to believe that his farming operations, so widely reported in the press during the seventies, were magnified both as to size and results by his desire to sell the lands of the KP and the Katy Railroads and thereby increase his commissions.[74] Henry's boastful claims as to the size and

[71] Joseph C. McCoy, *Historical Sketches of the Cattle Trade of the West and Southwest* (Kansas City, 1874), pp. 357 ff.; James MacDonald, *Food From the Far West*, pp. 82–88.

[72] *Davis County Republican* (Junction City), June 15, 1883.

[73] It has not seemed wise to give all the numerous references to the deed records for the transactions in the preceding sections.

[74] James C. Malin, *Winter Wheat in the Golden Belt of Kansas* (Lawrence, 1944), has two chapters on the agricultural operations

production of his wheat fields, as well as the acreage of land that he sold and its value, are difficult to follow but are worthy of note. In one place he claimed to have sold $2,500,-000 worth of land, and in another he maintained that he had sold a million acres at an average price of $5 an acre.[75] Nearly as widely acclaimed for his extensive farm operations was John Taylor of Cincinnati. With 3,043 acres bought of the Katy and some 3,500 acres acquired elsewhere he created two great farms, on which he built stone houses, "large" barns, planted 1,600 acres of wheat (later increased to 3,000 acres), and developed a herd of shorthorn cattle.[76]

Kansans watched with concern this tendency of the railroad companies and of the United States to sell land in large blocks to speculative interests; but when such sales were accompanied by development of the land through extensive farming or cattle-ranching operations, they tempered their criticism.[77]

---

and booster activities of Henry. He mentions a purchase of 10,000 acres of Katy land by M. D. Herington and Henry and a 16,000-acre purchase of Katy land by Henry alone. *Ibid.*, p. 91. All these purchases were made for resale. I have used *Henry's Advertiser,* II, no. 1, published in Topeka, in 1878.

[75] *Chicago Commercial Advertiser* reprinted in *Kansas Gazette,* Jan. 11, April 12, 1878; *Abilene Gazette,* Jan. 9 and July 23, 1880. The latter citation is to a sketch of Henry clipped from the *Leavenworth Times.*

[76] *Kansas Gazette* (Enterprise), April 27, 1876; *Junction City Union,* May 6, 1876; *Abilene Gazette,* Sept. 30, Nov. 4, 1881; July 4, 1884. The R. A. Whiting ranch of 3,192 acres in Morris County, which was bought of the Santa Fe and Katy, remained in the hands of the same family until 1937, though it was leased to others as early as 1911 for an annual rent of $4,000. *Council Grove Republican and Democrat,* March 31, 1878; Morris County, Miscellaneous Record, C:268.

[77] Albert Crane's 10,000-acre Durham Park farm, the Christie Ranch of some 2,000 acres, both in Marion County, and the 30,000-acre Diamond Ranch owned by the Western Land and Cattle Com-

Sales of railroad land to William Scully contributed to the establishment of the largest family-owned estate of farm land and to the most controversial landlord-program of developing an estate in the United States. An Irish landlord who saw the handwriting on the wall in his famine-ridden country, Scully came to the United States in 1850 in search of investment opportunities. A tour of the country persuaded him to concentrate his investments in Illinois, where he shortly acquired 38,000 acres of rich prairie land. Later development of this property by tenants and the liquidation of his Irish lands provided large returns, which Scully invested in land in Kansas and Nebraska. From the Federal government he bought 41,420 acres in Nuckolls County, Nebraska; 14,060 acres in Marion County, Kansas; and 1,160 acres in Dickinson County, Kansas. He bought 560 acres from the Union Pacific, Central Branch, in Marshall County; and 8,782 acres from the Santa Fe in Marion and Butler Counties. He also acquired 3,200 acres of the Potwin lands which had come from the LL&G.

Scully's insistence that his tenants should make all the improvements on lands they rented assured the poorest of homes, lightly-constructed fencing or none at all, and bad management of the land to such a degree that the farms were called "Scully slums." Tenants were subjected to numerous petty regulations and penalized with fines for infractions. Since they were required to pay all the taxes and assessments on land they rented, they opposed increased expenditures for roads, schools, and other such purposes. Cash rent was required instead of the usual share rent. The tenants complained about these practices, and the neighbors criticized them. Scully's dictatorial policies were unpopular because they smacked of rack renting in Ireland and created a bad

pany of England were given frequent and favorable attention in the *Marion County Record* (Marion). See the same for May 7, June 25, 1875; Jan. 5, 1882; Sept. 28, 1883; Jan. 9, 1885.

reputation for the counties in which his land was centered. The result was a political attack upon him. Efforts were made to tax his rent roll, to compel the sale of his property, and to bar him from purchasing additional land. The attack upon Scully came at a time when his purchases were growing rapidly as a result of the substantial rents now available to him.[78]

Table 27. SCULLY PURCHASES IN KANSAS AND NEBRASKA

Location	Acres	Cost
Butler County, Kansas	8,605	$77,410
Dickinson County, Kansas	1,120	1,400
Gage County, Nebraska	22,288	290,254
Marion County, Kansas	55,666	179,197
Marshall County, Kansas	4,115	55,252
Nuckolls County, Nebraska	41,420	51,775
Total	134,214	$655,288

Local newspapers, farm journals, agrarian parties and western representatives in Congress took up the cry to bar aliens from holding land. The agitation was largely directed at Scully, who, despite his heavy investments in the United States, spent little time here and retained his British citizenship.[79]

[78] The *Marion Register* carried the brunt of the attack in Kansas upon Scully. See it for Feb. 2, 9, 16, 21, March 2, 4, April 20, 1887. See also *Marion Record,* Feb. 25, 1887; *Canada Arcade,* Feb. 8, 1887; *Peabody Gazette,* March 18, 1861; *Topeka Commonwealth* in *Marion Register,* Feb. 9, 1887; John Davis, "Alien Landlordism in America," in C. F. Taylor, *The Land Question from Various Points of View* (Philadelphia, 1898), p. 58. It should be added that before these attacks reached their peak in 1887 Scully had introduced farm practices that were distinctly modern and, indeed, probably well in advance of general landlord practice at the time.

[79] Paul Wallace Gates, *Frontier Landlords and Pioneer Tenants* (Ithaca, 1945), pp. 34 ff.; Homer E. Socolofsky, "The Scully Land

America was in ferment, in the eighties, over numerous issues relating to land. Henry George's single-tax theories were attracting wide attention, the movement to make railroad land-grants taxable and to forfeit unearned grants and even lands which had been earned but not sold was popular in the West, reformers were attempting to modernize an archaic and incongruous land-distribution system to safeguard the small man in his efforts to acquire farm ownership, conservationists in the East were calling for the establishment of controls over the use of natural resources and the end of the predatory practices of the past. Shrill cries for reform were voiced everywhere. In the midst of this ferment, the attack upon alien ownership and upon the highly-publicized Scully tenant-policies came to a head. In 1887 the Union Labor Party linked together demands for a graduated land tax on all large estates, especially "those held for speculative or tenant purposes," demands for the forfeiture of unearned land grants, and for legislation to bar corporations and aliens from acquiring land.[80] In Congress efforts to bar aliens from acquiring land in the territories were forwarded, appropriately enough, by Senator Preston B. Plumb of Kansas and Congressman Lewis E. Payson of Illinois, both of whom lived under the shadow of Scully land. They wrote into law, with the approval of President Grover Cleveland, a measure "to restrict the ownership of real estate in the Territories to American citizens." At the same time Illinois, Nebraska, Colorado, Wisconsin, and Minnesota closed the door to further alien purchases within their boundaries. The Kansas legislature considered it necessary to submit to the people the issue of barring alien ownership in the form of a constitutional amendment, which was overwhelmingly ap-

System in Marion County," *Kansas Historical Quarterly* (Nov., 1950), XVIII, 337 ff.

[80] *Marshall County Democrat* (Marysville), Sept. 8, 1887.

proved. In 1891 Kansas joined other states in preventing further accumulation of land by aliens.[81]

Scullyism might have come to Kansas even had there been no railroad grants, but the concentration of ownership in large estates during the early period was largely the result of railroad- and Indian-land sales. It provided another grievance against the railroads and their land policies.

Railroad land-grants contributed to an unwholesome pattern of land settlement, a fact which added to the criticism directed against them. Within the grants with their alternate sections held at relatively high prices by the railroads and the reserved government sections open to homestead and pre-emption, settlers sought out the cheap or free land first, were willing to go far afield for it, and only took up the railroad sections when public land was gone or too remote. A reporter writing from a community on the KP railroad where the one-hundreth meridian crosses commented, in 1880, on the "scattered, sparse and hazardous" settlement pattern he had seen.[82] With railroad lands paying no taxes and lying vacant and unimproved for years while the public lands around them were being developed, it is understandable that roads were slow to be laid out, that schools, local government and marketing centers came late. The mortgage indebtedness and emergence of tenancy to which railroad land policy contributed were further reasons tending to bring not only the grants but also the railroads into disrepute among many.

Resentment against the locking up of so much potentially valuable territory in unearned or unsold grants and in large speculative holdings, combined with the slowness of the railroads to take title and have their lands placed on the tax roll, led to a demand for restoring to the public domain lands

[81] 24 *Stat.*, 476; Gates, *Frontier Landlords*, pp. 57–59.
[82] *New York Tribune*, Dec. 27, 1880.

289

along the projected railroads which were making no progress. Other reforms proposed were that railroads not conforming to the provisions of the law forfeit their grants, that the cash-sale law be repealed, and that restrictions be adopted to prevent speculators and large investors from monopolizing or acquiring in the future large portions of the public lands. Efforts were also made to have land beyond the primary-grant area restored by administrative action or forfeited by congressional action.

In Kansas the demand that railroads forfeit their land grants and return lands improperly patented to them attracted much attention. Both Plumb and Anderson were leading spirits in introducing and supporting congressional bills to achieve these objects. The Joy lines were the most hated of all railroads in the state because they had tried to purchase the Neutral Tract, to extend the LL&G land-grant into the Osage-ceded tract, and to monopolize the Osage trust and diminished reserve; they had also engaged in sharp controversies with homesteaders on public lands. The conflict in Allen and Woodson Counties between homesteaders on the one hand and the Katy and LL&G lines on the other was matched by the efforts of homesteaders along the proposed line of the latter railroad between Lawrence and Leavenworth to gain title to unearned but reserved lands. In 1876 the Kansas legislature urged Congress to forfeit the LL&G grant on the ground that the terms of the grant had not been met, and to open the forfeited lands to pre-emption and homestead.[83] With surprising celerity, Congress provided for the forfeiture of some 30,000 acres of land along the proposed route from Lawrence to Leavenworth. No work had been done on this line nor was there any indication that any would be done.[84]

[83] *Kansas Laws,* 1876, p. 340.
[84] *Cong. Record,* 44 Cong., 1 Sess., IV, part 5, 4235; IV, part 6, 5028.

The second forfeiture of a railroad grant in Kansas was also of a Joy line, but in this instance forfeiture was made with the consent of the railroad officials. The grant had been made to the Kansas and Neosho, predecessor of the Fort Scott Line. When the grant was made in 1866 there was little public land along its line which might be selected—not more than 5,000 or 10,000 acres according to Senator Pomeroy—but to compensate for that, the railroad was authorized to "negotiate with and acquire from any Indian nation or tribe, authorized to dispose of its lands for railroad purposes" their reserve.[85] The principal reserves in Kansas that might be acquired under the act were those of the Miami (70,033 acres), the New York (10,215 acres), the Black Bob (24,138 acres), the Confederated Peorias (an estimated 60,000 acres) and the Cherokee Neutral Tract (800,000 acres). As things fell out, only the Neutral Tract was acquired, and the sale was accomplished presumably without the aid of the statute of 1866.

Instead of a land grant of 1,024,000 acres, the Fort Scott Line was able to claim only 21,341 acres. The joker in the act was that section which authorized the Fort Scott Railroad, in the event that it reached Indian Territory before the LL&G, to build on through that territory and to receive any land grant which Indian cessions might permit. This right had previously been given solely to the LL&G. A later section of the act opened this same privilege to the Union Pacific, Southern Branch, subsequently the Katy Railroad, thus setting up conditions for a fierce rivalry between all three railroads. But ostensibly and on its surface the measure was a simple bill to provide another land grant to a Kansas railroad and was so pictured by its sponsors, who, however, admitted that the amount of land directly involved was probably not more than a few thousand acres.

[85] *Cong. Globe,* 39 Cong., 1 Sess., III, 2738, 2852 and elsewhere; 14 *U.S. Stat.,* 236.

The Katy Railroad won the struggle, and all the Fort Scott Line had to show for its part in lobbying for the land-grant act of 1866 was ownership of 21,341 acres of land, which were still left after a decade of land-selection by squatters, speculators, and others. For this meager allotment the railroad had voluntarily subjected itself to the limitations the government prescribed for land-grant railroads including the much-disliked lower rates on government traffic. Furthermore, the railroad officials found that homesteaders had established on the 21,341 acres claims antedating those of the Fort Scott Line, and now put up the usual fight to maintain their rights. It was apparent that the land grant was in no way beneficial, for it required heavy legal expense to defend the railroad right to the grant, which appeared to have little value anyway, and merely assured smaller income on Federal traffic. Having lost in their struggle with the Katy for the right to build through Indian Territory, the Fort Scott Line found that the benefits of the land-grant act of 1866 which once were so prized were now transformed into liabilities. At this point the railroad officials urged Congress to forfeit the grant "in consequence of the antagonism and opposition of the people living on those lands. . . ." as Senator Ingalls put it. Forfeiture was accomplished in 1877. It did not affect the 89,691 acres the railroad acquired from the State as an aid in its construction.[86]

David Ellis has shown how the pressure for forfeiture of unearned railroad land-grants and for the return of withdrawn land to homestead entry swept through the West in the seventies and eighties, displacing other issues in the minds

[86] The only satisfactory treatment of railroad forfeiture is in the master's thesis by David M. Ellis, completed in 1939, in the Cornell University Library, "The Forfeiture of Railroad Land Grants," and the same author's "The Forfeiture of Railroad Land Grants, 1867–1894," *Mississippi Valley Historical Review* (June, 1946), XXXIII, 27 ff.

not only of homesteaders but of real-estate interests and other business groups. The first results were special forfeiture measures applying to individual railroads. Then, under the Cleveland administration, when excitement reached a high peak, the Commissioner of the General Land Office, who had notable reform tendencies, boldly restored to entry some 81,000,000 acres of public land. Finally, when the forfeiture movement [87] reached the greatest excitement, the conservative Senate gave way reluctantly to the militantly aroused House, and permitted the enactment of a series of measures that forfeited additional specific grants and culminated, in 1890, in an emasculated general forfeiture act.[88]

By the eighties the railroads everywhere had fallen from their high position into public disgrace. No economic institution had earlier been so pampered, so liberally showered with grants of charters, rights of way through public property, rights of eminent domain, imperial land donations, and financial subventions by Federal, state, county, and municipal governments. Railroad officers had been publicly fêted, their word had become law in many communities, legislatures and executive figures waited on their convenience, their power seemed invincible. The tide had turned against them in the West when their grab for land, their unwillingness to pay taxes, their efforts to extract every possible dollar from their holdings, brought them into conflict with the homesteader and with small-town business interests. Railroad land- and tax-policies were as important as the rate-structure, perhaps more so, in bringing about this revulsion

[87] In 1886 the Kansas Democrats demanded the forfeiture of unearned land grants and the reopening of the forfeited lands to settlement. They also condemned the General Land Office which had been controlled by Republicans from 1861 to 1885 for permitting aliens to acquire large acreages of land. *Atchison Champion,* Aug. 5, 1886.

[88] In addition to Ellis, previously cited, see John B. Rae, "Commissioner Sparks and the Railroad Land Grants," *Mississippi Valley Historical Review* (Sept., 1938), XXV, 224.

of opinion. The donations of land were now regarded by the agrarian-minded people as a serious mistake. The companies owning these grants were held responsible for retarding development of community enterprises by refusing to pay their share of taxes, for keeping down immigration by the high price-level they maintained for their land, for driving settlers to more remote areas where the elusive "free" land might be found, and for contributing to the creation of a debt-ridden class of farmers. It was a far cry from the time when James F. Joy could buy the Neutral Tract and Washington officialdom could brave the roar of protest, or when the Indian Office could sell the Christian, Delaware, Pottawatomie, and Kickapoo reserves with but slight opposition except from resident squatters.

Bibliographical Note

FOR any research in Kansas history the unrivaled collections of the Kansas State Historical Society are indispensable. Its manuscripts, official archives, and newspapers as well as the usual printed materials cover a wide range and show imagination and leadership in their assembling. The Society's *Collections* in seventeen volumes and especially its *Kansas Historical Quarterly,* now in its twentieth volume, are models of scholarship, combining skillful editing of documents and revisionist articles of substance.

In addition to the materials in Topeka, reliance has been placed on the correspondence of the Office of Indian Affairs and the General Land Office, abstracts of land entries, deed, mortgage, and probate records of numerous Kansas counties, and a number of manuscript collections of private individuals. Public and private published documents have also been drawn on heavily. Mention is made here only of collections materially useful for investigation of land problems in Kansas.

General Land Office Records.

Abstracts of cash, warrant, and scrip entries were used for all the Kansas land offices. Some use was also made of the volumes of declaratory statements and original filings of homestead entries. These records are now kept in the National Archives. For the statistics of sales, homesteads, etc., the *Annual Reports* of the Commissioner of the General Land Office are essential.

Office of Indian Affairs Records.

Correspondence concerning treaties, trust sales, private bids, and railroad purchase of reserves; petitions and letters opposed to large purchases, and requests that lands be withheld for settlers. Much of this correspondence was used before it was moved to the National Archives but the reference is given to that center.

Deed, Mortgage, Probate, and Other Court Records of Kansas Counties.

The deed and mortgage records for Kansas counties in existence during the territorial period were used. Research in these and the probate and court records was carried into the period of statehood and as late as 1890, though less intensively pursued than was the work in the earlier years. Some counties like Marion were studied with greater minuteness. Records of thirty-five counties were used in eastern and central Kansas, but this leaves a greater number of counties beyond the ninety-seventh meridian that were not touched.

Corcoran, William W., and Corcoran and Riggs Manuscripts, Library of Congress. Corcoran invested in Kansas lands in the territorial period.

Dodge, Grenville M., Manuscripts, Iowa State Historical and Art Department, Material on Leavenworth, Pawnee, and Western Railroad.

Easley and Willingham Manuscripts, University of Virginia. Valuable for farm loans, land speculation, and tax-title business in Illinois, Iowa, Wisconsin, and Kansas.

Emigrant Aid Company Manuscripts, Kansas State Historical Society. With the Lawrence papers these are useful for the land deals of the antislavery group.

English, William E., Indiana Historical Society. Useful for relations with the pro-southern leadership in the Democratic Party.

Ewing, Thomas, Jr., Manuscripts. Kansas State Historical Society. Thomas Ewing, Jr., and his brother, Hugh Boyle Ewing, were early interested in land investments in Leavenworth, and afterward the former went into railroad promotion. Thomas Ewing, Jr., was a big-time lobbyist.

Ewing, William G., and George Washington Ewing Manuscripts. Indiana Historical Library. Fort Wayne and Logansport traders whose relations with the Miami and Pottawatomie Indians gave them a keen interest in Kansas in the fifties and early sixties.

Joy, James F., Manuscripts. Burton Historical Collections, Detroit Public Library. Indispensable for Kansas railroads, the conflict over the sale of the Neutral Tract, and the attempted sale of the Osage reserve.

Joy, James F., Historical Files. Originally used at the Grosse Pointe home of Henry B. Joy but since transferred to the Michigan Historical Collections, University of Michigan. Particularly useful were the typescripts and photostats of newspaper comment on the sale of the Neutral Tract to James F. Joy. In the assembling of this collection, Stephen Gilchrist was primarily concerned with Joy's relations with Lincoln, his part in the "River Roads" controversy, and his leadership in developing the railroad network in the Missouri Valley.

Lawrence, Amos, Manuscripts. Kansas State Historical Society. Lawrence's Kansas correspondents were on occasion extremely frank.

Leonard Collection of Thomas E. Durant Papers, State Historical Society of Iowa. Useful for story of lobbying for Indian reserves and land grants.

Pratt, John G., Manuscripts. Kansas State Historical Society. Contains a number of letters useful for this study.

Robinson, Charles, Manuscripts. Kansas State Historical Society. An influential politician who dabbled in lands and railroads.

Newspapers

Most Kansas newspapers for the period to 1890 that have been preserved by the Kansas State Historical Society and the Library of Congress were used. The collection in Topeka is remarkable for its size and coverage. *History of Kansas Newspapers,* (Topeka, 1916), is both a history of and a guide to this collection. It makes unnecessary listing in detail the newspapers used for this study. Very helpful was the nearly complete file of the *Atchison Champion* in the Cornell University Library.

Public Documents

All the pertinent Federal, state, and territorial documents were used for the period from 1854 to 1890. Included are the *Annual Reports* of the Commissioner of the General Land Office, the Commissioner of Indian Affairs, and the Secretary of the Interior; *Congressional Globe* and *Record, Senate Executive Journal, Senate* and *House Executive Documents* and *Reports, United States Statutes at Large, United States Supreme Court Decisions, Kansas Session Laws, Kansas Documents.* The compilation of Indian treaties edited by Charles J. Kappler, *Indian Affairs, Laws and Treaties* (2 Vols., Washington, 1904) is easier to use than the *Statutes at Large.*

Corporation Documents

Annual Reports and land advertising and settlement promotion pamphlets of the Atchison, Topeka, and Santa Fe; Kansas Pacific; Missouri, Kansas, and Texas; Leavenworth, Lawrence, and Galveston; and Missouri River, Fort Scott, and Gulf Railroads.

Because this study rests so largely on published and unpublished source materials it has not seemed wise to include a list of books that have been consulted. Those which proved to be useful have been given proper attention in the footnotes. A few items that have been particularly helpful are here mentioned. Anna H. Abel, "Indian Reservations in Kansas and the Extinguishment of their Title," Kansas State Historical Society, *Transactions,* VIII, (Topeka, 1904), 72–109, has not been displaced. G. Raymond Gaeddert, *The Birth of Kansas* (University of Kansas *Publications, Social Science Studies,* Topeka, 1940), is important. Lula Lemmon Brown, *Cherokee Neutral Lands*

Controversy (Pittsburg, Kansas, 1930), is a courageous attempt to deal with the sale of the Neutral Tract, prepared when few students were concerned with land problems. David M. Ellis, "The Forfeiture of Railroad Land Grants, 1867–1894," *Mississippi Valley Historical Review* (June, 1946), XXIII, 27–70, a compression of a master's thesis in the Library of Cornell University, is indispensable.

Index

Mix, Charles E., 131
Money lenders, interest rates of, 94-95
Montgomery, John, 40
Morris, Isaac N., 178, 187
Mortgages, 99; interest on, 100, 240
Munsee, *see* Christian Indians

Nebraska: people infuriated at sales policy, 90; Republican stronghold, 105
Neutral Land League, Cherokee: organization of, 171; raid land office, Ft. Scott Line, 172; *Manifesto,* 172n.; appeal to the people against Joy, 173; Laughlin, representative of, 174; Kansas legislature supports, 184
Neutral Tract, *see* Cherokee Neutral Tract
Nevins, Allan, 72
New England Emigrant Aid Co., 51
New York Indian Reserve: harassment of squatters on, 32; Indian rights in, upheld, 33-34; Missourians on, 57; claim warfare on, 61
New York Tribune, 106, 272, 273
Northrup & Chick, 147

Obrig, G. J., 99
Occupying claimants act, 186
Officers, military, claims of, 54
Opdyke, George, 146
Osage cession: Katy and LL&G confirmed in, 212; confirmation reversed by Supreme Court, 220; opened to squatters, 220-21; settlers' difficulty in purchasing, 224
Osage Co., 135
Osage Indians, 14
Osage reserve: effort to acquire, 1863, 195-96; treaty of 1865 confirmed, 196-97; LL&G tries to buy, 197; treaty for sale of, 198-99; condemnation of sale of, 203-6
Oto & Missouri, 14
Ottawas, 229

Pairo, Charles W., 50
Panic of 1857, 78

Parker, Nathan H., 24
Parkville & Grand River R.R., 115
Parrott, Marcus J., 24
Pawnee, 14
Payson, Lewis E., 279, 288
Peorias: allotments and trust lands of, 34; lands ordered surveyed, 49; allotments on timbered lands, 54; Missourians on, 56; sale of, 70-71, 229
Perry, A., 173n.
Phillips, William A., 52n.
Piankeshaws, 70
Pierce, Charles W., 146
Plumb, Preston B., senator, 86, 278-79, 288
Polk, O. H. P., 131n.
Pomeroy, Daniel C., 138
Pomeroy, Samuel C.: interested in Kansas half-breed allotments, 40; owner of float, 45n.; materialism of, 107, 108; sparkplug of Atchison, 115, 133; graft charges against, 123; suggested settlement on Delaware reserve, 126; aid of, Pottawatomie negotiations, 129; boodle of, 130; divided patronage with Lane, 133; Atchison as a railroad center, 134; secures land grants, 134-35; attends Kickapoo council, 137; negotiates for Pottawatomie reserve, 143; share in Pottawatomie lands, 146; suspicion of his railroad connections, 160; denounced by Neutral Land League, 171; a "blatherskite," 178; favored railroad claims in Osage cession, 213; disclosure of use of bribery by, 258; defeated for re-election, 259
Pottawatomie reserve: sought by LP&W, 128; treaty for sale of, 129-31; allotments located on timbered land, 131; purchase of, rejected by UPED, 132; acquired by Santa Fe, 143-44
Potwin, Charles, 283
Pratt, John G., 121
Pre-emption: on Miami reserve, 30; on public land, 81

 **Atheling books**

In the Social Sciences

THE NAZI MOVEMENT
Theodore Abel *($3.75)*

EGO & MILIEU
John Cumming and Elaine Cumming *($3.95)*

NATION-BUILDING
Karl W. Deutsch and William J. Foltz *($1.95)*

TABOO TOPICS
Norman L. Farberow *($1.95)*

HERBERT SPENCER'S SOCIOLOGY
Jay Rumney *($3.95)*

THE SOCIAL THEORY OF GEORG SIMMEL
Nicholas J. Spykman *($3.50)*

AN ANTHROPOLOGIST AT WORK
Writings of Ruth Benedict
Margaret Mead *($3.45)*

FIFTY MILLION ACRES
Conflicts over Kansas Land Policy, 1854-1890
Paul Wallace Gates *($2.95)*

In Education

FOUNDATIONS OF JOHN DEWEY'S EDUCATIONAL SYSTEM
Melvin C. Baker *($2.75)*

JOHN DEWEY: MASTER EDUCATOR
William W. Brickman and Stanley Lehrer *($1.95)*

THE DEWEY SCHOOL
Katherine Camp Mayhew and Anna Camp Edwards *($3.95)*

EDUCATION BETWEEN TWO WORLDS
Alexander Meiklejohn *($3.75)*

AUTHORITY, RESPONSIBILITY, AND EDUCATION
R. S. Peters *($1.95)*

CRISIS AND HOPE IN AMERICAN EDUCATION
Robert Ulich *($2.95)*